Corporate and Governmental Deviance

Corporate and Governmental Deviance

Problems of Organizational Behavior in Contemporary Society

Fifth Edition

M. David Ermann
University of Delaware

Richard J. Lundman
The Ohio State University

New York   Oxford
OXFORD UNIVERSITY PRESS
1996

Oxford University Press

Oxford   New York
Athens   Auckland   Bangkok   Bombay
Calcutta   Cape Town   Dar es Salaam   Delhi
Florence   Hong Kong   Istanbul   Karachi
Kuala Lumpur   Madras   Madrid   Melbourne
Mexico City   Nairobi   Paris   Singapore
Taipei   Tokyo   Toronto

and associated companies in
Berlin   Ibadan

Published by Oxford University Press, Inc.,
198 Madison Avenue, New York, New York 10016

Library of Congress Cataloging-in-Publication Data

Corporate and governmental deviance : problems of organizational
behavior in contemporary society / [edited by] M. David Ermann,
Richard J. Lundman.—5th ed.
p. cm.
Includes bibliographical references.

1. White collar crimes—United States   2. Political crimes and
offenses—United States.   I. Ermann, M. David.   II. Lundman,
Richard J., 1944– .
HV6769.C667   1996
364.1'68'0973—dc20   95–18505
CIP
ISBN 0-19-509487-5

9 8 7 6 5 4 3 2 1
Printed in the United States of America

To
Marlene, Michael, and Natalie Ermann
and
Julie and Bob Lundman

Preface

This book is for courses on deviance, social problems, criminology, organizations, and business and society. In these courses, reading assignments frequently include a comprehensive text and supplemental works focusing on specific topics. Whether comprehensive or supplemental, the assigned readings usually direct attention to the actions of individuals. This book provides an important balance by directing attention to the deviant actions of organizations. We believe that students who read our "Overview" and a sampling of the essays in this book will come away with an appreciation of when, how, and why organizations and the people in them commit deviant acts.

As with previous editions, we kept the student reader in mind while writing our introductory materials and making our selections. We have tried to maximize reader interest while simultaneously introducing students to the very best ideas and materials currently available.

This book is the result of our experience teaching courses that concentrate on the deviance of organizations. Over the past 25 years, students in our classes listened and responded as our ideas took shape. We greatly appreciate their enthusiasm, interest, and frequently helpful suggestions. We thank our departmental colleagues for their encouragement and our office staff for their skillful help.

Every aspect of this book is the product of our joint efforts. We shared equally in its creation and are equally responsible for the result.

Newark, Delaware   M.D.E.
Columbus, Ohio   R.J.L.
September 1995

Contents

I
Overview

1
Corporate and Governmental Deviance
Origins, Patterns, and Reactions
M. David Ermann and Richard J. Lundman

This essay is about the deviant acts of business corporations and governmental agencies. We begin by challenging common images of deviance. We then show that large organizations themselves, not just the people in them, can commit deviant acts. Next, we explain why and how organizations commit deviant acts. Finally, we analyze social reactions to corporate and governmental deviance.

Common Images of Deviance

Common images of deviance focus on people acting individually or in small groups. They rarely include organizational actors.[1] When people think about the financial losses associated with theft, for example, the probable image is of being burglarized, not of being the victim of illegal corporate price-fixing. When they think about being physically injured, most people imagine being assaulted, perhaps by someone high on or desperate for drugs, not about dying in the crash of a plane caused by a known safety defect. And when people act to protect their privacy, they are much more likely to install a dead-bolt lock than to insist on meaningful restraints on local police, the FBI, or the CIA.

These common images of deviance are unnecessarily limiting, however. The organizational actions these images exclude are fre-

1. Allen E. Liska, *Perspectives on Deviance*, 2nd ed. (Englewood Cliffs, N.J.: Prentice-Hall, 1987), p. 157; J. L. Simmons, "Public Stereotypes of Deviants," *Social Problems* 13 (1965): 223–24.

quently more personally and socially important[2] than the individual deviance on which most people concentrate. In addition, organizational deviance is often more interesting to study because it takes us inside the large corporations and governmental agencies that are so prominent in and important to contemporary society. We therefore emphasize that organizations—not just individuals—commit deviant acts.

Organizations as Acting Units

At first glance, it may appear difficult to study the deviance of businesses and government agencies while largely ignoring the individuals who make up these organizations. After all, organizations do not think or act.[3] Individuals must think and act for there to be corporate or governmental deviance. How is it possible to study the deviance of big business and big government apart from particular organizational members?

One answer is that a large organization can be viewed as "a collection of jobs or social positions, each with its own skills, power, rules, and rewards."[4] These organizational positions include chief executive officers or agency directors, workers, secretaries, and vice presidents or deputy administrators. Together with other positions, they are the building blocks from which all large organizations are constructed.

Large organizations thus are not mere collections of people. They are collections of positions that powerfully constrain the work-

2. Keith Schneider, "Judge Rejects $100 Million Fine for Exxon in Oil Spill as Too Low," *New York Times*, April 25, 1991, p. 1; Marshall B. Clinard, *Corporate Corruption: The Abuse of Power* (New York: Praeger, 1990); Tim Weiner, *Blank Check: The Pentagon's Black Budget* (New York: Warner Books, 1990); Robert F. Meier and James F. Short, Jr., "The Consequences of White-Collar Crime," in Herbert Edelhertz and Thomas D. Overcast (eds.), *White-Collar Crime: An Agenda for Research* (Lexington, Mass.: Heath, 1982), pp. 23–49.

3. Katherine M. Jamieson, *The Organization of Corporate Crime: Dynamics of Antitrust Violation* (Thousand Oaks, Calif.: Sage, 1994), p. 3; James William Coleman, "Toward an Integrated Theory of White-Collar Crime," *American Journal of Sociology* 93 (1987): 409–14; Lawrence W. Sherman, *Scandal and Reform: Controlling Police Corruption* (Berkeley: University of California Press, 1978), p. 6.

4. Jerald Hage and Michael Aiken, *Social Change in Complex Organizations* (New York: Random House, 1970), p. 11. Also see Richard H. Hall, *Organizations: Structures, Processes and Outcomes*, 4th ed. (Englewood Cliffs, N.J.: Prentice-Hall, 1987), pp. 42–43.

related thoughts and actions of the replaceable people who occupy these positions.

People Are Replaceable

People occupying positions within large organizations are replaceable.[5] Large organizations routinely replace their workers, managers, and top-level members with little effect on the organization. Such turnover is not threatening because the recruitment and training of replacements are well organized.[6] New organizational members quickly learn what is expected of them, by following formal work rules and job descriptions as well as the informal understandings associated with particular positions. Except in unusual circumstances, particular people regularly come and go while the organization continues to operate in an orderly fashion.

Consider what happened to the basketball programs at five universities in a single year:

> Follow these bounding coaches. When Joe B. Hall retired . . . from the head job at Kentucky, Eddie Sutton, at the time the head man at Arkansas, sought out Hall's old position. . . . With Sutton gone from Arkansas . . . the winning applicant was Nolan Richardson . . . the head . . . at the University of Tulsa. Richardson's move left the Tulsa spot open and along came J. D. Barnett from Virginia Commonwealth University to fill it. Into the Virginia job went Mike Pollio, head at Kentucky Wesleyan, and . . . into Pollio's slot moved Wayne Chapman.[7]

Despite these changes in the persons occupying the position of coach, each school still fielded a basketball team. And the young men played their games, even though the coaches who recruited them had moved on.

5. James S. Coleman, "The Rational Reconstruction of Society," *American Sociological Review* 58 (1993): 1–15; James S. Coleman, *Foundations of Social Theory* (Cambridge, Mass.: Harvard University Press, 1990), p. 427; James S. Coleman, *The Asymmetric Society* (Syracuse, N.Y.: Syracuse University Press, 1982), pp. 19–30; James S. Coleman, *Power and the Structure of Society* (New York: Norton, 1974), pp. 35–54.

6. Robert Jackall, *Moral Mazes: The World of Corporate Managers* (New York: Oxford University Press, 1988), pp. 41–46; Hall, *Organizations*, pp. 42–46; Rosabeth Moss Kanter, *Men and Women of the Corporation* (New York: Basic Books, 1977), pp. 47–68; Diane Rothbard Margolis, *The Managers: Corporate Life in America* (New York: Morrow, 1979).

7. Murray Sperber, *College Sports Inc.: The Athletic Department vs. the University* (New York: Holt, 1990), p. 159.

Similarly, students come and go on a regular basis with little or no effect on their colleges or universities. Each spring during commencement ceremonies, universities solemnly bid farewell to about one-quarter of their undergraduate student population, and each fall a new class is warmly welcomed as its members take the places of those who graduated. So too with professors. Each year some quit and go elsewhere, a handful are fired, and others retire or die. Search committees quickly find replacements, and the universities continue to operate as if nothing had happened.

For social scientists who study large organizations, then, particular people are replaceable. Sociologist James S. Coleman observes:

> The . . . structure exists independently of the persons occupying positions within it, like a city whose buildings exist independently of the particular persons who occupy them. . . . In an organization that consists of positions in a structure of relations, the persons who occupy the positions are incidental to the structure. They take on the obligations and expectations, the goals and the resources, associated with their positions in the way they put on work clothes for their jobs. But the obligations and expectations, the goals and resources, exist apart from the individual occupants of the positions.[8]

Organizations Constrain Thoughts and Actions

Large organizations constrain the work-related thoughts and actions of the people in them. Most people in large organizations occupy positions with circumscribed information and responsibility.[9] Their jobs require only limited knowledge, and their work makes only a small contribution to the overall activity of the organization. They are told what to do and usually do as they are told.

Of course, people occupying top-level positions tell other people what to do. But even these organizational elites are constrained by their past experiences and current positions.[10] Elites have been

8. Coleman, *Foundations*, p. 427.

9. Jackall, *Moral Mazes*, pp. 43–44; Hall, *Organizations*, p. 43.

10. Henry Rosovsky, *The University: An Owner's Manual* (New York: Norton, 1990), pp. 40–45; Jackall, *Moral Mazes*; James Q. Wilson, *Bureaucracy: What Government Agencies Do and Why They Do It* (New York: Basic Books, 1989), pp. 113–232; David R. James and Michael Soref, "Profit Constraints on Managerial Autonomy: Managerial Theory and Unmaking of the Corporation President," *American Sociological Review* 46 (1981): 1–18; Theodore Caplow, *Managing an Organization*, 2nd ed. (New York Holt, Rinehart and Winston, 1983), pp. 158–85; Warren Bennis, *The Unconscious Conspiracy: Why Leaders Can't Lead* (New York: American Management Association, 1976).

socialized by the powerful experiences of working for decades in the world of the large organization. In addition, they are paid to think and act for an organization that can easily replace them should they consistently fail in their efforts to advance its interests.

In sum, it is useful to conceive of a large organization as a real acting unit because the people within it can be replaced, and because the positions they occupy constrain their thoughts and actions.

Origins of Corporate and Governmental Deviance

The structure and operation of large organizations can produce organizational deviance in at least three ways. First, deviance can be traced to the limited information and responsibility available to people occupying positions in large organizations. Second, organizational elites can indirectly cause deviant actions by establishing norms, rewards, and punishments that encourage people occupying lower-level positions to produce deviant outcomes. Third, elites can consciously initiate a deviant action and use hierarchically linked positions to implement it.

Deviance Traceable to Limited Information and Responsibility

Large organizations typically divide tasks into small component parts. Each person makes only a limited contribution, and no single person can complete any job alone. Moreover, people generally are discouraged from doing other than their assigned jobs or undertaking actions independent of their supervisors.

Thus, employees may do their jobs well and nevertheless produce deviant outcomes. This is because no one person has the knowledge, responsibility, incentive, time, or skill to collect, analyze, and use the information needed to alter organizational actions before problems begin. Writing well in advance of the Three Mile Island and Chernobyl nuclear accidents, law professor Christopher Stone provided a chillingly accurate preview of how organizational positions, each with limited information and responsibility, can produce a deviant act:

Suppose . . . the case of an electric utility company that maintains a nuclear power plant. We can readily imagine that there might be knowledge of physics, evidence of radiation leakage, information regarding temperature variations, data related to previous operation runs in this and other plants, which if gathered in the mind of one single person, would make . . . continued operation of that plant, without a shutdown, wanton and reckless—that is, if an explosion resulted, strong civil and criminal liability could and would be brought to bear. . . . But let us suppose what is more likely to be the case in modern corporate America: that the information and acts are distributed among many different employees engaged in various functional groups within the corporation. The nuclear engineer can be charged with bit of information a, the architect knows b, the night watch . . . knows c, the research scientist task force knows d. Conceivably there will not be any single individual who has . . . such knowledge and intent as will support a charge against [that person] . . . individually.[11]

One of the coeditors of this book (Ermann) had a similar experience with how limited information and responsibility can lead to deviance. Twenty-five years ago, as a recently graduated financial analyst working in Detroit for a major automobile corporation's international division, his name, for no special reason, was on the routing list for documents about a transmission developed by a British subsidiary of the company. The transmission used a new and more efficient technology that forced gears onto shafts under great pressure. The gears were expected to fit on the shafts tight enough so that no additional steps would be needed to prevent slippage. The new design passed testing with flying colors, and the company put it into production.

As luck would have it, though, unexpected problems appeared when tens of thousands of British drivers gave the design what was, in effect, its final road test. A fraction of 1 percent of the gears slipped on their shafts, causing friction that in turn caused transmission parts to heat, expand, and eventually jam. The cars careened off the road and killed enough people to attract public attention. The company recalled the British vehicles and modified their transmissions.

The documents explained that the responsible American executives intended to withhold knowledge of this hazard from owners

11. Christopher D. Stone, *Where the Law Ends: Social Control of Corporate Behavior* (New York: Harper and Row, 1975), pp. 51–52.

of American automobiles with the same transmissions, on an untested hunch that the heavier American vehicles would have enough momentum to break and drop their locked transmissions. The cars, company engineers hoped, would then coast safely to a stop. Fortunately, a savvy Detroit reporter used trade reports about the British experience to ask publicly whether the company would recall and repair the American vehicles, a question the company quickly answered in the affirmative.

The troublesome transmission was not planned deviance. Decision-makers had incomplete knowledge when they tested and adopted a new design. But they could not wait for complete knowledge before proceeding. No amount of testing could have determined whether in widespread use their new transmission would be hazard-free. They could not know that their product had a design fault that produced failures at a rate so low that it would not become apparent during extensive initial testing. Only after putting the transmission in use was sufficient data available to identify its risk to users.

Later, when the transmission was placed in service, decision-makers did begin to receive failure data, but these data were deeply embedded among other bits of important and unimportant information. Furthermore, responsible employees were not in a constant state of alertness to possible gear slippage (or any other issue). They had no reason to suspect a problem. Even if they could have recognized that the slippage problem existed, they could not have known how common it was.

However, when the data flow gradually reached a point where decision-makers could know the dimensions of the danger, they chose concealment. They were more likely to conceal information at this time because they and others had committed themselves to this particular design when they tested it and decided to use it. Their earlier decisions encouraged them to escalate their commitment[12] to a course of action they did not envisage when they began. (Readers who have bid or bought more at an auction than they originally planned can understand this process.) As is often the case, human activity continued for reasons unrelated to why it began.

12. Barry M. Staw and Jerry Ross, "Behavior in Escalation Situations: Antecedents, Prototypes, and Solutions," *Research in Organizational Behavior* 9 (1987): 39–78.

Deviance Indirectly Traceable to Organizational Elites

Other organizational acts are less the result of limited information and responsibility, and more the incidental and unintended result of elite initiative. Top-level managers regularly confront opportunities and problems for which they must devise organizationally beneficial solutions. They respond to these opportunities and problems by establishing goals and then delegating to subordinates the day-to-day responsibility for attaining these goals. Occasionally delegated responsibility and routine procedures and rewards yield unintended results.

Let us look at two examples of how organizational practices can produce unintended deviance. The first recounts the Ford Motor Company's design, testing, and release of its Pinto, and the second involves Beech-Nut's "apple juice" for babies.

Ford Motor Company and the Pinto.[13]   In the mid-1960s, the Ford Motor Company faced a serious problem. The corporation was starting to lose sales to small, fuel-efficient foreign imports. Ford's vice-president, Lee Iacocca, and his allies in the corporation devised a solution: Ford would enter the small car market. To avoid further erosion in sales, it would do so no later than the 1970 model year. Mr. Iacocca eventually became president of Ford and, along with supportive colleagues, pushed through a crash plan to build the Pinto in two-thirds the time normally required to design, build, test, and market a new car. As a result, tooling had to be accomplished simultaneously with design and testing. By the time a fuel tank safety problem was discovered, therefore, tooling was well under way.

Initially, no one took the problem to corporate elites because, in the words of one engineer, "Safety wasn't a popular subject around Ford in those days."[14] In addition, Mr. Iacocca had established an

---

13. Dennis A. Gioia, "Pinto Fires and Personal Ethics: A Script Analysis of Missed Opportunities," *Journal of Business Ethics* 11 (1992): 379–89 (reprinted as Selection 7); Nancy Frank, "Unintended Murder and Corporate Risk-Taking: Defining the Concept of Justifiability," *Journal of Criminal Justice* 16 (1988): 17–24; Brent Fisse and John Braithwaite, *The Impact of Publicity on Corporate Offenders* (Albany: State University of New York Press, 1983), pp. 41–54; Frank Camps, "Warning an Auto Company About an Unsafe Design," in Alan F. West (ed.), *Whistle Blowing! Loyalty and Dissent in the Corporation* (New York: McGraw-Hill 1981), pp. 119–29; Mark Dowie, "Pinto Madness," in Jerome H. Skolnick and Elliot Currie (eds.), *Crisis in American Institutions*, 4th ed. (Boston: Little, Brown, 1979), pp. 23–41.

14. Dowie, "Pinto Madness," p. 27.

inflexible "Rule of 2,000" to ensure that the Pinto would be competitive with foreign imports. He insisted that the Pinto was not to weigh an ounce over 2,000 pounds and was not to cost a penny over $2,000. Consequently, "even when a crash test showed that . . . [a] one pound, one dollar piece of metal stopped the puncture of the gas tank, it was thrown out as extra cost and weight."[15] The car was sold with the fuel tank safety problem unresolved.

Nobody at Ford, including Mr. Iacocca, ordered that a car with a serious design defect be built. Instead, Mr. Iacocca perceived a problem, devised a solution, established goals and operating rules, and delegated to others the day-to-day responsibility for design, building, and testing. The unintended result of these routine procedures was an unsafe product.

Beech-Nut's "Apple Juice" for Babies.[16] Beech-Nut was founded in upstate New York in 1891 as a purveyor of smoked hams and bacon. By the mid-1960s, the company had diversified and offered many familiar products, including Tetley Tea, Life Savers, gum, and baby food. In late 1968 Squibb merged with Beech-Nut to form Squibb Beech-Nut. Squibb, in turn, spun off the baby foods product line and sold it in 1973 to Frank Nicholas, a Pennsylvania attorney and entrepreneur. Mr. Nicholas, who paid $16 million, sold the company three years later to Nestle, the Swiss food conglomerate, for $35 million. In late 1989, Nestle sold it to Ralston Purina for an estimated $65 million.

One of Beech-Nut's three plants, in Canajoharie, New York, just west of Albany, abuts the New York Thruway. Drivers can easily see the big Beech-Nut sign and the stacks of empty crates they might assume were used to deliver apples and other fruits Beech-Nut uses for its baby juices. Indeed, a factory making fruit juice would seem

---

15. Ibid., p. 28.

16. Standard and Poor's Corporation, *Standard Corporate Description* (New York: McGraw-Hill, 1990), p. 2485; "Bad Apples in the Executive Suite," *Consumer Reports*, May 1989, pp. 294–96; Robert C. Cole, "Ralston Purina to Buy Beech-Nut Baby Food," *New York Times*, September 16, 1989, p. 37; James Traub, "Into the Mouths of Babes," *New York Times Magazine*, July 24, 1988, pp. 18–20, 37–38, 52–53; Chris Welles, "What Led Beech-Nut Down the Road to Disgrace?" *Business Week*, February 22, 1988, pp. 124–28; "Former Beech-Nut Execs Guilty," *Columbus Dispatch*, February 18, 1988, p. 4A; "Beech-Nut Admits It Sold Bogus Apple Juice," *Columbus Dispatch*, November 14, 1987, p. 2A; "Beech-Nut: The Case of the Ersatz Apple Juice," *Newsweek*, November 17, 1986, p. 66; Bernice Kanner, "Into the Mouths of Babes: Jar Wars," *New York*, November 14, 1986, pp. 27–31.

to require fruit, or at least fruit juice. The crates suggested the
Canajoharie plant was receiving shipments of fruit.

Closer inspection, however, revealed that the crates were badly
weathered and many had deteriorated. Moreover, most juices,
including Beech-Nut's, are now made from concentrate:

> [By] the time apple juice reaches the store, the typical juice has been
> screened, filtered, blended with apples from other orchards, and
> perhaps dosed with a little ascorbic acid to help maintain its clar-
> ity. Then it has been concentrated, reconstituted with water, and
> pasteurized. . . . Apple juice . . . is best understood as a manufac-
> tured product . . . brewed in the bottler's plant.[17]

The weathered crates at the back of the Canajoharie plant were
perhaps a throwback to an earlier time. In any case, the crates had
not contained apples for many years.

Neither did Beech-Nut's apple juice for babies between late 1977
and the middle of 1982. Although Beech-Nut advertisements told
parents: "Our nutritionists prepare fresh-tasting vegetables, meats,
dinners, fruits, cereals and juices without artificial flavorings, preservatives or colorings,"[18] Beech-Nut's apple juice consisted of sugar
water colored brown to look like apple juice. The product brewed
at the Canajoharie plant and labeled as "100 percent apple juice"[19]
contained many things, including beet sugar, cane sugar, corn
syrup, and caramel for color. The one thing it did not contain was
apple juice.

There was no apple juice because each time Beech-Nut was
merged, spun off, or sold, the price of the company went up. New
owners had invested millions of dollars in Beech-Nut and understandably insisted that the Canajoharie plant show a profit: "Beech-
Nut was under great financial pressure and using cheap, phony
concentrate saved millions of dollars."[20] In addition, Beech-Nut was
in intense competition with Gerber, the market leader with 70
percent of baby-food sales.

Also, detecting adulterated juice is surprisingly difficult. Even
after Beech-Nut had been prosecuted, chemists who specialize in

17. "Bad Apples," p. 295.
18. Ibid., p. 294.
19. "Beech-Nut," p. 66.
20. Welles, "What Led Beech-Nut," p. 125.

testing food samples estimated in late 1993 that 10 percent of fruit juice sold in the United States is adulterated with, among other things, sugar, pulp wash (watery residue from soaking squeezed oranges in water and squeezing them again), difficult-to-detect preservatives such as natamycin, and preservatives not approved as safe for use in juices or even banned outright as hazardous (e.g., diethyl pyrocarbonate). Even if the Food and Drug Administration or state agencies had adequate enforcement budgets, adulteration would be difficult to detect.[21] It is not easy to find clear evidence of apples even in juice that does contain apples.

Neither Mr. Nicholas when he owned Beech-Nut nor Nestle after it bought the company ordered corporate officers or plant managers to make bogus juice. The new owners only made it clear that they expected a return on their investment. They then delegated profit making to the people in Canajoharie. Charged with showing a profit, these people cut corners. One of the corners cut was leaving apple juice out of the apple juice.

Deviance Directly Traceable to Organizational Elites

Not all organizational actions are accidents in the sense implied by Professor Stone's hypothetical nuclear plant, or unintentional as illustrated by Beech-Nut's "apple juice." Organizational elites sometimes knowingly use the hierarchy of organizational positions to command deviant actions. The relocation of Japanese Americans during World War II is a good example of deviance directly traceable to elite decisions.

Relocation of Japanese Americans During World War II.[22]   Prejudice against Japanese Americans had been part of American life long

---

21. Diana B. Henriques, "10% of Fruit Juice Sold in U.S. Is Not All Juice, Regulators Say," *New York Times*, October 31, 1993, p. 1.

22. "Japanese Wait, Trustfully, for Overdue Checks," *Columbus Dispatch*, March 27, 1990, p. 8A; John Hersey, "Behind Barbed Wire," *New York Times Magazine*, September 11, 1988, pp. 56–59, 73–74, 76, 120–21; Peter Wright and John C. Armor, *Manzanar* (New York: Times Books, 1988), with wonderfully insightful photographs of Manzanar and its people by Ansel Adams; Commission on Wartime Relocation and Internment of Civilians, *Personal Justice Denied* (Washington, D.C.: U.S. Government Printing Office, 1982); Roger Daniels, *The Decision to Relocate the Japanese Americans* (Philadelphia: Lippincott, 1975); Roger Daniels, *Concentration Camps, U.S.A.: Japanese Americans and World War II* (New York: Holt, Rinehart and Winston, 1972).

before December 1941. For example, in May 1905, the San Francisco School Board put all Japanese students in a single "Oriental School" because "our children should not be placed in any position where their youthful impressions may be affected by association with pupils of the Mongolian race."[23] California's Alien Land Law of 1913 prohibited Japanese immigrants, many of whom were farmers, from owning land. In 1924 the federal government changed the immigration laws specifically to exclude Japanese. Even President Franklin Delano Roosevelt was not above such "yellow peril" prejudice. Before his 1932 presidential election, Mr. Roosevelt had shown himself entirely capable of strong "anti-Oriental racism,"[24] and as president he showed himself to be equally capable of harsh discrimination.

In 1941, before the start of the World War II, approximately 120,000 Japanese Americans lived in Washington, Oregon, California, and Arizona, with three-quarters living in California. Seventy percent were citizens because they were born in the United States; American law prohibited the 30 percent born overseas from ever becoming citizens. By any measure, "Japanese Americans were model members of society."[25] The 120,000 Japanese Americans living on the West Coast in December 1941 also were fiercely patriotic.[26]

By June 1942, no Japanese Americans lived on the West Coast. All had been forced to store or quickly sell their possessions (often at a steep discount) and report to train and bus stations, bringing only what they could carry. Once there, they were taken to "assembly centers, most of which were located at fairgrounds and racetracks . . . [surrounded by] barbed wire and searchlights, and the guard of guns."[27] From these centers, the American government moved them to ten "relocation camps" where most spent the next three years.

At the time of this forced evacuation, no evidence suggested that Japanese Americans supported Japan's imperial war efforts. And no credible evidence surfaced in the days and weeks following the

---

23. Commission, *Personal Justice*, p. 3.

24. Daniels, *Concentration Camps*, p. 9.

25. Ibid., p. 4.

26. Commission, *Personal Justice*, p. 61.

27. Hersey, "Behind Barbed Wire," p. 59.

attack on Pearl Harbor. As the war progressed, the *nisei* (second-generation Japanese Americans) released from the camps to join the U.S. Army quickly distinguished themselves in battle and returned home the "most decorated and distinguished combat unit of World War II."[28] In terms of sheer numbers, the millions of German Americans and Italian Americans posed a greater threat, yet no serious consideration was given to their internment.

Many individuals and organizations—with a wide variety of contradictory positions—had knowledge that might affect the decision to put Japanese Americans into concentration camps. Without exception, the United States intelligence community opposed internment because it could find no credible grounds for such a massive and repressive action. Even the consistently conservative FBI dismissed claimed threats, unambiguously stating that it had "no evidence of planned sabotage."[29] Indeed, in a report that went directly to the president, intelligence analyst Curtis B. Munson simply stated: "There will be no armed uprising of Japanese. . . . [T]he local Japanese are loyal to the United States. . . . We do not believe that they would be . . . any more disloyal than any other racial group in the United States with whom we went to war."[30] Most cabinet members also opposed internment. Secretary of War Henry L. Stimson correctly worried that the forced relocation of Japanese Americans would "make a tremendous hole in our constitutional system."[31]

Some others, however, advocated exclusion. Army General John L. De Witt was responsible for West Coast security and a staunch supporter of relocation. In February 1942 he wrote:

> The Japanese race is an enemy race and while many second and third generation Japanese born on United States soil, possessed of United States citizenship, have become "Americanized," the racial strains are undiluted. . . . It . . . therefore . . . follows that along the vital Pacific Coast . . . potential enemies, of Japanese extraction, are at large today.[32]

Los Angeles Mayor Fletcher Bowron observed in a radio address: "Right here in our city are those who may spring to action at an

28. Commission, *Personal Justice*, p. 3.

29. Daniels, *Concentration Camps*, p. 48.

30. Ibid., p. 54.

31. Ibid., p. 79.

32. Ibid., p. 6.

appointed time . . . wherein each of our little Japanese friends will know his part in the event of any possible invasion or air raid."[33] There also were self-serving hate groups that used the war to further their economic interests. One such group, the Grower-Shipper Vegetable Association, stated its position unambiguously: "If all the Japs were removed tomorrow, we'd never miss them. . . . [W]hite farmers can take over and produce everything the Jap grows. And we don't want them back when the war ends, either."[34]

In the end, though, only one person could make such a decision. That person was the president, and the decision was really quite simple, for he had only two viable choices. He could side with the intelligence experts and cabinet members who told him that there was no threat and that the concentration of Japanese Americans was unnecessary and undesirable. Or he could appear decisive in a season of defeat by siding with the voices of fear, hatred, and hysteria. On February 19, 1942, Franklin Roosevelt signed Executive Order 9066 authorizing the secretary of war to relocate "any or all persons . . . [at] his discretion . . . [and] to provide . . . transportation, food, shelter, and other accommodations as may be necessary."[35] Following the order, only Japanese Americans were relocated; 120,000 spent most of the war years isolated in hastily built relocation centers under armed military guard (see Box 1).

Decades passed before the U.S. government finally admitted that the internment of Japanese Americans was unjust. In 1976, President Gerald Ford asked Congress to investigate the internment, and in 1980 Congress established the Commission on Wartime Relocation and Internment of Civilians. The commission reported in 1982 that the internment had been wrong. In 1988, Congress passed and President Reagan signed a bill specifying $20,000 in compensation for each person unnecessarily interned and a formal letter of apology from the U.S. government. Finally, in November 1989 President George Bush signed a separate bill authorizing payment. Checks and formal apologies were sent in three waves, with the third and final set sent in 1992.

33. Daniels, *Concentration Camps*, p. 41.

34. Commission, *Personal Justice*, p. 69.

35. Daniels, *Concentration Camps*, p. 113.

BOX 1 THE RELOCATION CENTERS

Eleven relocation centers were built, starting with the camp at Manzanar, California, in June 1941. That camp eventually held 10,200 Japanese Americans. The other camps (along with their estimated populations) were Gila River, Arizona (13,400); Granada, Colorado (7,600); Heart Mountain, Wyoming (11,100); Jerome, Arkansas (8,600); Mindoka, California (9,990); Poston, Arizona (18,000); Rohwer, Arkansas (8,500); Topaz, Utah (8,300); and the two camps at Tule Lake, California (18,800). Following the release of the Japanese Americans from these camps at the conclusion of World War II, several were maintained on a standby basis through 1971, including those at Tule Lake, California.

Sources: John Hersey, "Behind Barbed Wire," *New York Times Magazine,* September 11, 1988, pp. 56–59, 73–74, 76, 120–21; Peter Wright and John C. Armor, *Manzanar* (New York: Times Books, 1988); Commission on Wartime Relocation and Internment of Civilians, *Personal Justice Denied* (Washington, D.C.: U.S. Government Printing Office, 1982); Roger Daniels, *The Decision to Relocate the Japanese Americans* (Philadelphia: Lippincott, 1975); Roger Daniels, *Concentration Camps, U.S.A.: Japanese Americans and World War II* (New York: Holt, Rinehart and Winston, 1972).

Stages of Corporate and Governmental Deviance

Long-standing episodes of organizational deviance generally go through three stages. In the first or "introduction of deviance" stage, one or more individuals authorize or commit deviant actions. In the second stage, "institutionalization of deviance," the behavior takes on a life of its own, often continuing for reasons unrelated to why it started. Participants typically think little about its consequences for themselves or their organization. The third stage, "reactions," is reached if the public somehow finds out about the behavior. Courageous insiders may blow the whistle and alert the rest of us, or suspicious outsiders may take a careful look and reveal what they found.

Introduction of Deviance

In this first stage, individuals or groups define a new situation as organizationally problematic. These problems vary greatly, including designing an automobile quickly to compete with foreign imports or responding to fears of disloyalty in times of war.

Faced with such problems, organizational members try to devise solutions. They may establish guidelines to which subordinates must adapt, such as the "Rule of 2000" at Ford. Alternatively, they may mandate a specific action such as concentrating Japanese Americans. Their initial actions may not even be deviant. Participants in a long-running price-fixing conspiracy among companies making electrical equipment (see Selection 5) built cooperative networks and learned to trust one another when they worked together, with government prompting, to develop standards for interchangeable parts. Their links were strengthened when government again asked them to cooperate with one another, this time to keep prices from plummeting during the Great Depression. This early legal cooperation to solve problems established the personal contacts, experiences, and trust that later encouraged illegal cooperation to fix prices. In the words of one participant, fixing prices for these companies was "as easy as falling off a log."[36]

To illustrate how deviance is introduced, we will now describe one governmental agency's abuse of its unique investigative powers. The agency is the FBI, and the behavior in question violated basic First Amendment rights (see Box 2).

FBI Investigation of CISPES.[37]   In the early 1980s, many Americans were upset by the Salvadoran government's violence against its political opponents and by U.S. support for that government. They had good reasons to be upset. Right-wing "death squads" had murdered many people, including four religious missionaries. Despite these atrocities, the American government continued to provide financial aid to the El Salvadoran government.

In opposition to American policy, a group of Americans and their organizations joined in late 1980 to form the Committee in Solidarity with the People of El Salvador (CISPES). The FBI responded by launching a series of investigations of CISPES that were not

36. Richard Austin Smith, *Corporations in Crisis* (New York: Anchor, 1966), p. 121.

37. U.S. Congress, House, Subcommittee on Civil and Constitutional Rights of Committee on the Judiciary, *CISPES and FBI Counter-Terrorism Investigations* (Washington, D.C.: U.S. Government Printing Office, 1988); U.S. Congress, Senate, Select Committee on Intelligence, *The FBI and CISPES* (Washington, D.C.: U.S. Government Printing Office, 1989).

BOX 2 FIRST AMENDMENT RIGHTS

The First Amendment gives American citizens the right to disagree publicly with their government. While carrying out its domestic investigative responsibilities, the FBI therefore is required to avoid actions so extensive or intrusive that they violate the First Amendment rights of those who dissent. To investigate groups simply because they oppose policies of people who currently happen to control foreign policy or government agencies is to discourage free speech and the expression of political opinion:

> The mere collection of publicly available information can have a significant adverse effect . . . on people's exercise of their constitutional rights. The fear of possible government surveillance can . . . [discourage] people from participating in certain activities. It is impossible to know how, or even if, the information collected may come back to haunt someone who has done absolutely nothing wrong. But experience has shown . . . that in cases involving the intelligence surveillance of political organizations, the potential for abuse tends to outweigh the benefit of the information.

Source: U.S. Congress, House, Subcommittee on Civil and Constitutional Rights of Committee on the Judiciary, *CISPES* and *FBI Counter-Terrorism Investigations* (Washington, D.C.: U.S. Government Printing Office, 1988), p. 11.

productive, violated the law, and contradicted the letter and spirit of its own policies.

FBI actions began routinely enough. In January 1981, the FBI learned from the U.S. Park Service that CISPES planned a large demonstration. In June, it sent Frank Varelli to infiltrate the Dallas chapter of CISPES. It also launched an investigation to determine whether CISPES was an agent of a foreign government and thus required to register. Its conclusions were negative; CISPES was not a foreign agent. Up to this point, the FBI had violated no laws or internal policies except for sending Mr. Varelli before it had obtained official authorization.

Beginning in March 1983, however, the FBI launched a massive investigation of CISPES that gradually involved all 59 of its field offices. Initial efforts produced 178 spin-off investigations, some of which lasted into 1988. But, despite clear evidence that Mr. Varelli was unreliable, and ignoring its own conclusion that CISPES was not a foreign government agent, the FBI devoted 20,000 employee hours to the project, collecting information on 2,375 people and 1,330 organizations. As recounted during congressional hearings:

> The FBI undertook . . . photographs during demonstrations, surveillance of rallies on college campuses, and attendance at a mass at a local university. . . . In one case a Xavier University professor was investigated on the basis of an exam question and a speaker invited to the class. Spin-off investigations were apparently initiated solely on the basis of attendance at the showing of a CISPES-sponsored film, the appearance of names on lists of participants at CISPES conferences, and similar associations [with CISPES] having no other relevance to the purpose of the original investigation.[38]

According to the Congress and FBI Director William Sessions,[39] three things were wrong with the agency's actions. First, the FBI launched its investigation on the basis of allegations that were not credible. Though it claimed to base some of its actions on assertions that the Nicaraguan government was directing CISPES actions, the FBI actually had no such evidence.

Second, the FBI's investigations were far broader than would have been justified even if the allegations had been true. Professors' exams and college students attending mass, the Congress contended, should not be the basis for terrorist investigations. Nor should automobile bumper stickers critical of U.S. policy in El Salvador. Consider a cable sent by the Louisville field office to FBI headquarters in Washington, D.C.:

> On November 7, 1983 a vehicle described as a 1976 Datsun, 4-door, green, bearing the Kentucky vehicle tag KXM-498, and bumper sticker "US OUT OF EL SALVADOR" was observed in front of University of Louisville School of Law at 12:20 p.m., at which time Nicaraguan judges Mariano Barahona and Humberto Obregon were speaking on "Justice and the Legal System in Nicaragua" at a public lecture sponsored in part by CISPES.[40]

Third, the FBI continued its investigation, even though the information it gathered did not meet its own criteria for continua-

38. U.S. Congress, House, *CISPES*, p. 11.

39. U.S. Congress, Senate, *The FBI*, p. 1.

40. Ibid., p. 243.

tion. Very early in its investigation, FBI agents and administrators should have known that CISPES was a group of Americans exercising their First Amendment rights. The FBI, however, continued to investigate CISPES. Among the reasons given were complaints that critics of government policy were "pressuring legislators," an entirely legal activity that most of us call lobbying.

No single leader or decision therefore caused the introduction of deviance into the FBI in the CISPES case. Instead, the deviance was the result of a combination of people, events, and procedures. An FBI informant and employee initially provided distorted information. Domestic protest against El Salvador attracted the FBI's attention and apparently personally offended some FBI officials.

In addition, the FBI's internal administrative procedures were flawed in at least three ways. The agency provided inadequate organizational control over the employee in the Terrorism Section who made such decisions. It accepted, without serious questioning, material from ideologically motivated outside groups, and converted unsubstantiated assertions into postulates for future action. Orders and actions that originally justified by the FBI's antiterrorist responsibilities lost their purpose, focusing instead on simple public disagreement with U.S. government policy.

The FBI lacked the resources needed to avoid initiating this deviance. It had no in-house expertise on Central America or international politics generally, although it was conducting investigations in these areas. Further, two busy upper-level administrators were responsible for protecting First Amendment rights, and both failed to monitor the CISPES investigation.

Institutionalization of Deviance

Deviant solutions to organizational problems often become part of the fabric of institutional life. Participants no longer think very much about their deviance, save for necessary but taken-for-granted precautions. In fact, even their motives can change as their involvement continues.

Consider the changing motives that cause some executives to conceal known drug hazards. The drug development process takes five to ten years and involves a wide variety of specialists in many technical and administrative areas. During this time, important relationships and commitments develop among the participating people and departments. Hiding hazards is not planned in advance. Instead, it results from a process of increasing commitments, as illustrated by one pharmaceutical executive's description of how his scientists' motives change:

> The chemist who synthesizes a new compound is very possessive about it. It is his offspring, and he defends it like a son or daughter. Also the pharmacologist who shows that this new compound has certain effects of therapeutic value sees it as his baby. It is not so much that they will lie and cheat to defend it, but they will be biased.[41]

In all organizations, employees who initiate deviance move on to new positions as time passes. Their replacements find that deviant behavior is an expected part of their new positions. These new members conclude that they must either comply with role expectations or be replaced by people more willing to do as they are told. Thus, once deviant actions are institutionalized, they become intertwined with legitimate ones, and both become routine.

We have already presented several examples of deviance that became institutionalized. Beech-Nut passed bogus apple juice as the real thing for five years, and the U.S. government continued its internment of Japanese Americans virtually without challenge. In the following section, we analyze in detail one example of institutionalized deviance—Gulf Oil's illegal political campaign contributions.

Gulf Oil's Illegal Campaign Contributions.[42]   For more than fifteen years, Gulf Oil Corporation laundered and distributed corporate funds to American politicians. The system worked well, and those who ran it hardly thought about what they were doing, even though their actions were blatantly illegal (see Box 3).

Routine orders and illegal cash moved along the following path. When the head of Gulf's Government Relations Office in Washington, D.C., needed money, he called Gulf's headquarters in Pittsburgh. There, the company's comptroller authorized its treasurer

41. John Braithwaite, *Corporate Crime in the Pharmaceutical Industry* (London: Routledge and Kegan Paul, 1984), pp. 93–94.

42. *Securities and Exchange Commission, Plaintiff,* v. *Gulf Oil Corporation, Claude C. Wild, Jr., Defendants, Report of the Special Review Committee of the Board of Directors of Gulf Oil Corporation,* United States District Court, District of Columbia, December 30, 1975.

BOX 3 CORPORATE CAMPAIGN CONTRIBUTIONS

Corporate campaign contributions have been illegal for almost ninety years. In 1907 the Congress passed what came to be known as the "Corrupt Practices Act," a law that bans corporations from providing funds to people campaigning for federal office. The states then quickly passed similar laws outlawing the contribution of corporate funds to candidates for state and local office.

The logic behind these laws is straightforward. The resources of America's largest corporations far exceed those of individuals, so corporations are in a position to make large monetary contributions to candidates and unduly influence the actions of those elected. Corrupt practices acts are intended to limit corporate influence on the electoral process.

Corporations nonetheless have considerable clout when it comes to financing political campaigns. They are allowed to use corporate funds to administer political action committees (PACs), which collect voluntary donations from employees and give this money to people running for public office. But corporations are not allowed to contribute corporate funds.

Sources: James Ring Adams, *The Big Fix: Inside the S & L Scandal* (New York: Wiley, 1990); Brooks Jackson, *Honest Graft: Big Money and the American Political Process* (New York: Knopf, 1988); Amitai Etzioni, *Capital Corruption: The New Attack on American Democracy* (San Diego: Harcourt Brace Jovanovich, 1984); Larry Sabato, *PAC Power: Inside the World of Political Action Committees* (New York: Norton, 1984).

to transfer money to a nearly inactive Gulf subsidiary in the Bahamas. A Gulf employee in the Bahamas then laundered the money by passing it through several Bahamian bank accounts. The cleaned cash was then taken to Washington, where employees in Gulf's Government Relations Office secretly distributed it to politicians. This system operated for nearly 15 years, distributing slightly more than $5 million to hundreds of politicians at the national, state, and local levels.

What made Gulf's system of laundering and distributing so elegant was its use of employees who did not have, need, or probably want complete information or responsibility. They simply made small contributions to the overall system by quietly doing what was defined for them as part of their jobs. Consider the role of Gulf's comptrollers. After the comptroller who helped develop the system left, three other people sequentially occupied his position. None of them had to make any difficult decisions, much less consciously involve themselves in criminal activities. They merely were told that they would receive requests for money. All they did was write notes to treasurers asking that the money be provided. Easy to do and easy to live with.

Gulf's treasurers also did little and could choose to know very little. They were simply told that the account in the Bahamas "was highly sensitive and confidential."[43] All they did was send money to that account on receipt of a note from a comptroller. Tens of other Gulf employees engaged in similar actions, knowing or choosing to know very little and making small contributions to the overall system as part of their work. The actions and attitudes of one Gulf employee who delivered cash clearly illustrate the limited knowledge and responsibility required of individuals in organizations in which deviance is institutionalized:

> Most often delivery would be at an airport or at the recipient's office, but occasionally it would be at a place suggestive of a desire for secrecy. . . . [H]e handed an envelope to Representative Richard L. Roudebush of Indiana . . . in the men's room of a motel in Indianapolis. . . . Time and again, asked whether he knew what was in the envelope he had delivered, he replied, "I do not," or "I have no knowledge." A minor figure, . . . [he was] apparently content to spin constantly above the cities, plains, and mountains of America, not knowing why, not wanting to know why.[44]

It is important to recognize that institutionalized deviance at Gulf existed alongside normal organizational activities. Some Gulf employees did spend some of their working days moving money, but even these people could rationalize that they spent the rest of their time on legal activities. Most people spent their time moving oil and gas.

Reactions to Corporate and Governmental Deviance

Institutionalized deviance typically continues until challenged from inside or outside the organization. In some situations, internal

---

43. Ibid., p. 223.

44. John Brooks, "The Bagman," in Rosabeth Moss Kanter and Barry A. Stein (eds.), *Life in Organizations: Workplaces as People Experience Them* (New York: Basic Books, 1979).

whistle-blowers step forward with accusations and evidence of wrongdoing. At other times, the media, prosecutors, or victims challenge organizational actions.

Organizations have their own versions of events and respond to accusations of deviance with accusations and assertions of their own. In the exchange of claims and counterclaims, whether an organizational action actually comes to be seen as deviant is fundamentally a matter of definition.

The Organizational Deviance-defining Process[45]

Many sociologists who study marijuana use, prostitution, and other actions by individuals assert that no behavior is intrinsically deviant.[46] Instead, they argue that actions are deviant only if they are defined as deviant. They suggest that the deviance-defining process happens in the following way:

> For deviance to become a social fact, somebody must perceive an act, situation, or event as a departure from social norms, must categorize that perception, must report that perception to others, must get them to accept this definition of the situation, and must obtain a response that conforms to their definition. Unless all these requirements are met, deviance as a social fact does not come into being.[47]

We believe that a similar view of the deviance-defining process should be taken for organizational actions. When viewed through this lense, no organizational action is intrinsically deviant. Instead, organizational actions are deviant only to the extent that they are perceived, reported, accepted, treated, and defined as deviant.

This perspective emphasizes the disagreement that typically surrounds definitions of organizational deviance. Whereas some voices insist that what an organization is doing is wrong, other voices insist that nothing improper is taking place. Members of the general public hearing both voices may be confused by the contradictory assertions. Even when there does appear to be a consensus, as with

45. For an earlier statement see M. David Ermann and Richard J. Lundman, *Corporate Deviance* (New York: Holt, Rinehart and Winston, 1982), pp. 16–30.

46. A classic statement of this position is by Howard S. Becker, *Outsiders: Studies in the Sociology of Deviance* (New York: Free Press, 1963).

47. Earl Rubington and Martin S. Weinberg (eds.), *Deviance: The Interactionist Perspective*, 2nd ed. (New York: Macmillan, 1973), p. vii.

a corporation that knowingly releases an unsafe product, there are still important differences in reporting, perception, acceptance, and definition. Agreement on broad generalities does not necessarily yield a consensus on what is to be defined as deviant.

Consider the Department of Justice's accusations of price-fixing directed against some of the nation's most visible colleges and universities, including Harvard, Princeton, and Yale, at the start of the 1990s.[48] Over 50 colleges and universities allegedly conspired to fix financial aid and tuition fees for students and salaries for faculty. Following the accusations, some of the accused institutions acknowledged membership in what they called the "Overlap Group," admitted fixing financial aid offers made to students who had been accepted for admission by more than one institution, and defended their actions. Here are the words of former Williams College President Francis Oakley: "Overlap . . . exchange[s] information about family and student resources of students accepted by more than one Overlap school. . . . Were Overlap to disappear, colleges and universities . . . would come under increasing pressure . . . to . . . use financial aid to try to 'buy' particularly attractive applicants."[49]

Many people agreed because they saw nothing wrong with colleges and universities fixing offers of financial aid. They believed that colleges and universities already charge outrageous fees, especially the tony institutions that were the targets of Department of Justice accusations. They argued that if Overlap and similar arrangements[50] were eliminated, the price of education at these places would be even higher. They rejected efforts at labeling.

48. Herschel Grossman, "Rebirth of the Ivy Cartel," *Wall Street Journal*, January 26, 1994, p. A15; William Honan, "M.I.T. Wins Right to Share Financial Aid Data in Antitrust Accord," *New York Times*, December 23, 1993, p. A13; Anthony DePalma, "M.I.T. Ruled Guilty in Antitrust Case," *New York Times*, September 3, 1992, p. A1; Rohit Menezes, "The Anti-Trust Saga: Williams' Future Hangs in the Balance," *The Williams Observer*, November 14, 1990, p. 1; Robert Weisberg, "Justice Department Opens Investigation of Williams," *The Williams Record*, September 12, 1989, p. 1; "U.S. Price Fixing Probe Said to Add Hopkins and Goucher," *Evening Sun*, September 15, 1989, p. F4; Robert Weisberg, "Wesleyan Senior Files Lawsuit Against Williams, 11 Others," *The Williams Record*, September 26, 1989, p. 1; Francis Oakley, "The Antitrust Inquiry and Higher Education," *Williams Reports* (Williams College, Office of Public Information), October 1989; Mike Elliot, "Justice Department Suspects Schools of Price-Fixing, Antitrust Violations," *U: The National College Newspaper*, December 1989, p. 1.

49. Oakley, "The Antitrust," pp. 4–5. Francis Oakley is now professor of history at Williams College.

50. For a similar organization ("The Augmented Seven") involving Harvard and seven other universities, see Rosovsky, *The University*, p. 54.

But others defined Overlap agreements as deviant. They asserted that colleges and universities, like businesses, should be bound by free-market forces. Without competition, institutions would be free to make artificially low financial aid offers, denying students a full range of financial aid possibilities while saving money that could then be spent in other areas, including salaries for administrators.

Among those defining Overlap agreements as deviant were the attorneys working inside the Antitrust Division of the Justice Department. They pushed their definition and threatened legal action. Most of the institutions decided not to take their chances in court or experience the negative publicity that would accompany it. They signed consent decrees indicating that while they had not necessarily been in the business of fixing financial aid offers, they would stop communicating with each other about such offers.

Massachusetts Institute of Technology (MIT) resisted the Antitrust Division's definitions of its actions, went to court, and lost. MIT then appealed and the higher court instructed the lower court to reconsider the case. By then, however, Antitrust attorneys were under considerable pressure to abandon the case,[51] so they settled with MIT. The agreement stipulated that institutions must practice need-based financial aid and can talk to each other via computer only after independent auditors report "gross discrepancies" in financial aid offers.

In the wake of the agreement, MIT and Antitrust attorneys both claimed their definition of Overlap and other financial aid practices had been vindicated. They were both correct because both definitions were recognized by the settlement. The only actors who clearly did not emerge victorious were students applying for financial aid. Without competition, institutions are free to make artificifially low financial aid offers, denying students the full range of financial aid possibilities.

In these and many other situations, individuals and groups attempt to hold organizations to their own particular normative expectations. When people or groups feel that an organization has violated those norms, they may try to label the organization and its actions deviant.

---

51. For examples see these editorials: "Drop the MIT Case," *Washington Post*, October 14, 1993, p. A30; "The MIT Case: Time to Back Off," *New York Times*, December 27, 1993, p. A12.

Organizations do not stand passively to the side and allow their fate to be shaped by others' definitions and reactions. Instead, nearly all organizations work very diligently to escape a deviant label. They build reservoirs of goodwill and provide alternative accounts of their behavior to interested audiences. Organizations also sometimes play verbal hardball as they pitch words at their accusers and audiences.

Goodwill. Organizations try to build goodwill long before anyone has accused them of specific deviant acts. Writing about business organizations, sociologist Edwin H. Sutherland (see Box 4) observed in 1949: "The corporation attempts not only to 'fix' particular accusations against it, but also to develop good will before accusations are made."[52]

Mobil Oil is an especially good example of a corporation that has worked hard to develop goodwill.[53] For almost 25 years, Mobil has been a generous contributor to the Public Broadcasting Service (public television), prominent for its sponsorship of public television's Masterpiece Theater. Mobil's actions are an important part of its overall public relations effort to reach the "loyal, affluent, and well-educated audience, particularly the elusive . . . 'light viewers' who prefer 'Masterpiece Theater' to 'Melrose Place.'"[54] A Mobil executive responsible for public relations explained that being "associated with excellence helps present the company view." He continued: "A reader sees a Mobil message and associates it with Big Oil. So he may be wary. But he also associates it with the company that brings him [Public Broadcasting Service programs] so maybe he's a little more open-minded and a little more receptive."[55] A middle-level Mobil executive stated that the purpose of sponsoring public television programs was "to win credibility and . . . provide access to, and rapport with, key groups and special publics—

52. Edwin H. Sutherland, *White Collar Crime* (New York: Dryden, 1949), p. 32.

53. M. David Ermann, "The Operative Goals of Corporate Philanthropy: Contributions to the Public Broadcasting Service, 1972–1976," *Social Problems* 25 (1978): 504–14.

54. Laura Bird, "Public TV Plugs Getting Closer to Network Ads," *Wall Street Journal*, August 10, 1992, p. B4. Also see Elizabeth Kolbert, "A New 'Good Evening' From 'Masterpiece Theater,'" *New York Times*, February 24, 1993, p. C13.

55. Quoted in Irwin Ross, "Public Relations Isn't Kid-Glove Stuff at Mobil," *Fortune* 94 (1976): p. 110.

BOX 4 EDWIN H. SUTHERLAND, 1883–1950

Edwin H. Sutherland received his Ph.D. in sociology from the University of Chicago in 1913 and spent most of his academic career at Indiana University. He made many important contributions to the sociological study of crime. To us, his most important contribution was his analysis of what he called "white-collar crime." Professor Sutherland coined the phrase and most contemporary researchers in the field trace their work to his pioneering efforts.

In 1939, Professor Sutherland presented a paper at the annual meeting of the American Sociological Society. He spoke as president of the society and entitled his address "White Collar Criminality." In his paper, he demonstrated that crime in the suites was as worthy of sociological attention as was crime in the streets.

Professor Sutherland followed his presidential address with a book, *White Collar Crime,* in 1949. This book was the culmination of nearly a quarter century of frequently single-handed research. Although not permitted to identify the corporations because his publisher feared libel suits and because his university feared a reduction in corporate funding, Professor Sutherland reported that seventy of the nation's largest corporations had been convicted of a total of 980 illegal actions and that many of the corporations had been convicted more than once. Of those with at least one conviction, the average was four, making them "habitual offenders" under then existing laws in most states and eligible for contemporary "three strikes and you are out" sentencing.

In 1983, the "uncut version" of *White Collar Crime* was published, restoring the integrity of the original book by identifying the corporations studied.

Sources: Edwin H. Sutherland, *White Collar Crime* (New York: Dryden, 1949); Edwin H. Sutherland, with an introduction by Gilbert Geis and Colin Goff, *White Collar Crime: The Uncut Version* (New Haven, CT: Yale University Press, 1983).

legislators and regulators; the press; intellectuals and academics."[56] The next-level Mobil executive said, "These programs, we think, build enough acceptance to allow us to get tougher on substantive issues."[57]

56. Quoted in Phillis S. McGarath, *Business Credibility: The Critical Factors* (New York: The Conference Board, 1976), p. 30.

57. Ross, "Public Relations," p. 110.

Mobil is not alone among corporations in building goodwill in anticipation of difficult times. Each Friday evening, "Wall Street Week with Louis Rukeyser" on public television begins and ends with acknowledgments of financial support from major corporations. Internationally based corporations seek to Americanize their image by supporting U.S. Olympic teams, with Subaru providing automobiles for the skiers. Still others, like McDonald's and its Ronald McDonald Houses, use high-visibility charitable activities to garner goodwill.

Building goodwill is not limited to the world of business. The Internal Revenue Service provides a toll-free 800 number in an effort to keep taxpayers happy. Colleges and universities make their facilities available to community organizations, and faculty members regularly leave campus to talk to community groups about their research. Police departments have community relations officers who speak to groups about crime prevention, organize neighborhood crime watches, run "safety city" programs for small children, and dare older children to stay away from drugs.

Alternative Accounts.　　When accused of deviance, organizations provide alternative accounts of their behavior. These accounts differ very little from those offered by accused individuals.[58] Organizations attribute troublesome actions to particular individuals ("scapegoating"), assert that no one was injured ("denial of injury"), and accuse attackers of being dishonest and self-serving ("condemnation of the condemners").

Immediately following the Valdez oil tanker disaster, for instance, Exxon was unprepared to offer anything more than traditional accounts of what had happened,[59] and so it initially directed attention to the tanker's captain. The corporation also asserted that the environmental damage was minimal, and it suggested that the Coast Guard was responsible for the delay in starting to clean up the mess.

58. See especially Gresham M. Sykes and David Matza, "Techniques of Neutralization: A Theory of Delinquency," *American Sociological Review* 22 (1957): 664–70. Also see C. Wright Mills, "Situated Actions and Vocabularies of Motive," *American Sociological Review* 5 (1940): 904–13; Lawrence Nichols, "Reconceptualizing Social Accounts: An Agenda for Theory Building and Empirical Research," *Current Perspectives in Social Theory* 10 (1990): 113–44.

59. William J. Small, "Exxon Valdez: How to Spend Billions and Still Get a Black Eye," *Public Relations Review* 17 (1991): 9–25; Allana Sullivan, "Rawl Wishes He'd Visited Valdez Sooner," *Wall Street Journal,* June 30, 1989, p. B3; John Holusha, "Exxon's Public-Relations Problem," *New York Times,* April 21, 1989, p. C1.

Audiences.   Observing this process of accusation and response are audiences. These audiences are large and diverse, and they can cause significant damage to successfully labeled organizations. The general public may avoid purchasing products from deviant businesses, or Congress may reduce public funding for colleges and universities. Regulatory agencies may force corporations to undertake expensive remedial actions. Consumers may sue for past injuries, and Civilian Review Boards may be instituted to monitor police actions.

However, audiences typically have two significant weaknesses. First, audience members lack the knowledge to independently assess the accuracy of accusations and responses. According to attorneys representing families of people killed and injured in General Motors pickups, the side-saddle gasoline tanks on the 6 million trucks sold between 1973 and 1987 are gasoline bombs waiting for side-collision ignitions.[60] According to GM, the trucks are safe. For most of the rest of us who serve as audience members, we cannot possibly know who to believe because we cannot gather or interpret the information needed to make independent assessments.

Equally important, accused organizations typically are more powerful than their accusers; they can craft more compelling accounts and disseminate them more effectively. Accuser's voices typically are more muted, less frequent, less well crafted, and appear less appealing. Audience members therefore hear and see much more of what accused organizations want heard and seen.

In sum, organizational deviance is the result of public interactions between accusers and responding organizations, with interested audiences as final arbiters. Whether a perceived departure from social norms comes to be widely labeled and penalized as deviant depends on the power of the accusers to make their labels stick, as compared with the power of the organizations to resist labeling. Because audience members cannot independently assess what comes their way, and because organizations almost always are more powerful than their accusers, audiences rarely label or penalize organizations. We shall now illustrate these points by looking at accusations of deviance directed at the Central Intelligence Agency (CIA).

60. James Bennet, "U.S. and G.M. End Truck Case Without Recall," *New York Times*, December 3, 1994, p. A1; Douglas Lavin and Joseph B. White, "Agency Opens Safety Probe of GM Pickups," *Wall Street Journal*, December 9, 1992, p. A3.

Deviance and the CIA.[61]   In the early 1970s, the Central Intelligence Agency was experiencing another of its periodic rounds of attack and accusation by outsiders. Foremost among the numerous accusations was the assertion that the agency gathered domestic intelligence information. Despite legislation banning internal spying, the CIA was accused of gathering information on antiwar and other dissident groups. Some accusers asserted that as much as one-third of the officially listed CIA work force of 18,000 was involved in domestic intelligence gathering, that CIA personnel had infiltrated over 250 domestic political groups, and that the agency had assembled secret files on thousands of Americans.

Congress and the president responded to these accusations by establishing separate investigative bodies. Both attracted an audience, although their final reports sponsored very different versions of CIA activities. A Senate Special Subcommittee on Intelligence strongly supported accusations of misconduct. In contrast, the Rockefeller Commission concluded that no widespread pattern of deviant activity existed, and that accusations of domestic intelligence gathering were largely unfounded.

The CIA did not stand idly by and permit its fate to be determined by accusers or investigative bodies. Instead, it used its considerable organizational power to turn away accusations of deviance. It first scapegoated by arguing that it did not bear full responsibility for the infrequent, objectionable activities that may have occurred, noting that government agencies seldom question the orders of executive branch officials. It thus asserted that if it had done something wrong, it did so because others with more power had ordered these actions.

It also promoted alternative interpretations of the extent and importance of domestic spying operations. One top-level CIA official denied that any substantial injury had taken place, observing that domestic operations may have involved "some violations of rights, but nothing earth-shattering."

Bolder tactics were used against the agency's critics. The most prominent example involved journalist Daniel Schorr, who had disseminated classified CIA material in order to document accusa-

---

61. Weiner, *Blank Check*, pp. 111–42; William Waegel, M. David Ermann, and Alan M. Horowitz, "Organizational Responses to Imputations of Deviance," *Sociological Quarterly* 22 (1981): 43–55.

tions of agency misconduct. CIA officials argued that Mr. Schorr's action jeopardized the safety of agency personnel, with one former CIA official labeling him "Killer Schorr." Similar attempts were made to condemn vocal accusers in the House of Representatives, by noting their role in releasing secret testimony. How, the CIA asked, could the audience trust accusers who risked the lives of others by releasing information that was supposed to be secret?

These and other CIA responses to accusations of deviance succeeded. Congress imposed no meaningful constraints. In the wake of accusations of deviance, the CIA's structure, operational authority, and autonomy remained essentially unchanged.

One way to understand how little was accomplished is to examine the CIA's activities in the wake of the scandals of the early 1970s.[62] At the start of the 1980s, the CIA used "secret funds . . . hidden from Congress"[63] to develop weapons delivery and money laundering operations that helped support the *mujaheddin* resistance to the Soviet Union's occupation of Afghanistan. In the mid-1980s, the CIA covertly sold antitank missiles to Iran in violation of a federal law requiring congressional approval. Toward the end of the decade, it diverted money from arms sales to Iran to the *contras* in Nicaragua, again violating the congressional mandate. In the early 1990s, a mole inside the CIA, Aldrich H. Ames, finally surfaced after providing the Soviet Union with information on CIA double agents and agency actions for at least eight years, in clearly the "worst security breach in the agency's history."[64] By the mid-1990s, members of Congress once again called for investigation of the CIA.[65]

In sum, individuals and groups accused the CIA of departing from important social norms by engaging in domestic intelligence gathering. They alerted others to their perceptions and argued that something needed to be done. The CIA used its considerable power to respond to accusations and shape audience reactions. It scapegoated, denied that serious injury had occurred, and con-

---

62. "Frontline," PBS, April 21, 1991; Weiner, *Blank Check*, pp. 143–213.

63. Weiner, *Blank Check*, p. 164.

64. Tim Weiner, "Congress Decides to Conduct Study of Need for C.I.A.," *New York Times*, September 28, 1994, p. A17. Also see Tim Weiner, "Report Finds Ames's Sabotage More Vast Than C.I.A. Admitted," *New York Times*, September 24, 1994, p. A1; Anthony Lewis, "Maurice the Waiter," *New York Times*, December 14, 1992, p. A17.

65. Weiner, "Congress Decides."

demned those accusing the agency of misconduct. Although it did experience some very rough times, the agency continued with business pretty much as usual. Deviant labels have repeatedly been directed at the CIA, but few have stuck.

Punishing Organizational Deviance

Punishment of organizational deviance is relatively rare. The reasons are several (see Box 5), but one is most important. Organizations are wealthy and powerful actors, and they use their resources well. Consider the United States Sentencing Commission that Congress established in 1984.[66] The commission's goal was to increase the certainty and uniformity of punishment for both individuals and corporations convicted in federal courts. The commission began with individuals and submitted its recommendations to Congress in 1987. There was little sustained reaction, and so the Commission turned its attention to sentencing guidelines for corporations.

When the commission publicly circulated its draft guidelines in 1990, a storm of self-serving corporate protest ensued. Corporate representatives described the proposals as "extremely harsh," "critically flawed," and "overwhelmingly intrusive." Corporate lobbying was not only intensive, it was also very effective. The Department of Justice withdrew its previous support for the guidelines. The White House instructed the commission to recall, revise, and resubmit its guidelines. In 1992, the commission's more timid guidelines went into effect.[67] Recent efforts at expansion have met the same corporate resistance.[68]

Even when guidelines and laws are in place, organizations use their resources in other ways. For example, an organization, the Industrial Crisis Institute, and a journal, *Public Relations Review,* shape corporate responses in the minutes and hours following major crises. Industrial Crisis Institute president Paul Shrivastava

---

66. Amitai Etzioni, "Going Soft on Corporate Crime," *Wilmington News Journal,* April 15, 1990, p. G1.

67. Joseph E. Murphy, "Protections, Incentives for Self-Policing Lacking," *National Law Journal,* March 8, 1993, p. S12.

68. Richard B. Schmitt, "Plan for Tough Pollution Penalties Sparks Opposition from Business," *Wall Street Journal,* March 14, 1994, p. B4; David Hanson, "New Guidelines Would Dictate Corporate Fines," *Chemical and Engineering News* 72 (February 7, 1994): 18.

BOX 5 PUBLIC OPINION AND
ORGANIZATIONAL DEVIANCE

Public indifference is *not* among the explanations for the infrequent punishment of organizational deviance. Public opinion surveys consistently reveal strong condemnation of organizationally deviant actions, especially when the behavior causes illness, injury, or death. In a survey of members of the public, participants were asked to assign penalties to forty-one offenses: "Knowingly manufacturing and selling contaminated food that results in death" was given the third highest sentence (behind "assassination of a public official" and "killing of a police officer in the course of a terrorist hijacking of a plane"). This offense was punished more severely than "killing someone during a serious argument," "forcible rape of a stranger in a park," and "armed robbery of a bank."

Other findings also reveal strong public reaction to organizational deviance. Research has consistently shown that the general public believes that white collar criminals are treated too leniently. Similarly, the public considers corporations that harm innocent people to be more reckless and morally wrong, and deserving of more serious punishment, than individuals who commit identical acts under identical circumstances.

Sources: Peter Grabosky, John Braithwaite, and P. R. Wilson, "The Myth of Community Tolerance Toward White-Collar Crime," *Australia and New Zealand Journal of Criminology* 20 (1987): 34; Valerie P. Hans, "Factors Affecting Lay Judgments of Corporate Wrongdoing." Paper presented at the Third European Conference of Law and Psychology, University of Oxford, Oxford, England, September 19, 1992; John Braithwaite, "Challenging Just Deserts: Punishing White Collar Criminals," *Journal of Criminal Law and Criminology* 73 (1982): 723–63; Valerie P. Hans and M. David Ermann, "Responses to Corporate Versus Individual Wrongdoing," *Law and Human Behavior* 13 (1989): 151–66.

notes that all "crises have a window of opportunity to gain control of 45 minutes to 12 hours. If you don't move in that time you might as well go back to sleep."[69] The Institute helps corporations find the high ground. It recommends sending the CEO to the scene to signal corporate interest and concern and to ensure that the

69. Holusha, "Exxon's Public-Relations Problem," p. C1.

corporation's position is a visible part of the news. Papers in *Public Relations Review* agree.[70]

When the crisis intervention fails, Litigation Services and Metricus, Inc., may be able to help.[71] Sociologists, psychologists, marketers, graphic artists, and technicians at both firms predict and shape jury decisions using pretrial opinion polls, profiles of "ideal" jurors, mock trials, shadow juries, and courtroom graphics.[72]

Two other factors also are important. Even in the best of circumstances, investigating organizational deviance is extraordinarily complex and time-consuming because organizations hide their actions.[73] During the Iran-Contra episode, hard cash came from a variety of interesting sources, including a secret Pentagon budget, a Saudi prince, and a Texas billionaire.[74] After careful laundering, conspirators used the money to purchase antitank missiles sent to Iran via Israel. The conspirators then laundered the profit from the illegal sales and used it to purchase and ship weapons for the *contras*. Despite exhaustive investigations, only a small fraction of the overall conspiracy has been brought to light.

Equally important, punishment is difficult to assign fairly. Should attention be directed at the people who committed the deviance for the organization or at the organization itself? Individuals claim that they should not be punished because the organization pressured or directed them to act as they did. Student athletes at major universities who remain eligible by cheating on examinations and submitting fraudulent summer school courses point to the extraordinary time commitments that their sport requires.[75] Corporations

70. Samuel Coad Dyer, Jr., M. Mark Miller, and Jeff Boone, "Wire Service Coverage of the Exxon Valdez Crisis," *Public Relations Review* 17 (1991): 27–36; Falguni Sen and William G. Egelhoff, "Six Years and Counting: Learning from Crisis Management at Bhopal," *Public Relations Review* 17 (1991): 69–83.

71. American Sociological Association, *Employment Bulletin*, February, 1995, p. 6, contained an opening for a position at Metricus, Inc.; Junda Woo, "Legal Beat," *Wall Street Journal*, April 14, 1993, p. B1; Stephen J. Adler, "Consultants Dope Out the Mysteries of Jurors for Clients Being Sued," *Wall Street Journal*, October 24, 1989, p. A1.

72. Adler, "Consultants Dope," p. A1.

73. Michael Benson, William J. Maakestad, Francis T. Cullen, and Gilbert Geis, "District Attorneys and Corporate Crime." Paper presented at the annual meeting of the American Society of Criminology, Montreal, 1987.

74. Weiner, *Blank Check*, pp. 199–213.

75. Sperber, *College Sports*, pp. 302–6; Peter Golenbock, *Personal Fouls: The Broken Promises and Shattered Dreams of Big Money Basketball at Jim Valvano's North Carolina State* (New York: Carroll and Graf, 1989), pp. 167–68.

and governmental agencies argue that an entire organization should not be punished for the actions of a few "bad apples" who deliberately or carelessly misunderstand what is being asked of them. Universities under NCAA investigation for improper payments to student athletes ask for leniency on the grounds that a handful of overzealous alumni boosters are responsible.[76]

In the end, though, punishment must be directed at either individuals or organizations, for there are no other choices. We therefore conclude by looking first at the punishment of individuals and then at the punishment of organizations.

Punishing Individuals.   Punishment seldom is directed at the people responsible for corporate crime in the United States. Consider the Occupational Safety and Health Administration (OSHA), created by Congress in 1970. OSHA can seek prison sentences for convicted offenders. By the end of 1988, however, only fourteen persons had been prosecuted for risking their employees' safety, health, and lives, and none had been sentenced to prison.[77]

Recent OSHA responses to workplace deaths suggest continued avoidance of prison sentences for employers. When a tire-making machine at Bridgestone's Dayton, Ohio, factory crushed Robert Julian to death, OSHA fined the corporation for its "unjustifiable and offensive" failure to provide padlocks and warning signs ("lockout/tagout") to secure equipment before employees get in them to make repairs.[78] No corporate officials were prosecuted. When a scrap-metal compaction and cutting machine sliced Mario Barraza in half while he was working inside it, OSHA took no action against managers of Acme Iron and Metal of Albuquerque, New Mexico. The company was merely fined for the absence of lockout/tagout equipment.[79]

Marshall Clinard (see Box 6) and Peter Yeager's data indicate that reluctance to direct attention to the individuals responsible for

76. Frederick C. Klein, "No Bowl for Auburn," *Wall Street Journal,* November 22, 1993, p. A12.

77. William Glaberson, "Court Says Job Hazards May Be a Crime," *New York Times,* October 17, 1990, p. Bl.

78. Kevin G. Salwen, "Bridgestone Unit Is Fined $7.5 Million by Labor Department in Worker Death," *Wall Street Journal,* April 19, 1994, p. A4.

79. Barbara Marsh, "Workers at Risk: Chance of Getting Hurt Is Generally Far Higher at Smaller Companies," *Wall Street Journal,* February 2, 1994, p. A1.

organizational actions has long existed. Professors Clinard and Yeager specifically report that only 1.5 percent of all federal enforcement efforts directed at corporations in 1975 and 1976 produced a conviction of a corporate officer.[80] Jail sentences for those convicted of offenses in the course of "normal" business activity rarely exceeded 30 days, and monetary fines generally were small.

Some individuals are punished for white-collar crime, although in the instances we have isolated the punishment has been meted out by state courts rather than federal agencies. When Stefan Golab died in 1983 from inhaling cyanide gas at the now closed Film Recovery Systems plant in Elk Grove Village, Illinois, a state court found officials guilty of homicide two years later. This decision marked "the first prosecution of corporate officials for a work-related employee death."[81] The convictions, however, were overturned and the case was finally scheduled for a second trial in 1993. Before the trial began, all three targets of the second prosecution pleaded guilty to involuntary manslaughter. Two were sentenced to prison while the third was sentenced to probation.[82] In the wake of the fire that killed 25 and injured 56 at the Imperial Food Products factory in Hamlet, North Carolina, in 1992 (see Selection 14), three corporate officials were charged in state court with homicide, including the owner and his son.[83] The owner pleaded guilty to involuntary manslaughter in exchange for the dropping of the charges against his son and the other corporate official and is now serving a 20-year prison sentence.

Punishing Organizations.   Organizations cannot be imprisoned, and they rarely are given "death sentences" forcing them to dis-

80. Marshall B. Clinard and Peter C. Yeager, *Illegal Corporate Behavior* (Washington, D.C.: U.S. Government Printing Office, 1979).

81. Dana Milbank and James P. Miller, "Legal Beat," *Wall Street Journal*, September 9, 1993, p. B7. Also see William Presecky, "3rd Guilty Plea in Worker's Death," *Chicago Tribune*, September 10, 1993, p. 2L.; Garth L. Magnum, "Murder in the Workplace: Criminal Prosecution v. Regulatory Enforcement," *Labor Law Journal* 39 (1988): 220–31; William J. Maakestad, "States's Attorneys Stalk Corporate Murderers," *Business and Society Review* 56 (1986): 21–25.

82. Presecky, "3rd Guilty Plea."

83. "Meat-Plant Owner Pleads Guilty in a Blaze That Killed 25 People," *New York Times*, September 15, 1992, p. A20; Laurie M. Grossman, "Owner Sentenced to Nearly 20 Years Over Plant Fire," *Wall Street Journal*, September 15, 1992, p. B2; "Victims of Poultry Plant Fire to Get $16.1 Million," *New York Times*, p. A40; "Chicken Plant Operators Indicted," *New York Times*, March 10, 1992, p. A14.

BOX 6 MARSHALL B. CLINARD

Marshall B. Clinard received his Ph.D. in sociology from the University of Chicago in 1941 and is now emeritus professor of sociology at the University of Wisconsin. He currently holds, as well, a distinguished research professorship in sociology at the University of New Mexico.

Professor Clinard has made four distinctive contributions to the study of white-collar and corporate crime. The first was a 1952 book entitled *The Black Market: A Study of White Collar Crime.* In this book, Professor Clinard examined corporate violations of price regulations during World War II. He reported that even during times of national emergency, corporations did not hesitate to maximize their profits illegally.

In 1980, Professor Clinard and his colleague's important book *Corporate Crime* was published. It revealed that in 1975 and 1976 the nation's 582 largest corporations had accumulated 1,553 violations of federal law. Of the 582 corporations, 350 (60.1 percent) had at least 1 violation, and of those with at least 1 violation, the average was 4.4 per corporation. Professor Clinard and his colleagues thus established that corporate crime was just as common as when it was first studied by Professor Sutherland a quarter of a century earlier.

Professor Clinard's 1983 book *Corporate Ethics and Crime* probed the origins of corporate crime by conducting lengthy interviews with 68 retired middle-management executives of Fortune 500 corporations. Not surprisingly, these middle-level managers portrayed corporate crimes as determined by top managers who pushed too hard and made demands that could be met only by breaking the law.

Professor Clinard's most recent contribution is his 1990 book entitled *Corporate Corruption,* about the many ways in which major corporations abuse their enormous power. Professor Clinard recounts familiar and important examples, along with those that are less well known, in order to reveal patterns of corporate corruption.

Sources: Marshall B. Clinard, *The Black Market: A Study of White Collar Crime* (New York: Holt, Rinehart and Winston, 1952); Marshall B. Clinard and Peter C. Yeager, with the collaboration of Ruth Blackburn Clinard, *Corporate Crime* (New York: Free Press, 1980); Marshall B. Clinard, *Corporate Ethics and Crime* (Beverly Hills, CA: Sage, 1983); Marshall B. Clinard, *Corporate Corruption: The Abuse of Power* (New York: Praeger, 1990).

band.[84] The commonly imposed punishments are monetary, including regulatory fines, criminal fines, and damages from private suits. For the most part, these financial penalties fail to exceed or even equal the gains from corporate violations of the law. Thus, the Sentencing Commission found that federal courts fined only two corporations in its sample more than $500,000. The average fine was $141,000.[85]

This is a lot of money for most individuals, but it is insignificant for most corporations. To get a sense of the impact of an average fine for a corporation, we calculated the equivalent fine for a person earning $35,000 per year.[86] If a "small" corporation with annual sales of $500 million—a firm approximately one-tenth the size of Apple Computer—were fined $141,000, it would be the equivalent of $10 for a person earning $35,000.

Professor Clinard and Yeager's data for the nation's 582 largest corporations in 1975 and 1976 indicate that fines for corporations violating federal law have long been without significant impact. Only 328 of the 1,860 violations of federal law actually resulted in regulatory fines.[87] Over 80 percent of the regulatory fines corporations of all sizes paid were less than $5,000; less than 5 percent exceeded $50,000.

Some laws impose penalties that appear far greater than the ones we have examined thus far. The Sherman Antitrust Act[88] permits civil suits by victims for financial damages because of price-fixing.

The experiences of the corporations convicted in the school milk price-fixing conspiracies show how corporations can usually treat both criminal penalties and civil fines as merely a cost of doing business.[89] Consider Borden. Between 1987 and 1990,

84. For an exception see "Corporate Death Sentence," *Wall Street Journal*, May 20, 1994, p. B6.

85. Mark A. Cohen, "Corporate Crime and Punishment: A Study of Social Harm and Sentencing Practice in the Federal Courts," *American Criminal Law Review* 26 (1989): 605–60.

86. Our comparison is based on one first advanced by Professor Gilbert Geis. See Selection 5 where he observes that for "General Electric, a half million dollar loss was no more unsettling than a $3 parking fine would be to a [person earning] $175,000 a year."

87. Clinard and Yeager, *Illegal Corporate Behavior*, p. 143.

88. Ermann and Lundman, *Corporate Deviance*, pp. 85–86.

89. "U.S. Charges Borden Again," *New York Times*, October 10, 1993, p. D6; "Borden Milk-Bidding Settlement," *Wall Street Journal*, March 26, 1992, p. A4; "School Milk Bid-Rigging Probe Spreads," *Washington Post*, September 6, 1991, p. A9; "Southland Corp., Borden Inc. Admit Guilt in Milk Case," *Wall Street Journal*, March 2, 1990, p. C2.

Borden paid slightly over $21 million in criminal penalties to the courts and civil fines to the school districts it victimized.[90] During those same years, however, Borden's total operating revenues were $28.9 billion,[91] making the criminal and civil fines the equivalent of $101.43 for a person earning $35,000 per year during each of those years.

Some Modest Exceptions.   There are some exceptions to the general rule of light punishments for corporate crimes. These actions have yielded significant, but not lasting, financial and other consequences for large organizations. Union Carbide's experience in the wake of the deaths and injuries in Bhopal, India, is one example, and the environmental disaster in Alaska's Prince William Sound caused by the *Exxon Valdez* is a second.

In December 1984, Union Carbide's Bhopal plant released a deadly cloud of liquid methyl isocyanate that quickly spread through nearby residences.[92] The Indian government puts the official toll at 3,415 killed and 200,000 injured, 50,000 of them seriously. Others advance even higher estimates, putting the deaths near 8,000 and injuries over 400,000.[93] Bhopal is easily the "world's worst industrial accident."[94]

Initially, Union Carbide was barely hanging on.[95] Following Bhopal, the firm's profit decreased and its stock took a nosedive.

90. Ibid.

91. Standard and Poor's Corporation, *Standard and Poor's Industry Surveys* (New York: Standard and Poor's, 1993), p. F40.

92. Warren Getler, "Union Carbide Shares Are Gobbled Up by Insiders," *Wall Street Journal*, January 4, 1995, p. C1; Molly Moore, "Bhopal Gas Leak Victims Caught in Cycle of Despair," *Washington Post*, September 13, 1993, p. A1; Edward Felsenthal, "Legal Beat," *Wall Street Journal*, January 27, 1993, p. B2; Robert D. Kennedy, "Kicked Us When We're Down, But Getting Up" (letter to the editor), *Wall Street Journal*, March 6, 1992, p. A9 (Mr. Kennedy is CEO of Union Carbide and wrote in response to the next article); Scott McMurray, "Wounded Giant: Union Carbide Offers Some Sober Lessons in Crisis Management," *Wall Street Journal*, January 28, 1992, p. A1; Clinard, *Corporate Corruption*, pp. 137–41; Alyssa A. Lappen, "Breaking Up Is Hard to Do "*Forbes*, December 10, 1990, pp. 102–6; Subrata N. Chakravarty, "The Ghost Returns," *Forbes*, December 10, 1990, p. 108; Russel Mokhiber, *Corporate Crime and Violence: Business Power and the Abuse of the Public Trust* (San Francisco: Sierra Club Books, 1988), pp. 86–195; Dan Kurzman, *A Killing Wind* (New York: McGraw-Hill, 1987); David Weir, *The Bhopal Syndrome* (San Francisco: Sierra Club Books, 1987).

93. Moore, "Bhopal."

94. Clinard, *Corporate Corruption*, p. 87.

95. Standard and Poor's Corporation, *Standard NYSE Stock Reports* (New York: Standard and Poor's, 1991), p. 2276; Lappen, "Breaking Up"; Chakravarty, "The Ghost."

In 1985, GAF tried to buy Union Carbide because its stock was undervalued. To repel the GAF takeover and prevent others, Union Carbide made its stock unattractive by selling Prestone antifreeze, Eveready batteries, and Glad bags, and by deliberately going deeply in debt by buying back its own stock. In February 1989, Union Carbide settled nearly all claims, including those by the Indian government, for $480 million. For Union Carbide, Bhopal was a human tragedy of unprecedented proportions and a corporate catastrophy. By the early 1990s, there was real doubt that the corporation could survive.[96]

By the mid-1990s, however, Union Carbide was in the midst of a remarkable corporate resurgence. Its stock was one of the top performers among the 30 corporations that make up the Dow Jones Industrial Average.[97] Its top-level administrators were buying Union Carbide shares in anticipation of even better corporate profits.[98] Despite the remarkable financial hits that came its way in the wake of the deaths and injuries in Bhopal, Union Carbide is once again a financially healthy major corporation.

The people of Bhopal had a different experience.[99] The Indian government was understandably overwhelmed by the thousands who were killed and the many more thousands who continue to suffer. Local hospitals cannot respond to the needs of the ill, and less than 1 percent of the money Union Carbide paid to settle claims has been dispersed. Some analysts argue that 20 years may pass before all death and injury claims are processed.[100]

Exxon's experiences following the Valdez oil spill have been mixed.[101] On March 24, 1989, the Exxon tanker *Valdez* veered off

96. McMurray, "Wounded Giant."

97. Getler, "Union Carbide's Shares."

98. Ibid.

99. Moore, "Bhopal."

100. Ibid.

101. Caleb Solomon, "Exxon Is Told to Pay $5 Billion for Valdez Spill," *Wall Street Journal,* September 19, 1994, p. A3; Schneider, "Judge Rejects"; Allanna Sullivan, Charles McCoy, and Paul M. Barrett, "Judge Rejects Exxon Alaska-Spill Pact; Net Income Rose 75% in First Quarter," *Wall Street Journal,* April 25, 1991, p. A3; "Judge Rejects 'Exxon Valdez' Settlement," *Columbus Dispatch,* April 25, 1991, p. 3; Peter Nutty, "Exxon's Problem: Not What You Think," *Fortune,* April 23, 1990, pp. 202–4; Bryan Hodgson, "Alaska's Big Oil Spill: Can the Wilderness Heal?" *National Geographic* 177 (1990): 4–42.

course, hit Bligh Reef, and dumped almost 11 million gallons of crude oil into the waters of Alaska's Prince William Sound. From day one, Valdez was a public relations nightmare for Exxon.[102] Its CEO, Lawrence Rawl, failed to go to the scene, and the disaster's environmental consequences therefore dominated the news. Exxon went from sixth on the *Fortune* list of Most Admired Corporations to 110th, and industry sources described morale inside the giant corporation as very low.[103]

Exxon's future was never in doubt, however. The Valdez spill did hold down profits and stock prices for a time, but it left operations unaffected.[104] There were no unfriendly takeover attempts, and Exxon accumulated no unusual debts. The corporation did take some financial hits. By April 1990, Exxon had paid $2 billion in penalties and cleanup costs.[105] In April 1991, Exxon entered a negotiated misdemeanor plea bargain in exchange for dropping felony charges. The company agreed to pay a $100-million fine and provide an additional $1 billion in cleanup funding spread across the next ten years. But the Alaskan federal district court judge hearing the case rejected the deal as "too lenient."[106] A new decision in September 1994 directed Exxon to pay an additional $5 billion in punitive damages. Exxon, however, is appealing that decision, so a final determination is not expected for at least three years.[107] One sign of the perceived final impact on Exxon was registered by the New York Stock Exchange: Exxon shares went up.[108]

For Exxon, Valdez was an environmental disaster with serious public relations and morale consequences. In contrast to the Union Carbide case, however, Exxon's survival was never in doubt.

102. Dyer, "Wire Service"; Sullivan, "Rawl Wishes"; Holusha, "Exxon's Public-Relations Problem."

103. Nutty, "Exxon's Problem," p. 202.

104. Standard and Poor's, *Standard NYSE*, p. 846F; Nutty, "Exxon's Problem," p. 203.

105. Nutty, "Exxon's Problem."

106. Sullivan, McCoy, and Barrett, "Judge Rejects Exxon Alaska-Spill Pact."

107. Solomon, "Exxon Is Told."

108. Ibid.

Summary

This essay on corporate and governmental deviance has made three major points. First, large organizations can originate deviant actions. Second, episodes of corporate and governmental deviance follow a pattern. Third, reactions to the behavior of big business and big government vary in both the amount of deviant labeling and the financial and other penalties they produce. The readings in the sections that follow expand and illustrate these major points.

II
Organizational Framework

Preview of the Readings

Large organizations are profoundly important because they are the societal places where individuals spend much of their time. As children, adolescents, and young adults, educational institutions help shape our futures. As adults, many of us play out these futures at work in the world of large organizations. The readings in this section establish the organizational framework for our book by isolating the enormous power of large organizations and by focusing on the nature of life inside organizations for individuals.

In Selection 2, "The Asymmetric Society," James S. Coleman begins by tracing the growth of large organizations in contemporary society. He then examines the asymmetries in power between organizations and individuals and emphasizes that corporate actors are wholly independent of natural persons. Professor Coleman thus directs our attention to the corporate and governmental actors that are the focus of this book. James S. Coleman was University Professor of Sociology at the University of Chicago until his death in March 1995.

Selection 3, Robert Jackall's "Moral Mazes," describes the nature of life for the people who manage large business organizations. Professor Jackall richly details the mazes that corporate managers negotiate with a special focus on how large organizations cause managers to lose their moral compass. We believe that episodes of corporate deviance frequently are directly traceable to these moral mazes. Robert Jackall is a professor of sociology at Williams College.

Annotated Bibliography

Barker, Thomas, and Julian Roebuck. *An Empirical Typology of Police Corruption: A Study in Organizational Deviance.* Springfield, Ill.:

Thomas, 1973. An early examination of the concept of organizational deviance.

Blankenship, Michael B. (ed.). *Understanding Corporate Criminality.* New York: Garland, 1993. A good collection of scholarly papers about corporate crime.

Bernard, Thomas J. "The Historical Development of Corporate Criminal Liability." *Criminology* 22 (1984): 3–17. Traces the development of the legal doctrine that corporations can be held liable for criminal actions.

Coleman, James S. *Power and the Structure of Society.* New York: Norton, 1974. Details the emergence of organizational actors and the implications for individuals.

——. *Foundations of Social Theory.* Cambridge: Harvard University Press, Belknap Press, 1990. About rational choice theory generally, with a sustained examination of organizational actors (see especially pp. 325–577).

——. "The Rational Reconstruction of Society." *American Sociological Review* 58 (1993): 1–15. Professor Coleman's 1992 presidential address to the annual meeting of the American Sociological Association. Offers more on corporate actors and, especially, their rational reconstruction to better fit the needs of the individuals in them.

Coleman, James W. *The Criminal Elite: The Sociology of White Collar Crime,* 3rd ed. New York: St. Martin's, 1994. A description and analysis of organizational and occupational crimes.

Cressey, Donald R. "The Poverty of Theory in Corporate Crime Research." In William S. Laufer and Freda Adler (eds.), *Advances in Criminological Theory.* Vol. 1. New Brunswick, N.J.: Transaction Books, 1989. Sharply criticizes the notion of organizational actors and argues that individuals are responsible for episodes of corporate crime. Professor Cressey (1919–1987) was Edwin H. Sutherland's last Ph.D. student at Indiana University.

Ermann, M. David, and Richard J. Lundman. *Corporate Deviance.* New York: Holt, Rinehart and Winston, 1982. A description and analysis of corporate deviance.

Farrell, Ronald A., and Victoria L. Swigert. "The Corporation in Criminology: New Directions for Research." *Journal of Research in Crime and Delinquency* 22 (1985): 83–94. A review of research on corporate crime and specification of directions for future research.

Geis, Gilbert. "From Deuteronomy to Deniability: A Historical Perlustration on White-Collar Crime." *Justice Quarterly* 5 (1988): 7–32. Starts with the legal background of efforts to control commercial power and ends with the Iran-Contra affair.

——. "Towards a Delineation of White Collar Offenses." *Sociological Inquiry* 32 (1962): 160–71. A description of the various types of white-collar crime and a critique of the notion of organizational deviance by one of the leading students of white-collar crime. Professor Geis asserts that a focus on organizational actors is sociological nonsense, arguing that we should study individuals rather than organizations.

Geis, Gilbert, Robert F. Meier, and Lawrence M. Salinger (eds.). *White Collar Crime: Classic and Contemporary Views*, 3rd ed. New York: The Free Press, 1994. The best of the earliest works, with new analyses of major types of white collar crime.

Hirschi, Travis, and Michael Gottfredson. "Causes of White-Collar Crime." *Criminology* 25 (1987): 949–74. Develops a general theory of crime that the authors believe is applicable to both ordinary and white-collar crime.

Reiss, Albert J., Jr., "The Study of Deviant Behavior: Where the Action Is." *Ohio Valley Sociologist* 32 (1960): 60–66. An early and important call for a "more general theory that encompasses the deviant character of organizations as well as individuals."

Rosovsky, Henry. *The University: An Owner's Manual.* New York: Norton, 1990. To understand organizational deviance, it is first necessary to understand how large organizations are managed. Professor Rosovsky's focus here is the management of large universities.

Shapiro, Susan P. "Collaring the Crime, Not the Criminal: Reconsidering the Concept of White-Collar Crime." *American Sociological Review* 55 (1990): 346–65. Argues that sociologists have spent far too much time studying white-collar criminals and far too little time examining their trust-violating criminal actions.

Snider, Laureen. *Bad Business: Corporate Crime in Canada.* Scarborough, Ont.: Nelson Canada, 1993. Emphasizes competing explanations of corporate crime and Canadian attempts to control it.

Stone, Christopher D. *Where the Law Ends: The Social Control of Corporate Behavior.* New York: Harper and Row, 1975. Professor Stone is the most prominent American lawyer in the study of corporate crime and its control.

Tonry, Michael, and Albert J. Reiss, Jr. *Beyond the Law: Crime in Complex Organizations.* Chicago: University of Chicago Press, 1993. Case-oriented discussion of organizational crimes.

Wilson, James Q. *Bureaucracy: What Govermental Agencies Do and Why They Do It.* New York: Basic Books, 1989. Well-written and -researched description and analysis of governmental agencies.

2

The Asymmetric Society
Organizational Actors, Corporate Power,
and the Irrelevance of Persons

James S. Coleman

[Organizational Actors]

[T]he law has facilitated, and technological developments have
motivated, an enormous growth of a new kind of person in society, a person not like you and me, but one which can and does act,
and one whose actions have extensive consequences for natural
persons like you and me.

Something of the character and nature of that growth can be seen
by a few charts. Figure 2.1 gives an indication of the growth in
numbers of profit-making corporations in the United States since
1917. The chart shows the numbers of corporations paying taxes
in each year since 1917, a growth from 1917 to 1969 of more than
five times. There was, to be sure, population growth among natural persons in the United States during this period, but far less than
the fivefold growth shown in the chart.

Two other charts show something about the actions of corporate
actors and persons. The first of these, Figure 2.2, covering all actions
in the New York State Appellate Court from 1853 to 1973, shows
the proportion of persons—or agents of corporate actors (the two
were combined, because it was difficult to tell whether a person
was a party to a case as a natural person or as an agent of a corporation)—and the proportion that were corporate actors. The proportion was highly skewed in the direction of natural persons in

FIGURE 2.1
Growth in Numbers of Corporations in the United States, 1916–1968

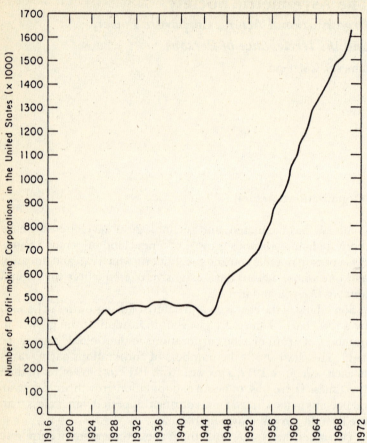

Source: From Shi Chang Wu, "Distribution of Economic Resources in the United States," mimeographed (Chicago, Ill.: National Opinion Research Center, 1974).

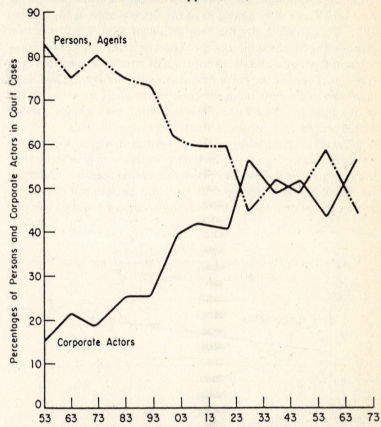

FIGURE 2.2
Participation of Persons and Corporate Actors in Court Cases, New York State Court of Appeals, 1853–1973

Source: From Naava Binder Grossman, "A Study of the Relative Participation of Persons and Corporate Actors in Court Cases," mimeographed (Chicago, Ill.: National Opinion Research Center, 1974).

1853 (85 percent to 15 percent); by 1930, it became about even and
has remained that way through 1973.

Figure 2.3 shows . . . actions reported on the front page of the
New York Times, over a portion of the same period, from 1876 to
1972. This chart shows the proportion of front page attention
given—either as the subject of the action or as the object of action—
to natural persons and the proportion of attention given to corporate actors—either the corporate actors or their agents. Again the
chart shows a reduction in the proportion of all attention on the
stage of the *New York Times* given to natural persons: from about
40 percent in 1876, down to about 20 percent in 1972.

What these changes suggest is a structural change in society over
the past hundred years in which corporate actors play an increasing role and natural persons play a decreasing role. It is as if there
has been extensive immigration over this period, not of persons
from Europe or Asia or Africa or South America, but of [people]

FIGURE 2.3
Attention to Persons and Corporate Actors on the Front Page
of the *New York Times,* 1876–1972

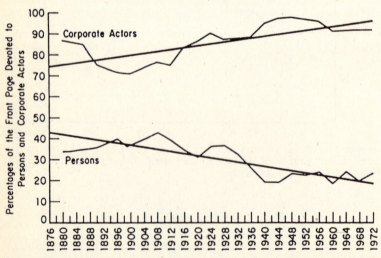

Source: From Ronald S. Burt, "Corporate Society: A Time Series Analysis of Network Structure," mimeographed (Chicago, Ill.: National Opinion Research Center,
1975).

from Mars—a race of persons unknown in history. And this new race of persons has come to crowd out natural persons from various points in the social structure—at least some of those points that take part in activities which end up in appellate court or on the front page of the *New York Times*.

Yet these new persons are not Martians. They employ natural persons as agents, they have natural persons as their chief executives, they are governed by boards of directors made up of natural persons,[1] natural persons are their owners. Or so it once was; not even all these things are now true. The stockholders are, with increasing frequency, themselves corporate actors, either other business corporations or other forms of corporate actors: pension funds or insurance companies. Members of their boards of directors may be agents of other corporate actors who are large stockholders.

These corporate actors are different from those that have gone before in a fundamental way. In the earlier structure of societies, the family was the nucleus of the corporate structure, and the component elements of the family were natural persons. The family had a place in the larger structure, and through the family, each person did as well. That person had a fixed station and was an intrinsic part of the structure of society. As Marc Bloch (1961) wrote about the manor in the Middle Ages, "In the days when vassalage was developing, or when it was in its prime, the manor was first and foremost a community of dependents who were by turns protected, commanded, and oppressed by their lord to whom many of them were bound by a sort of hereditary link, unconnected with possession of the soil or place of abode" (p. 279). There were, to be sure, various devices to cope with the fact that persons were mortal, and one person's function might have to be taken over by another. But the central and overriding fact was that all social organization was

---

1. The practice in industrial firms of having executives of other firms or of financial institutions as members of boards of directors does not involve agency. These persons are board members in their capacities as persons, and their other positions are relevant only as they have acquired skills or knowledge from those positions. This points to a central difficulty of sociological studies of "interlocking directorates," which show the "interlock" created by an executive officer of one firm being a member of a board of directors of another firm. Because the board member does not come as an agent but as a natural person, there is no interlock in the sense ordinarily meant. It is for this reason that such studies have never proved very useful for the study of the functioning of society. The end point of such studies is ordinarily simply a demonstration of the "interlocks," with the implicit assumption that the interlock has significance for the functioning of society.

organization of persons, and that those forms of organization which were fruitfully conceptualized as corporate actors were structures themselves composed of persons.

But the conception of the corporation as a legal person distinct from natural persons, able to act and be acted on, and the reorganization of society around corporate bodies made possible a radically different kind of social structure than before. So long as society was seen as a single fixed organic whole, then the existence of social differentiation of activities as it was emerging in the Middle Ages (merchants, crafts, agriculture, churches) implied a rigid differentiation of persons in fixed positions—as in caste India, but with less continuity through generations. But as this differentiation of activities increased, a new form of social organization slowly came to be invented, and the law reflected this invention. This form involved the corporation as a functional element in social organization; a juristic person which could substitute functionally for a natural person. It could act in a unitary way, it could own resources, it could have rights and responsibilities, it could occupy the fixed functional position or estate which had been imposed on natural persons (and later it too could be partially freed from that fixed position). Natural persons, in turn, came to be free from the fixed estates, gaining mobility, as the structural stability of society was provided by the new fixed functional units, the corporations or corporate bodies. Persons needed no longer to be "one dimensional" but could occupy several positions in the structure at once and could change positions freely. It was the positions, as components of the new elements of society, the corporate actors, which provided the continuity and stability of structure.

The emergence of this new structure for society has had and continues to have extensive consequences for the lives of the natural persons within it. . . .

The Asymmetry of Relations

The first and perhaps most compelling [consequence] is the *asymmetry* of a large portion of its relations. I can best describe this asymmetry to you by asking you to look at the diagram of Figure 2.4.

FIGURE 2.4

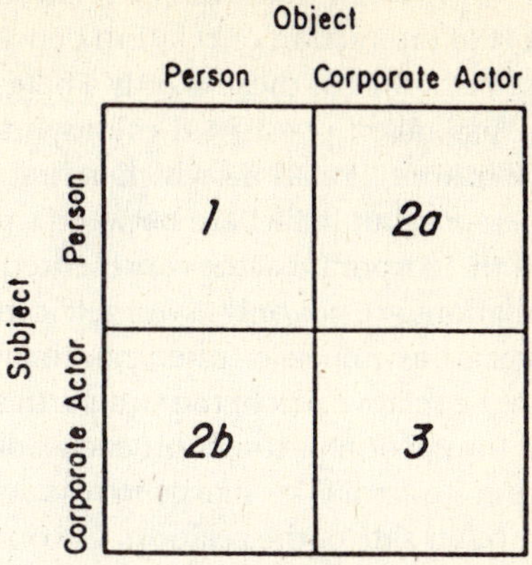

Object

What I have done here is to start with the recognition that there are two fundamentally distinct types of actors in modern society, natural persons and corporate actors. Then I have classified actions according to whether the *subject* of action is a person or corporate actor, and according to whether the *object* of action is a person or corporate actor. The result is four kinds of action, which I have labeled 1, 2a, 2b, and 3. Actions of type 1 are actions to which we have all been socialized as children: actions of one person toward another person. Actions of type 3 are actions of a corporate actor toward another corporate actor, for example an action of one corporation toward another, or an action of the state (i.e., the government) toward a corporation or a trade union. Actions of types 2a and 2b, however, are actions in which the two parties to an action are of *different* types: one is a person and one is a corporate actor. And because a relation involves both parties as subject and object of action, we may speak of a relation of type 2, involving actions of types 2a and 2b. This, in contrast to the other two types of relations, is asymmetric. And with the enormous growth in numbers of corporate actors in modern society, this asymmetric form of relation has come to proliferate throughout the social structure. Some of the growth in appearances of corporate actors in court cases which I presented earlier is growth in this kind of relation, a person and a corporate actor opposed in court. Some of the growth in attention to corporate actors in the *New York Times,* which I also presented earlier, is growth in this kind of relation, that is, articles involving some sort of interaction or relation between a person and a corporate actor. Yet either of these is only a pale reflection of the total growth that has taken place in these asymmetric relations.

Increasingly, there are . . . relations which at first glance appear to be between two persons, but in fact are between a person and a corporate actor, with the corporate actor represented by its agent. . . . [M]any of these relations are not only asymmetric in the types of parties they involve, but are asymmetric—often extremely so—in two other respects as well: in the relative *sizes* of the two parties, and in the *numbers* of alternative transaction partners on each side of the relation. Typically, the corporate actor is very large in resources, compared to the person on the other side of the relation. On one side may be the telephone company, a corporate actor, and on the other side, a customer, a person. Or on the one side may be the United Steelworkers' Union, a corporate actor, and on the other side a union member, a person. Or on the one side may be the U.S. government, a corporate actor, and on the other side, a citizen, a person.

And typically, on the corporate actor side there are only a few other parties as alternative transaction partners. . . . On the person side there are typically hundreds, thousands, or even millions. These two asymmetries have extensive consequences for the nature of the relation. One consequence is that the corporate actor nearly always controls most of the conditions surrounding the relation. The corporate actor controls much of the information relevant to the interaction—typically by advertising, propaganda, market research, public opinion research, credit ratings of customers, and dossiers of other sorts. Information expressly designed to serve the interests of the person is far less in evidence. And as with information, so with other of the conditions. The end result is that two parties beginning with nominally equal rights in a relation, but coming to it with vastly different resources, end with very different actual rights in the relation.

These asymmetries of power in relationships have led to extensive attempts by persons to redress the balance, using as their instrument the state. Thus the principle of *caveat emptor,* let the buyer beware, in a social structure which was not asymmetric between buyers and sellers, has been replaced, in the asymmetric society, with sharp restriction of the seller's rights and expansion of the means of redress for persons. The [1970s] alone saw a whole spate of such legislation at both the state and federal levels, ranging from truth in lending laws to privacy acts, designed to protect natural persons from corporate actors' use of information about them in ways antagonistic to their interests.

The asymmetry, however, has other consequences in the behavior of the two parties to the relation. The person, if unconstrained by internal moral constraints, may steal from or cheat a corporate actor, protected by the anonymity provided by numbers. A person angry at the telephone company might rip the cord from a public phone, or a customer or employee in a store may shoplift, or may fail to notify a cashier if too much change has been returned. Yet these same persons might never do any of these things in relations with other *persons,* where actions are subject to the other's constant surveillance.

In short, the asymmetry of the relation gives power to the corporate actor and at the same time gives opportunities for malfeasance to the person. On both counts, the relation functions less well than the personal relations of which social structures have long been composed, and for which normative systems of constraints have arisen. . . .

The Irrelevance of Persons

Persons have become, in a sense that was never before true, incidental to a large fraction of the productive activity in society. This is most evident when the person who occupies a position in a corporate actor is replaced not by another person but by a machine. Then the general irrelevance of persons is clear. But the invention which made this possible was not a technological invention which replaced [people with machines]; it was a social invention which created a structure that was independent of particular persons and consisted only of positions. Once this was done, it became merely a matter of ingenuity to devise machines that could carry out the activities which those positions required.

The irrelevance of persons in the structure is not a question of machines, it is a question of the *form* of the structure. In management training programs in many firms, there is a game that is used as part of the training program: the in-basket game. In this game [manage-ment trainees are] asked to assume that [they] unexpectedly replaced the previous plant manager over the weekend and [are] confronted with the unanswered mail in [their] predecessor's in-basket. The task is to respond appropriately to the various items of correspondence. A few are personal, and [they are] expected to distinguish between those and the correspondence that is intended for the plant manager as manager, that is, as agent of the firm. The aim of the in-basket exercise is to make the transition from one manager to the next unnoticeable—to make the manager *as a person* irrelevant to the func-tioning of the plant. This is good for the smooth functioning of the organization; but it takes away something of central importance to each of us: the sense of being *needed*. It is this which makes the fam-ily—which is an anachronism from another age in the modern social structure we have created—an important element in our lives. A fam-ily member is a part of that family as a person, not as an occupant of a position; and no answers to correspondence in an in-basket can make a family's loss of a member unnoticeable. . . .

Is this a desirable state of affairs for society? I think not. Yet it is a state of affairs which follows directly from the structure of corporate action which we have invented for ourselves and under which we live.

Reference

Bloch, Marc. 1961. *Feudal Society*, vol. 1. Chicago, Ill.: University of Chi-cago Press.

Editors' Postscript

The trends Professor Coleman identified continue. Among lawsuits filed in federal courts between 1985 and 1991, the largest number of them (191,000) involved business contract disputes between two or more firms. These suits were far more common than personal injury lawsuits filed by natural persons against companies. (See Milo Geyelin, "Suits by Firms Exceed Those by Individuals," *Wall Street Journal*, December 3, 1993, p. B1.)

3
Moral Mazes
Managerial Work and Personal Ethics
Robert Jackall

Sooner or later . . . almost all managers experience clashes between
the requirements of their world and aspects of their valued self-
images. Such tensions arise most predictably when organizational
upheavals cause an unraveling of the social and moral ties that
secure one's status and social identity or when public attacks
on one's organization call one's organizational morality into question. But even the everyday ambiguities and compromises of
managerial work often pose invitations to jeopardy. Some of the
recurring dilemmas that managers face test their own preferred self-
definitions. All of these revolve in one way or another around the
meaning of work. Those managers who respond fully to the organizational premiums on success are especially important here because their ambition not only drives themselves but continually
regenerates the structure of their world. . . .

[Interpersonal Behavior]

[S]ome of the fundamental requirements of managerial work clash
with the normal ethics governing interpersonal behavior, let alone
friendship in our society. Our egalitarian ideology couples here with
remnants of Judeo-Christian beliefs counseling honesty, loyalty, and
compassion toward other people. But at bottom, a great deal of
managerial work consists of ongoing struggles for dominance and

From *Moral Mazes: The World of Corporate Managers*, pp. 194–204. Copyright ©
1988 by Oxford University Press. Reprinted by permission.

status. Real administrative effectiveness flows, in fact, from the prestige that one establishes with other managers. Prestige in managerial hierarchies depends not only on position as determined by the crucial indices of rank, grade, title, and salary, and the external accoutrements that symbolize power. Even more fundamentally, it consists of the socially recognized ability to work one's will, to get one's way, to have the say-so when one chooses in both the petty and large choices of organizational life. At one level, the superordination and subordination of bureaucratic hierarchies guarantee clashes between the egos of men and women who "like to control things," whose choice of occupation, in fact, has been at least partly shaped by their orientation and habituation to control. For instance, an administrative coordinator describes the daily battles between Beach, the president of one of Weft's divisions,* and Schultz, his talented vice-president:

> I feel every knife turn between [Beach] and [Schultz]. [Beach] enjoys lording it over [Schultz]. For instance, in a dispute, [Beach] will say: "I'll make the final choices." And this drives [Schultz] crazy. And then the whole department is drawn up on either side of the battle. . . . [I]n the morning, I'll come in and try to cope with the latest issue. I'll be thinking: "What did [one] mean about this? How will the other guy react when he finds out?" The way things are now is that [Schultz] can work heavily toward influencing things, but if [Beach] felt that he could make some decision which would turn out well and would at the same time be against [Schultz], he would make it in a minute.

At another level, the struggle for dominance is an inevitable by-product of the pyramidal construction of bureaucracies that fuels managers' driving competitiveness. A divisional vice-president at Weft comments:

> There just aren't that many places to go when you get up as high as I am. . . . [T]he competition that does occur is within the division. You're not competing for jobs with another division.
> Now within the division, there's a limited number of positions, of spots, and after you're here for awhile and know the score, you don't have three guys after one spot. . . . [T]he competition is not necessarily for the jobs that open up, since they are so few. Rather the ongoing competition is *for your way of doing things.* We all want

---

*ED. NOTE: Professor Jackall studied two corporations in detail. Weft is a textile corporation and Alchemy manufactures chemical products.

things to go our way and the competition, dilemmas, and problems
are when it doesn't go my way but somebody else's. I've competed
and lost on that issue. . . . That's where there is real pressure. It's in
the competitiveness in trying to have it your way. You have to be
able to swallow the defeat.

Defeat at the middle and upper-middle levels produces in the los-
ers feelings of frustration and of being "boxed in." Such disappoint-
ments must be concealed and the ideology of team play often
affords a convenient cover for defeat, one that might even be translated later into organizational credit. But one cannot, of course,
lose too often without risking permanent anonymity. At the top of
an organization, the loss of prestige occasioned by a major policy
defeat leaves the loser with the hard choice between resignation or
the daily humiliation of cheerfully doing something someone else's
way. Defeat in such circumstances seems especially difficult when
the victor insists on being magnanimous. In such a case, the victor
enjoys plaudits for big-hearted sensitivity while his defeated
opponent often finds such generosity more oppressive than vindictiveness. On the other hand, winning carries with it the knowledge
of others' envy and the fear that one's defeated opponents are lying
in wait for an opportunity to turn the tables. One adopts then a
stance of public humility, of self-effacing modesty that helps dis-
guise whatever sense of triumph one might feel. Moreover, winning,
say, on a policy dispute, carries the burden of implementation,
sometimes involving those whom one has defeated. One must then
simultaneously protect one's flanks and employ whatever wiles are
necessary to secure requisite cooperation. Here the disarming social
grace that is a principal aspect of desirable managerial style can be
particularly useful in making disingenuousness seem like "straight
arrow" behavior. Finally, winning sometimes requires the willingness to move decisively against others, even though this might mean
undermining their organizational careers. These may be neighbors
on the same block, members of the same religious communion,
longtime work colleagues, or, more rarely, members of the same
club. They may be good, even excellent, employees. In short, managerial effectiveness and others' perceptions of one's leadership
depend on the willingness to battle for the prestige that comes from
dominance and to make whatever moral accommodations such
struggles demand. In the work world, those who adhere either to

secular democratic precepts as guides rather than guises or, even more, to an ethic of brotherly love run the risk of faltering in those struggles. But those who abandon the ethics of *caritas* and hone themselves to do what has to be done must accept the peculiar emotional aridity that is one price of organizational striving and, especially, of victory. . . .

[Inequalities]

[M]anagers at the middle levels in particular also have to come to grips with the peculiar inequities of the corporate world that call the meaning, purpose, and value of their work into question. They take for granted, of course, the material and symbolic inequities embedded in their bureaucratic hierarchies, hoping as they do that they themselves will one day benefit from the opportunities to appropriate credit from subordinates, command others' deference, and enjoy the generous salaries, company cars, year-end bonuses, big offices, attractive secretaries, and golden parachutes and golden handcuffs (financial ties that bind) that are seen to be the prerogatives of high rank, prestige, and power. However, the institutionalized inequities that result from what managers see as a pervasive mediocrity in big organizations do pose dilemmas. One measure of the troublesome character of such mediocrity is the widespread emotional resonance tapped by the recent widely heralded managerial consultant slogan of "excellence in management."[1]

As managers see it, mediocrity emerges out of the lack of fixed criteria within an organization to measure quality, whether of products or performance. In a world where criteria depend entirely on the interpretive judgments of shifting groups in an ever-changing social structure, where everyone's eyes are fixed on each other and

1. The stress on excellence in management boomed with the publication of Thomas J. Peters and Robert H. Waterman, Jr., *In Search of Excellence: Lessons from America's Best-Run Companies* (New York: Warner Books, 1982), a book that is another classic paradigm of managerial consultant writing, complete with a handy list of eight attributes of excellence. Two years later, a follow-up study by *Business Week*, November 5, 1984, pp. 76–83, argues that at least fourteen of the forty-three corporations cited by Peters and Waterman as excellent had "lost their luster." The article notes that Peters at least is undeterred by such troubling news and is planning other works showing managers how to implement the attributes of excellence.

on market exigencies, the construction of notions of quality becomes highly political since individual fates depend on the outcome. Clearly, skillful leadership and mobilization of organizational resources can impose a consensus about appropriate standards. However, to do so, one has to: resist pressures for short-term expedient solutions to problems that compromise one's notion of desirable standards; be willing to confront others, both in private and in public, who espouse or embody in some way variant, undesirable standards; and enforce one's judgment with organizationally approved sanctions. But given the bureaucratic ethos, such insistence on standards of excellence can quickly earn one enemies and the feared label of being "inflexible." As it happens, when it is socially difficult to extol or uphold high standards, a kind of leveling process occurs that produces a comfortable mediocrity, a willingness to settle for, say, whatever the market will bear, or to tolerate shoddiness of products or performance, provided there is no undue social disruption. In such situations, among those managers who wish for clearer, higher standards, quasifictional images of the supposed superiority of different organizations or of the purported technical and managerial prowess of the Japanese often abound, usually invoked with wistful longing and sometimes with rueful envy.

Perceptions of pervasive mediocrity breed an endless quest for social distinctions even of a minor sort that might give one an "edge," enable one to "step out of the crowd," or at least serve as a basis for individual claims to privilege. More specifically, an atmosphere of mediocrity erodes the hope of meaningful collective achievement and encourages, at least among more aggressive managers, a predatory stance toward their organizations, that is, a search for private deals, a working of the system for one's own personal advantage. This may mean, variously, winning the assignment of a valued account, product, or client; wrangling one of the coveted discretionary places on a bonus scheme; or getting the inside track on promotions through the exposure gained by chairing a crucial committee or task force. A system of deal making places a premium on maximizing one's organizational leverage in order to make claims on those with power to dispense perquisites. In such a system, "big numbers" may help reduce organizational vulnerability but do not necessarily help maximize leverage. Rather, the social factors that bind managers to one another, whether in conflict or

in harmony, are the chief sources of deals. Such a system is thus
principally characterized by the exchange of personal favors and
the dispensation of patronage to seal the alliances that give one
"clout"; by the systematic collection of information damaging to
others and particularly about deals struck and favors won in order
to argue more effectively the propriety and legitimacy of one's own
claims; and, on the part of those in power, by pervasive secrecy,
called confidentiality, that attempts to cordon off the knowledge
of deals already made lest the demands on the system escalate
unduly. It is worth noting that most middle managers' general
detestation of affirmative action programs, apart from their resentment at yet another wild card in the corporate deck and at being
asked to bear cheerfully the burdens of others' neglect and mistakes,
is rooted in the perception that such arrangements symbolically
legitimate the perceived inequities of their world, cloaking simply
a new kind of expedient favoritism with self-righteous ideologies.
Seen from this perspective, the corporation resembles for many a
jerry-built structure, like a boardwalk erected on pilings of different heights, that, when viewed from a distance over sandy stretches
in baking summer heat, shimmers rickety and swaying to the eye.

In such a world, notions of fairness or equity that managers might
privately hold, as measures of gauging the worth of their own work,
become merely quaint. One fluctuates between a frustrated resentment at what seems to be a kind of institutionalized corruption and
systematic attempts to make oneself a beneficiary of the system.
Being a "good soldier" may carry for some the private satisfactions
of work well done, of bargains kept, or of organizational goals
attained through one's best efforts. But such dedication may also
make one unfit for the maneuvers that can bring organizational
privilege and reward. . . .

[The Meaning of Work]

[M]anagers at every level face puzzles about the overall meaning of
their work in a business civilization in which the old notion of stew-
ardship has been lost and in which work in business is alternately
regarded with at times adulation, at times tolerant condescension,

and at times outright suspicion. Sooner or later, most managers realize, as Thorstein Veblen did many years ago, that there are no intrinsic connections between the good of a particular corporation, the good of an individual manager, and the common weal. Stories are legion among managers about corporations that "devour" individuals, "plunder" the public, and succeed extravagantly; about individual managers whose predatory stances toward their fellows, their organizations, and society itself only further propel their sky-rocketing careers; about individual managers desiring to harness the great resources of private enterprise and address social ills only to end up disillusioned by their colleagues' attention to exigencies; and about corporations that have espoused noble public goals only to founder in competitive markets and endanger the occupational security of their employees by failing to concentrate on the bottom line.

Meaningful connections between organizational well-being, individual fates, and the common weal can, of course, be forged both by individual managers and by organizations at the level of policy. But, where they exist, such connections proceed from some ideological standpoint backed by institutional mechanisms. Law and regulation usually shape only the broad parameters of action and allowable public discourse in such matters. . . . [L]aw and regulation can be quite important in providing requisite appeals to inevitability on controversial issues that break political deadlocks within organizations. But typically such external compulsions cannot offer the meaningful rationales that sustain the hard organizational work of coordinating diverse, sometimes opposing, managerial interests. Properly enforced, assertions of values by top management can do this, at least for periods of time until organizational reshuffling alters organizational premiums. Some corporations, for instance, espouse policies of product responsibility, tying organizational rewards to sustained vigilance over the uses and possible uses to which a product might be put. Such programs thus try to link individual success, reduction of corporate liability, and consumer safety. These programs can, of course, never be wholly successful. As the several poisonings of over-the-counter drugs in early 1986 suggest, even relatively farsighted product safety policies cannot anticipate the potential depth of individual irrationalities, whether these proceed from psychopathology or, perhaps more disturbing, from the didactic self-righteousness of those privileged to receive some ideological enlightenment. Moreover, to sustain the links between the corporation, the individual, and the common good over the long haul, important conditions must obtain within an organization. Specifically, the ideology incorporating certain values must be continuously and forcefully articulated by key authorities who are ostensibly committed to its premises, and, at the same time, the ideological links between the good of the corporation and the common weal in particular must be plausible both to managers and to important external publics. As it happens, both conditions are difficult to meet. Day-to-day exigencies, the personnel transitions of large organizations, the endless circulation of new rhetorics of innovation among top managers, the entrenched cynicism of middle managers on whose backs the burdens for any such policies will fall, and, of course, the "take the money and run" ethos, make it difficult to sustain organizational commitment to goals defined as socially important.

Even more difficult is fashioning some working consensus about the meaning of "corporate social responsibility," a consensus that includes top management, external publics that top management is trying to appease, and middle management that must implement a policy. Here the precariousness of ideological bridges over the chasm between the interests of a corporation, individual managers, and the public are most apparent. Some years ago, for example, Alchemy Inc. was producing a food-grade chemical used principally as a meat preservative. The company was, in fact, one of the chief suppliers of the chemical to the processed food industry. Although the business was small in comparison to other company operations, its oligopolistic position in this particular market made the preservative a very lucrative commodity. Suddenly, a newly released government study fingered the food preservative as carcinogenic. The report received great and widespread publicity, coinciding as it did with a public debate about carcinogens in food and with a nationwide health food fad that stressed, among other things, natural diets uncontaminated with artificial ingredients. Moreover, Covenant Corporation* was recovering at the time from the bad publicity of an environmental catastrophe. In light of both developments, the

*ED. NOTE: Covenant Corporation is the parent company of Alchemy.

CEO of Covenant, who was nearing retirement, ordered the immediate sale of the preservative business, arguing that the recent scientific evidence made such a divestiture an act of corporate social responsibility. This position earned him plaudits from several environmental and health groups.

Alchemy managers, by contrast, argued privately that the CEO's real motivation was simply the avoidance of any further public relations hassles at that stage of his career. After the managers in charge of the preservative business had divested, they had more material grounds for their skepticism as they watched the company that bought the operation "make money hand over fist." They wondered whether the CEO had not simply "caved in." Is, they asked, "supine acquiescence" to special-interest groups or to suspect or perhaps even bogus government research the meaning of corporate responsibility? Of course, they discounted the animal tests that suggested the preservative's carcinogenicity. But so what, they argued, if the preservative did in fact pose some risk of cancer? Better, they said, the risk of a slight long-run increase in the rate of stomach and intestinal cancer than the certainty of a precipitous spurt in the incidence of botulism, particularly in the lower-income black and Hispanic groups that typically consume large amounts of processed meat and, both because of poverty and cultural practices, often leave food uncovered and unrefrigerated for considerable periods. Is corporate social responsibility, they asked, maintaining a private sense and public image of moral purity while someone else does necessary but tainted work? Or is real social responsibility the willingness to get one's hands dirty, to make whatever compromises have to be made to produce a product with some utility, to achieve therefore some social good, even though one knows that one's accomplishments and motives will inevitably be misinterpreted by others for their own ends, usually by those with the least reason to complain? Besides, they pointed out, consumers continue to purchase artificially preserved meats in large quantities. Is not the proper role of business "to give the public what it wants," adopting the market as its polar star, as the only reliable guide in a pluralistic society to "the greatest good for the greatest number," as the final arbiter not of values, which are always arguable, but, more importantly, of tastes, about which there can be no reasonable dispute?

In short, managers' occupational roles are such that they simply cannot please everybody, even fellow managers. What seems socially responsible from one perspective may seem irresponsible or just plain venal from another angle. In fact, exercises in substantive rationality—the critical, reflective use of reason—are not only subject to infinite interpretations and counterinterpretations but also invite fantastic constructions of reality, including attributions of conspiracy. Thus a major corporation provides a gift of $10 million to establish new foundations that will materially aid South African blacks and is promptly accused by a black American leader of bolstering apartheid.[2] Weft managers create an elaborate recreational complex for Weft employees in the corporation's southern community and are charged with perpetuating traditional textile company paternalism. Some executives at Images Inc.* donate their time to bring together several institutional sectors of a local town in which they live for community betterment and are charged with trying to grab headlines and line up future business. Managers often feel that, however genuine it may be, altruism is a motive that is always denied them by others. To complicate matters still further, the necessary self-promotional work of presenting private goals as public goods, or the self-defensive work within the corporation of presenting public goods as hardheaded business decisions, or managers' knowledge that bureaucracy insulates them from the real consequences of their actual choices, often make their protestations of socially responsible actions suspect even to themselves.

This context helps one understand why many managers feel, particularly as they grow older, that much of the actual work of management is senseless. Of course, big victories, pleasing deals, the seizure of capricious opportunities to accomplish something one thinks is worthwhile, the intrinsic pleasure, when it occurs, of harmonious orchestration, and, with personal success, the opportunity for leading roles in philanthropic, artistic, or social organizations of various sorts, trusteeships at elite colleges and universities, directorships in other corporations and the concomitant opportunity to mingle with other powerful peers, and the respectability that money and status afford, all punctuate and mitigate such

---

2. See Kathleen Telsch, "Coca Cola Giving $10 Million To Help South Africa Blacks," *New York Times*, March 24, 1986, Al 3, col. 2.

*ED. NOTE: Images Inc. is a public relations firm.

senselessness. But the anonymity that is the lot of most corporate managers exacerbates it. Moreover, the successful propagation of professional ideologies of service or truth-seeking by occupations like medicine or the professoriate often make businessmen view their own attention to the material world as base or crass.

Yet attention to the material world can anchor one's sense of self. In fact, the problem of the senselessness of managerial work increases as the work itself becomes more abstract, typically as one advances. With increasing seniority, one retreats from concrete tasks, say, overseeing the manufacture of sheets or shirting material or running the production of hydrofluoric acid. One thus loses immediate connections to tangible human or industrial needs. For those who came up through the plants, one also loses regular contact with the renewing drama of industrial work. A plant manager at one of Alchemy's largest and most troublesome operations, a man who regularly goes in at all hours "to fight the dragons," tells how often he does not even wait for trouble:

> Sometimes I'll wake up in the middle of the night thinking about the plant. And if I can't get back to sleep, I'll slip out of bed and walk over to the plant and just walk around the machinery and talk to the guys. I love the smell of the oil and the grease and the sound of the machines. For me, that's what life is all about.

But to advance, one must leave behind such a comforting concreteness, indeed the visible enactment of one's rational schemes, where materials, labor, and machinery are brought together to produce value.[3] One leaves behind as well the technical knowledge or scien-

---

3. Take, for instance, the scene that one encounters on the main floor of Weft's large finishing plant, called "The Bleachery." The cloth from the greige mills comes to loading docks at the rear of the building in huge rolls, tinted different colors to distinguish different weights—for instance, white for shirting material and pink for heavy trouser cloth. All of the cloth contains polyvinyl alcohol (pva), one agent that facilitates the weaving process. The first operation is to remove the pva by washing the cloth in "rope" form—that is, twisted into long strands. The cloth is then untwisted and run at incredibly high speeds in flat form through gas flames on both sides. This helps remove other impurities still left in the cotton part of the cloth. Then the cloth is put back into rope form and whipped by ropes and pulleys through holes in the wall into an adjacent room where it is put into huge vats with a biologically active enzyme that removes the "sizing," the starch that gives the yarn requisite tensile strength for weaving. After the cloth sits in the vats for four hours, it is once again pulled up in rope form into a series of baths, for instance, of hot water and of caustic soda, and at each stage is dried over drying cans. After this, the cloth is often mercerized, that is, put again in a caustic soda bath to heighten its receptivity to dyes. After drying, it then goes to the dyeing ranges, and perhaps later, to the printing ranges.

All of this is an astonishing sight. At any given moment, thousands and thousands of yards of cloth in rope form swirl overhead on pulleys moving from one operation to another; here

tific expertise of one's younger years, lore now more suited for the
narrower roles of technicians or junior managers. One must, in fact,
put distance between oneself and technical details of every sort or
risk the inevitable entrapment of the particular. Salesmen too must
leave their bags and regular customers and long boisterous evenings
that seal measurable deals behind them and turn to marketing strategies. Work becomes more ambiguous, directed as it is toward
maneuvering money, symbols, organizational structures, and especially people. The CEO at Weft Corporation, it is said, "doesn't
know a loom from a car." And the higher one goes, the more managers find that "the essence of managerial work is cronyism, covering your ass, [and] pyramiding to protect your buddies."

The more abstract work becomes, that is, the less one actually
does or oversees concrete tasks, the greater the likelihood that one's
rational efforts to improve an organization will meet with and even
beget various kinds of irrationality. One's rational systems, say, in
Weft Corporation for measuring loom efficiency, or in Covenant
for designing a grid appraising the relative strategic potentials of a
cluster of businesses, fall to others for implementation and become
hostage to their own private and organizational agendas, or become
the cross hairs of others' gunsights. One's best laid plans are always
subject to ambush by random events, fickle markets, recalcitrant
or, worse, well-intentioned but incompetent subordinates, rival
managers, or simply the weariness that work produces. One's best
intentioned schemes sometimes produce exactly the opposite of
what one wanted to achieve. One's best efforts at being fair, equi-
table, and generous with subordinates clash both with a logic that
demands choices between people, inevitably producing hatred, envy
and animosity, and with the plain fact that, despite protestations
to the contrary, many people do not want to be treated fairly. In
short, the increasingly abstract quality of managerial work as one
advances both symbolizes and exacerbates the structural fragmen-

---

cloth is racing through flames, here over drying cans, there entering the finishing ranges a
dull gray and emerging any of a series of muted or brilliant colors. At one level of their consciousness, those who work in the plant come to take for granted what seems extraordinary
to an outsider. At another level, they make connections between product and process—say,
the shirt that one wears and how it was made—generally unavailable to those outside a particular occupational community. Even after years of work in such a setting, some managers
still find their daily exposure to the drama of coordinating human toil with technology an
exhilarating experience.

tation of corporate, individual, and common goods. Such conun-
drums often produce nostalgic yearnings for simpler times, for the
concrete work of one's younger years, even for fabled crisis periods when "everyone pulled together and got the job done," and
perhaps especially for a society that unambiguously, it is thought,
extolled work in business as socially honorable and personally
salvific.

[The Main Chance]

For most managers, especially for those who are ambitious, the real
meaning of work—the basis of social identity and valued self-image—
becomes keeping one's eye on the main chance, maintaining and
furthering one's own position and career. This task requires, of
course, unrelenting attentiveness to the social intricacies of one's
organization. One gains dominance or fails depending on one's
access to key managerial circles where prestige is gauged precisely
by the relationships that one establishes with powerful managers
and by the demonstrated favor such relationships bring. Even
beyond their practical and crucial importance in furthering careers,
the social psychological lure of entrance into such select groups is,
of course, powerful and layers the drive to get ahead with complicated overtones. Such acceptance means, variously, no longer being
relegated to marginality; having one's voice heard and opinion
count in matters small and weighty; experiencing the peculiar bonds
with one's fellows produced by shared secrecy, hard decisions and
hard times, a sense of shared emotional aridity, and competition
with rival cliques; penetrating the many layers of consciousness in
the corporation that baffle outsiders and marginal managers alike;
and being able to dispense at times, usually in the heat of battle
and only within one's tried and trusted circle, with the gentlemanly
politesse and requisite public advocacy of high-minded beliefs and,
always with relief and sometimes with comic vulgarity, to get down
to brass tacks. What one manager calls "our surrender of ourselves
to groups" has its emotional touchstone in the sense of professional
intimacy that acceptance into a managerial circle affords. Group
intimacy, especially with powerful others, rewards and seals the self-

directed transformation of self that makes one come to accept the
ethos of an organization as one's own. But the process is rarely
simple, precisely because such acceptance depends on developing
and maintaining personal relationships with powerful others. Mas-
tering the subtle but necessary arts of deference without seeming
to be deferential, of "brown nosing" without fawning, of simultaneous self-promotion and self-effacement, and occasionally of the
outright self-abasement that such relationships require is a taxing
endeavor that demands continual compromises with conventional
and popular notions of integrity. Only those with an inexhaustible
capacity for self-rationalization, fueled by boundless ambition, can
escape the discomfort such compromises produce. . . .

But self-rationalization, even for those willing to open themselves
up fully to institutional demands, produces its own discomforts and
discontents. As in all professional careers, particularly those dependent on large organizations, managerial work requires a psychic
asceticism of a high degree, a willingness to discipline the self, to
thwart one's impulses, to stifle spontaneity in favor of control, to
conceal emotion and intent, and to objectify the self with the same
kind of calculating functional rationality that one brings to the
packaging of any commodity. Moreover, such dispassionate objectification of the self frames and paces the rational objectification
of circumstances and people that alertness to expediency demands.
In its asceticism, self-rationalization curiously parallels the methodi-
cal subjection to God's will that the old Protestant ethic counseled.
But instead of the satisfaction of believing that one is acquiring old-
time moral virtues, one becomes a master at manipulating personae;
instead of making oneself into an instrument of God's will to accomplish His work in this world, one becomes, variously, a boss's "hammer," a tough guy who never blinks at hard decisions, or perhaps, if
all goes very well, an "industrial statesman," a leader with vision.

On one hand, such psychic asceticism is connected to the nar-
cissism that one sees in executives of high rank. The simultaneous
need for self-abnegation, self-promotion, and self-display, as managers work their way through the probationary crucibles of big
organizational life, foster an absorption with self and specifically
with self-improvement. Managers become continually and self-
consciously aware of their public performances; they measure

themselves constantly against others; and they plot out whatever self-transformations will help them achieve desired goals. . . .

On the other hand, over a period of time, psychic asceticism creates a curious sense of guilt, heightened as it happens by narcissistic self-preoccupation. Such guilt, a regret at sustained self-abnegation and deprivation, finds expression principally in one's private emotional life. One drinks too much; one is subject to pencil-snapping fits of alternating anxiety, depression, rage, and self-disgust for willingly submitting oneself to the knowing and not knowing, to the constant containment of anger, to the keeping quiet, to the knuckling under that are all inevitable in bureaucratic life. One experiences great tensions at home because one's spouse is unable to grasp or unable to tolerate the endless review of the social world of the workplace, the rehearsals of upcoming conversations, or the agonizing over real or imagined social slights or perceptions of shifts in power alignments. One wishes that one had spent more time with one's children when they were small so that one could grasp the meanings of their adolescent traumas. Or one withdraws emotionally from one's family and, with alternating fascination and regret, plunges ever deeper into the dense and intimate relationships of organizational circles where emotional aridity signals a kind of fraternity of expediency. Many try at times to escape the guilt with Walter Mitty–like fantasies of insouciant rebellion and vengeful retaliation; but one knows that only if and when one rises to high position in a bureaucratic hierarchy does one have the opportunity to turn the pain of self-repression against one's fellows. . . .

However, for those with the requisite discipline, sheer dogged perseverance, the agile flexibility, the tolerance for extreme ambiguity, the casuistic discernment that allows one to dispense with shopworn pieties, the habit of mind that perceives opportunities in others' and even one's own misfortunes, the brazen nerve that allows one to pretend that nothing is wrong even when the world is crumbling, and, above all, the ability to read the inner logic of events, to see and do what has to be done, the rewards of corporate success can be very great. And, of course, those who do succeed, those who find their way out of the crowded, twisting corridors and into the back rooms where the real action is, where the big games take place, and where everyone present is a player, shape, in a decisive way, the moral rules-in-use that filter down through their organizations. The ethos that they fashion turns principles into guidelines, ethics into etiquette, values into tastes, personal responsibility into an adroitness at public relations, and notions of truth into credibility. Corporate managers who become imbued with this ethos pragmatically take their world as they find it and try to make that world work according to its own institutional logic. They pursue their own careers and good fortune as best they can within the rules of their world. As it happens, given their pivotal institutional role in our epoch, they help create and re-create, as one unintended consequence of their personal striving, a society where morality becomes indistinguishable from the quest for one's own survival and advantage.

III
Patterns

Preview of the Readings

Many social patterns found in corporations and government agencies nourish and sustain deviance. Job assignments and organizational routines can push employees to be so committed to their product that they fail to take action when they learn the product is hazardous. Bureaucracies and armies can provide resources, beliefs, and authorization that encourage their people to murder other people. Management pressures can influence employees to launch unsafe space shuttles. The readings in this section examine how patterns such as these are linked with corporate and governmental deviance.

Selection 4, "White-Collar Crime," is from Edwin Sutherland's book by the same title. Professor Sutherland was the first to define white-collar crime and one of the first to document that corporations frequently violate the law. His data were so novel when first presented that they gained front-page attention in the *New York Times*.

Selection 5, Gilbert Geis's "The Heavy Electrical Equipment Antitrust Cases," is a classic description and analysis of an important and well-publicized instance of price-fixing where prosecutors actually went after major corporations. Professor Geis describes how over a 20-year period General Electric, Westinghouse, 27 other corporations, and many more individuals illegally conspired to decide which of them would offer the low bid, and what that bid would be, when selling heavy electrical equipment to public utilities for use in generating and transmitting electricity.

Selection 6, Kermit Vandivier's "Why Should My Conscience Bother Me?" details how and why B. F. Goodrich Company built and released an aircraft brake that many employees knew was unsafe. In addition to providing a vivid account of his personal involvement in corporate deviance, the author shows how Goodrich's organizational structure and climate made the deviance more likely.

Selection 7, "Why I Didn't Recognize Pinto Fire Hazards," explains Dennis Gioia's role in the failure to recall the Pinto. He was of pivotal importance because he served as Ford's recall coordinator between 1973 and 1975. Looking back at that earlier time in his life, Professor Gioia argues that expected behaviors ("scripts") and belief systems ("schemas") kept him and other Ford employees from recognizing and correcting Pinto hazards.

Selection 8, "The Nazi Holocaust," focuses on the administrative and psychological obstacles that we might think would have hindered German participants in genocide. It explains how bureaucracies and people overcame these normal human obstacles. Agencies reformulated or ignored laws, some bureaucrats wrote intentionally passionless memos, others sought to efficiently define and concentrate the people who were to be murdered, and the entire structure helped participants at all levels repress and rationalize the problems that their participation raised in their minds.

Selection 9, "The My Lai Massacre," explains why American soldiers murdered over 100 unarmed women, children, babies, and old men in My Lai, Viet Nam. Professors Herbert Kellman and Lee Hamilton use this case to direct our attention to the organizational forces, especially authorization, routinization, and dehumanization, that lead to sanctioned massacres such as My Lai.

Selection 10, "The *Challenger* Disaster," traces events leading to the deaths of seven astronauts aboard the space shuttle *Challenger*. The authors show that managers had to decide in the absence of clear organizational launch criteria for a crucial component that ultimately failed. This is no excuse, however. The authors point out that while individuals are not "the locus of power and responsibility" in large organizations, individuals have and can make important choices.

Selection 11, "Rodney King and Use of Excessive Force," uses the Los Angeles police beating of Rodney King to show how the training and experiences of police officers could encourage their deviance. It shows that police departments, like other organizations, train new organizational members, enforce compliance with formal and informal norms, and ultimately influence how they deal with people outside the organization.

Annotated Bibliography

Adams, James Ring. *The Big Fix: Inside the S & L Scandal.* New York: Wiley, 1990. Why so many savings and loans went belly up.

Burnham, David. *A Law unto Itself: Power, Politics, and the IRS.* New York: Random House, 1990. Misconduct by the Internal Revenue Service, ranging from cashing checks that were not its to cash to helping presidents harass political enemies.

Burrough, Bryand, and John Helyar. *Barbarians at the Gate: The Fall and Rise of RJR Nabisco.* New York: Harper and Row, 1990. A richly textured account of the leveraged buyout of the giant tobacco and food conglomerate.

Clinard Marshall B., and Peter C. Yeager, with the collaboration of Ruth Blackburn Clinard. *Corporate Crime.* New York: Free Press, 1980. Violations of federal laws by the nation's 582 largest corporations. One of the most important books in the area of corporate crime.

Donner, Frank. *Protectors of Privilege: Red Squads and Police Repression in Urban America.* Berkeley: University of California Press, 1990. Repression by police in major U.S. cities.

Gamson, William A. "Hiroshima, the Holocaust, and the Politics of Exclusion." *American Sociological Review* 60 (1995): 1–20. How we define "we" and "they" can set in motion processes that can culminate in genocide and other forms of mass destruction.

Golenbock, Peter. *Personal Fouls: The Broken Promises and Shattered Dreams of Big Money Basketball at Jim Valvano's North Carolina State.* New York: Carroll and Graf, 1989. Corruption and misconduct during the late Jim Valvano's tenure as men's basketball coach.

Gordon, William. *The Fourth of May: Killings and Cover Ups at Kent State.* Buffalo, N.Y.: Prometheus, 1990. Events surrounding the shootings at Kent State University on May 4, 1970.

Grant, Nicole J. *The Selling of Contraception: The Dalkon Shield Case, Sexuality, and Women's Autonomy.* Columbus, Ohio: Ohio State University Press, 1992. Analysis of the corporate and governmental sexism that sustained release of the Dalkon Shield.

Hilberg, Raul. *Perpetrators Victims Bystanders: The Jewish Catastrophe, 1933–1945.* New York: Aaron Asher, 1992. A study of individuals who participated in the Holocaust, by the author of Selection 8.

Jamieson, Katherine M. *The Organization of Corporate Crime: Dynamics of Antitrust Violation.* Thousand Oaks, Calif.: Sage, 1994. Price-fixing by Fortune 500 corporations between 1981 and 1985.

Jamieson, Kathleen Hall. *Dirty Politics: Deception, Distraction, and Democracy.* New York: Oxford University Press, 1992. "Attack campaigning" across time, with an especially compelling chapter on the 1988 presidential campaign and the Willie Horton episode.

Jones, James. *Bad Blood: The Tuskegee Syphilis Experiment.* New York: Free Press, 1993. The U.S. Public Health Service "experiment" in which men with syphilis were left untreated in order to assess the long-term effects of the disease.

Kohn, Howard. "Service With A Sneer." *New York Times Magazine*, November 6, 1994, pp. 43ff. Explains racism at Denny's restaurants and what the company is doing to change things.

Kutler, Stanley. *The Wars of Watergate: The Last Crisis of Richard Nixon*. New York: Knopf, 1990. The Watergate burglary and the cover-up that followed.

Lowy, Martin. *Inside the Savings and Loan Debacle*. New York: Praeger, 1991. Origins of the savings and loan crisis.

Perry, Susan, and Jim Dawson. *Nightmare: Women and the Dalkon Shield*. New York: Macmillan, 1985. A. H. Robins's birth control device that killed and injured women.

Robins, Natalie. *Alien Ink: The FBI's War on Freedom of Expression*. New York: William Morrow, 1992. Description of FBI collection and use of information on prominent authors.

Rosenblatt, Roger. "How Do They Live with Themselves?" *New York Times Magazine*, March 20, 1994, pp. 34ff. How the people inside the tobacco and food conglomerate Philip Morris rationalize making and selling Marlboro and other cigarettes.

Rothmiller, Mike, with Ivan G. Goldman. *L.A. Secret Police: Inside the LAPD Elite Spy Network*. New York: Pocket Books, 1992. Description of the Organized Crime Intelligence Division that spied on almost everybody, sometimes even members of organized crime.

Sperber, Murray. *College Sports Inc.: The Athletic Department vs. the University*. New York: Holt, 1990. Corruption in college sport.

Wilkinson, Alec. *Big Sugar: Seasons in the Cane Fields of Florida*. New York: Knopf, 1989. A description of the workers who keep things sweet for major sugar companies.

4

White Collar Crime
Definition and the Statistical Record

Edwin H. Sutherland

[Definition]

The thesis of this [selection], stated positively, is that persons of the upper socioeconomic class engage in much criminal behavior; that this criminal behavior differs from the criminal behavior of the lower socioeconomic class principally in the administrative procedures which are used in dealing with the offenders; and that variations in administrative procedures are not significant from the point of view of causation of crime. The causes of tuberculosis were not different when it was treated by poultices and bloodletting than when treated by streptomycin.

These violations of law by persons in the upper socioeconomic class are, for convenience, called "white collar crimes." This concept is not intended to be definitive, but merely to call attention to crimes which are not ordinarily included within the scope of criminology. White collar crime may be defined approximately as a crime committed by a person of respectability and high social status in the course of his occupation. Consequently it excludes many crimes of the upper class such as most cases of murder, intoxication, or adultery, since these are not a part of the occupational procedures. Also, it excludes the confidence games of wealthy members of the underworld, since they are not persons of respectability and high social status. . . .

The Statistical Record

In order to secure more definite information regarding the crimes of persons of the upper socioeconomic class, an attempt has been made to tabulate the decisions of courts and administrative commissions against the 70 largest manufacturing, mining, and mercantile corporations.* The 70 largest corporations used in this analysis are, with two exceptions, included in each of two lists of the 200 largest nonfinancial corporations in the United States. One of these lists was prepared by Berle and Means in 1929 and the other by the Temporary National Economic Committee in 1938. From these lists were excluded the public utility corporations, including transportation and communications corporations, and also the petroleum corporations. This left 68 corporations common to both lists. To these were added two corporations which appeared in the list for 1938 but not in the list for 1929. One of these was Standard Brands, which was organized by the merger of preexisting corporations in 1929 and had grown to the dimensions of the other large corporations by 1938. The other was Gimbel Brothers, which was not far below the other corporations in 1929, and which was added to the present list in order to secure a larger representation of mercantile corporations. The list of 70 corporations is, therefore, unselected except as to size and type of specialization, with the two exceptions mentioned, and neither of these exceptions was selected with knowledge of its rank among large corporations as to violations of laws.

The present analysis covers the life careers of the 70 corporations. The average life of these corporations is approximately 45 years, but decisions as to the date of origin are arbitrary in a few cases. The analysis, also, includes the decisions against the subsidiaries of the 70 corporations, as listed in the standard manuals, for the period these subsidiaries have been under the control of the parent corporation.

The analysis is concerned with the following types of violations of laws: restraint of trade, misrepresentation in advertising; infringe-

*ED NOTE: In the original version of *White Collar Crime* published in 1949, Professor Sutherland's publisher (Dryden Press) would not permit identification of the corporations for fear of being sued. The version from which you are now reading was the first time the corporations studied by Professor Sutherland were publicly identified.

ment of patent, trademarks, and copyrights; "unfair labor practices" as defined by the National Labor Relations Board and a few decisions under other labor laws; rebates; financial fraud and violation of trust; violations of war regulations; and some miscellaneous offenses. All of the cases included in the tabulation are defined as violations of law, most of them may properly be defined as crimes, and the others are closely allied to criminal behavior. . . .

The sources of information regarding these violations of law are the decisions of the federal, state, and, in a few cases, municipal courts, as published in the *Federal Reporter* and the *American State Reports*; the published decisions of the Federal Trade Commission, the Interstate Commerce Commission, the Securities and Exchange Commission, the National Labor Relations Board, and, for the period 1934–37, of the Federal Pure Food and Drug Administration. These official reports have been supplemented, as to infringement, by the reports on infringement cases listed in the *Official Gazette* of the Patent Office, and as to violations of law in general by reports of decisions in newspapers. The *New York Times* has been used, especially, because its material has been indexed since 1913. The name of each of the 70 corporations and its subsidiaries was checked against the index of each of these series of reports and of the *New York Times*.

The enumeration of decisions as reported in these sources is certainly far short of the total number of decisions against these 70 corporations. First, many of the decisions of the lower courts are not published in the series of federal and state reports, and many of them are not published in the newspapers. Second, many suits are settled out of court and no outcome is reported in the series of reports or in newspapers. The number of suits initiated against the 70 corporations which dropped out of sight after preliminary motions and were presumably settled out of court is approximately 50 percent of the number included in the tabulation in this chapter. Presumably many of these involved violations of law and could have been tabulated as such if more complete information were available. Third, the Pure Food and Drug Administration has not published its decisions by names of offenders except during the years 1924–47. Fourth, many of the decisions are indexed under names such as "The John Doe Trade Association," or "John Doe et al." Consequently, many of the 70 corporations which have been defendants in those suits were not discovered because their names did not appear in the indexes, and often were not even mentioned in the published reports. Finally, many of the subsidiaries of these corporations are not listed in the financial manuals and could not be identified for the present study.

A decision against one of the 70 corporations is the unit in this tabulation. If a decision is made in one suit against 3 of the 70 corporations, that decision is counted three times, once against each of the 3 corporations. Also, if a criminal suit and an equity suit are initiated against one corporation for essentially the same overt behavior and a decision is made against the corporation in each of those suits, two decisions are counted. This, obviously, involves some duplication. On the other hand, one decision may contain scores of counts, each of which charges a specific violation of law and, also, may refer to a policy which has been in operation for a decade or longer. These are some of the reasons why these decisions are not an accurate index of the comparative amounts of illegal behavior by the several corporations.

The term "decision" is used here to include not only the formal decisions and orders of courts, but also the decisions of administrative commissions, stipulations accepted by courts and commissions, settlements ordered or approved by the court, confiscation of food as in violation of the Pure Food Law, and, in a few cases, which will be explained in the later chapters, opinion of courts that the defendant had violated the law at an earlier time even though the court then dismissed the suit.

The enumeration of the decisions which have been discovered is presented in Table 4.1. This shows that each of the 70 large corporations has 1 or more decisions against it, with a maximum of 50. The total number of decisions is 980, and the average per corporation is 14.0. Sixty corporations have decisions against them for restraint of trade, 53 for infringement, 44 for unfair labor practices, 43 for miscellaneous offenses, 28 for misrepresentation in advertising, and 26 for rebates.

Armour & Company and Swift & Company stand at the top of the list in the total number of adverse decisions, with 50 each. General Motors has third rank with 40, and Sears Roebuck ties with Montgomery Ward for fourth rank with 39 each. These five corporations are decidedly in excess of the other corporations in the

TABLE 4.1
Decisions by Courts and Commissions against 70 Large Corporations by Types of Laws Violated

Corporation	Restraint of trade	Misrepresentation in advertising	Infringement	Unfair labor practices	Rebates	Other	Total
Allied Chemical & Dye	7	1	—	5	—	—	13
Aluminum Co. of America	4	—	1	3	3	3	14
American Can	6	—	1	—	—	1	8
American Car & Foundry	1	—	6	2	—	1	10
Amer. Radiator & Stand. San.	—	—	—	2	—	—	2
American Rolling Mills	1	—	—	3	1	—	5
American Smelting & Refin.	2	—	1	4	2	5	14
American Sugar Refining	7	—	—	—	10	6	23
American Tobacco	19	—	2	—	2	2	25
American Woolen	1	1	1	—	—	—	3
Anaconda Copper	4	—	4	2	—	7	17
Armour & Company	12	6	2	11	6	13	50
Bethlehem Steel	3	—	2	5	4	—	14
Borden	7	2	1	—	1	1	12
Chrysler	1	3	1	1	1	2	9
Corn Products	3	4	1	—	1	1	10
Crane	3	—	1	1	1	—	6
Crown Zellerbach	5	—	—	—	—	—	5
Deere	—	—	2	2	—	—	4
DuPont	7	—	4	3	—	—	14
Eastman Kodak	5	—	3	—	—	—	8
Firestone	1	1	4	2	—	—	8
Ford	1	2	8	15	1	1	28
General Electric	13	2	9	—	—	1	25

TABLE 4.1 (continued)

Corporation	Restraint of trade	Misrepresentation in advertising	Infringement	Unfair labor practices	Rebates	Other	Total
General Motors	6	2	22	9	—	1	40
Gimbel	—	12	11	—	—	—	23
Glen Alden Coal	5	—	—	1	1	—	7
Goodrich	1	1	2	3	—	—	7
Goodyear	1	1	4	3	—	5	14
Great A & P	8	3	—	1	—	7	19
Inland Steel	1	—	—	3	1	3	8
International Harvester	11	—	3	2	3	—	19
International Paper	2	—	2	—	2	2	8
International Shoe	—	2	—	—	—	1	3
Jones & Laughlin	1	—	—	4	1	1	7
Kennecott Copper	2	—	1	2	—	—	5
Kresge	—	1	9	1	—	7	18
Liggett & Myers	1	—	—	—	—	1	2
Loew's	22	—	6	—	—	3	31
Macy & Company	—	5	13	—	—	—	18
Marshall Field	1	2	2	3	—	—	8
Montgomery Ward	1	12	15	5	—	6	39
National Biscuit	2	1	1	—	—	1	5
National Dairy Products	8	—	1	—	1	2	12
National Lead	3	—	3	5	—	1	12

National Steel	1	—	—	2	2	1	6
Paramount	21	—	4	—	—	—	25
Phelps Dodge	3	—	1	9	—	1	14
Philadelphia & Reading Coal	6	—	1	—	—	—	7
Pittsburgh Coal	1	—	—	—	—	—	1
Pittsburgh Plate Glass	6	—	3	3	4	1	17
Procter & Gamble	1	8	1	1	—	2	13
RCA	3	1	2	—	—	2	8
Republic Steel	3	—	—	7	1	—	11
Reynolds Tobacco	1	—	—	—	—	—	1
Sears Roebuck	—	18	20	1	—	—	39
Singer Mfg. Co.	—	—	5	2	—	—	7
Standard Brands	2	1	—	—	—	—	3
Swift & Company	12	1	1	10	5	21	50
Union Carbide & Carbon	—	—	5	—	—	2	7
United Fruit	3	—	1	—	—	1	5
United Shoe Machinery	1	1	3	—	—	1	6
U.S. Rubber	6	1	1	1	—	1	10
U.S. Steel	9	2	5	2	5	3	26
Warner Bros.	21	—	3	—	—	1	25
Westinghouse Electric	10	1	5	2	—	1	19
Wheeling Steel	2	—	1	1	2	—	6
Wilson & Company	4	—	1	9	3	2	19
Woolworth	—	—	10	1	—	4	15
Youngstown	2	—	3	—	2	1	8
Total	307	97	222	158	66	130	980

number of decisions, for Loew's in sixth rank has only 31. These totals, however, are not a precise measure of the comparative amounts of illegal behavior by these corporations. Armour and Swift, for instance, are subject to the Pure Food and Drug Law, which does not apply to many other corporations. If the laws explicitly declared that any defects in shoes, electrical equipment, tobacco, films, or automobiles were misdemeanors, as they do in regard to foods, the number of decisions against the other corporations might be as high as the number against Swift and Armour. Table 4.1 shows, however, that Armour and Swift would be in the highest ranks even if decisions under the Pure Food Law were disregarded. General Motors, which stands in third rank, has more than half of the decisions against it on charges of infringements, while Sears Roebuck and Montgomery Ward have decisions concentrated in "misrepresentation in advertising" and "infringements."

The corporations in one industry frequently cluster in one part of the distribution and have ranks which are not far apart, considering the possible spread of 70 ranks. Three meat-packing corporations in the list of 70 corporations have ranks of 1, 2, and 17. The two mail order corporations tie for fourth rank. The two dairy corporations tie for 33rd rank. The ranks of the three motion picture corporations are: Loew's 6th, and Paramount and Warner tied for 10th position. On the other hand, the corporations in one industry are sometimes scattered more widely. The four rubber manufacturers have ranks as follows: Goodyear 25th, U.S. Rubber 35th, Firestone 43rd, and Goodrich 48th. The nine steel corporations range between ninth and 58th positions.

Table 4.2 presents an analysis of the 980 decisions by types of jurisdictions of the courts and commissions which rendered the decisions. This shows that 158 decisions were made against 41 of the 70 corporations by criminal courts, 296 decisions against 57 of the corporations by civil courts, and 129 decisions against 44 corporations by courts under equity jurisdiction.This gives a total of 583 decisions which were made by courts. The administrative commissions made 361 decisions, and approximately one-fourth of these were referred to courts and were sustained by the courts. The commissions, also, confiscated goods in 25 cases as in violation of the Pure Food law. Eleven cases are tabulated as "settlements," and all

TABLE 4.2

Decisions by Courts and Commissions against 70 Large Corporations for Violations of Specified Laws, by Jurisdictions and Procedures

Corporation	Court			Commission			Total
	Criminal	Civil	Equity	Order	Confiscation	Settlement	
Allied Chemical & Dye	3	—	1	9	—	—	13
Aluminum Co. of America	3	3	3	4	—	1	14
American Can	2	3	2	2	—	—	8
American Car & Foundry	—	6	1	3	—	—	10
Amer. Radiator & Stand. San.	—	—	—	2	—	—	2
Amer. Rolling Mills	1	—	—	4	—	—	5
American Smelting	3	1	4	6	—	—	14
American Sugar	12	3	7	—	—	1	23
American Tobacco	10	10	2	1	—	2	25
American Woolen	—	1	1	1	—	—	3
Anaconda	6	4	4	3	—	—	17
Armour	18	4	4	17	7	—	50
Bethlehem	3	2	4	8	—	—	14
Borden	6	1	—	5	—	—	12
Chrysler	2	2	—	5	—	—	9
Corn Products	2	1	3	4	—	—	10
Crane	1	1	1	3	—	—	6
Crown Zellerbach	3	—	1	1	—	—	5
Deere	—	2	—	2	—	—	4
DuPont	4	4	1	5	—	—	14
Eastman	—	4	2	2	—	—	8
Firestone	—	4	—	4	—	—	8
Ford	2	8	—	18	—	—	28

TABLE 4.2 (continued)

Corporation	Court			Commission		Settlement	Total
	Criminal	Civil	Equity	Order	Confiscation		
General Electric	4	9	5	6	—	1	25
General Motors	1	23	4	12	—	—	40
Gimbel	—	12	—	11	—	—	23
Glen Alden Coal	1	—	4	2	—	—	7
Goodrich	—	2	—	5	—	—	7
Goodyear	2	5	—	5	—	2	14
Great A & P	7	4	—	6	2	—	19
Inland Steel	—	—	2	6	—	—	8
Intern. Harvester	10	3	1	5	—	—	19
Intern. Paper	3	4	1	—	—	—	8
Intern. Shoe	—	1	—	2	—	—	3
Jones & Laughlin	1	—	1	5	—	—	7
Kennecott	1	1	—	3	—	—	5
Kresge	2	9	5	2	—	—	18
Liggett & Myers	2	—	—	—	—	—	2
Loew's	—	15	13	3	—	—	31
Macy	—	13	—	5	—	—	18
Marshall Field	—	2	—	6	—	—	8
Montgomery Ward	—	18	2	19	—	—	39
National Biscuit	—	2	—	2	1	—	5
National Dairy Products	6	1	1	3	1	—	12
National Lead	1	5	1	5	—	—	12

							Total
National Steel	1	—	—	5	—	—	6
Paramount	—	11	10	4	—	—	25
Phelps Dodge	1	1	1	11	—	—	14
Phil. & Reading Coal	1	—	5	1	—	—	7
Pittsburgh Coal	—	—	—	1	—	—	1
Pittsburgh Plate	2	5	1	9	—	—	17
Procter & Gamble	1	1	1	9	—	1	13
RCA	—	3	1	3	—	1	8
Republic Steel	1	—	—	10	—	—	11
Reynolds Tobacco	1	—	—	—	—	—	1
Sears Roebuck	—	20	—	19	—	—	39
Singer	—	5	—	2	—	—	7
Standard Brands	—	—	—	3	—	—	3
Swift	18	3	6	10	13	—	50
Union Carbide & Carbon	—	6	—	1	—	—	7
United Fruit	—	4	1	—	—	—	5
United Shoe Mach.	—	5	1	—	—	—	6
U.S. Rubber	—	3	1	6	—	—	10
U.S. Steel	4	6	3	13	—	—	26
Warner Bros.	—	10	10	4	—	1	25
Westinghouse	3	6	3	6	—	1	19
Wheeling	—	1	1	4	—	—	6
Wilson	3	2	4	10	—	—	19
Woolworth	2	10	2	1	—	—	15
Youngstown	—	1	—	7	—	—	8
Total	158	296	129	361	23	11	980

of these were civil suits in which the settlements were approved or ordered by the courts. In hundreds of other cases, settlements were reached outside of courts but these have not been included in the tabulation in this chapter.

This analysis shows that approximately 16 percent of the decisions were made by criminal courts. . . . Even if the present analysis were limited to these decisions by criminal courts, it would show that 60 percent of the 70 large corporations have been convicted in criminal courts and have an average of approximately four convictions each. In many states persons with four convictions are defined by statute to be "habitual criminals." The frequency of these convictions of large corporations might be sufficient to demonstrate the fallacy in the conventional theories that crime is due to poverty or to the personal and social pathologies connected with poverty.

One of the interesting aspects of these decisions is that they have been concentrated in the last decade. The distribution of the decisions in time is presented by types of offenses in Table 4.3. In this analysis the date of the first adverse decision in a particular suit was used. The case was not counted, of course, unless the final decision was against the corporation. Relatively few cases initiated after 1944 have been included in this study. Consequently, it is approximately correct to conclude that 60 percent of the adverse decisions were rendered in the 10-year period 1935–44, while only 40 percent were rendered in the 35-year period 1900–34.

One possible explanation of this concentration is that violations of laws by large corporations have increased and are much more prevalent in recent years than in earlier years. Since several possible explanations may be equally significant, they are considered first.

First, the number of corporations has not remained constant during the period under consideration. Although the 70 corporations have had an average life of 45 years, only 63 of these corporations were in existence in 1920 and only 53 in 1910. This factor, however, seems to be relatively unimportant. A separate tabulation of the 53 corporations which originated prior to 1910 shows that 57.4 percent of the decisions were rendered in the period 1935–44, as contrasted with 59.7 percent for the entire list of 70 corporations.

Second, some of the laws which have been violated by these corporations were enacted during the last decade. The National Labor

TABLE 4.3
Decisions against 70 Large Corporations by Five-Year Periods and by Types of Laws Violated

Dates	Restraint of trade	Misrepresentation in advertising	Infringement	Unfair labor practices	Rebates	Other	Total	Percentages
1940–date	102	34	52	102	7	43	340	34.7
1935–39	59	42	59	50	15	20	245	25.0
1930–34	27	8	36	4	7	10	92	9.4
1925–29	28	1	26	–	–	23	78	8.0
1920–24	18	3	12	–	–	9	42	4.3
1915–19	20	7	5	–	6	7	45	4.6
1910–14	29	1	13	1	14	7	64	6.5
1905–09	17	–	9	1	14	5	46	4.7
1900–04	5	1	6	1	3	1	17	1.7
1890–99	2	–	1	–	–	3	6	0.6
Prior to 1890	–	–	3	–	–	2	5	0.5
Totals	307	97	222	158	66	130	980	100.0

Relations Law was enacted in 1935, with a similar law under the National Industrial Recovery Act of 1934, and decisions under this law are necessarily concentrated almost entirely in the period 1935–44. If this law is disregarded, 52.5 percent of the decisions under the other laws were made in the ten-year period 1935–44. The enactment and amendment of other laws applying to corporations provide some explanation of this concentration in the last decade. Although this influence cannot be measured with precision, it certainly accounts for a very small part of the concentration.

Third, vigorous prosecution of violations of law by corporations has been concentrated in the period since 1932. Budgets have been increased and additional assistants provided, so that violations were acted upon in the last decade which were neglected in the earlier decades. Probably both the enactment of laws and the enforcement of laws during this period are explained by the fact that businessmen lost much prestige in the depression which began in 1929. The increase in the number of decisions on restraint of trade and misrepresentation in advertising, especially, can be explained in this manner.

Fourth, businessmen are resorting to an increasing extent to "policies of social manipulation" in contrast with the earlier concentration on efficiency in production. With emphasis on advertising and salesmanship, as policies of social manipulation, have gone increased attention to lobbying and litigation. This is shown especially in the trend in decisions regarding infringements. Since these are civil suits, initiated by persons who regard their rights as infringed, they are not a direct reflection of governmental policies. They are, however, presumably affected somewhat by governmental policies in an indirect manner. The increase in the number of prosecutions on charges of restraint of trade, frequently involving patent manipulations, has given the general public and the owners of patents insight into the policies of these large corporations and has stimulated efforts of patent holders to protect their rights.

Of these possible explanations, the increased vigor of and facilities for prosecution are probably the most important. It is probable, also, that the frequency of violations of some of the laws has increased significantly, although this does not appear to be true of all laws.

Of the 70 corporations, 30 were either illegal in their origin or began illegal activities immediately after their origin, and 8 additional corporations were probably illegal in origin or in initial policies. Of the violations of law which appeared in these early activities, 27 were restraint of trade and 3 were patent infringements; of the 8 origins which were probably criminal, 5 involved restraint of trade, 2 patent infringements, and 1 fraud. The evidence for this appraisal of the origins of corporations consists in court decisions in 21 cases, and other historical evidence in the other cases.

5

The Heavy Electrical Equipment Antitrust Cases

Price-Fixing Techniques and Rationalizations

Gilbert Geis

An inadvertent bit of humor by a defense attorney provided one of the major criminological motifs for "the most serious violation of the antitrust laws since the time of their passage at the turn of the century."[1] The defendants, including several vice-presidents of the General Electric Corporation and the Westinghouse Electric Corporation—the two largest companies in the heavy electrical equipment industry—stood somberly in a federal courtroom in Philadelphia on February 6, 1961. They were aptly described by a newspaper reporter as "middle-class men in Ivy League suits—typical business men in appearance, men who would never be taken for lawbreakers."[2] Several were deacons or vestrymen of their churches. One was president of his local chamber of commerce, another a hospital board member, another chief fund raiser for the community chest, another a bank director, another a director of the taxpayer's association, another an organizer of the local Little League.

The attorney for a General Electric executive attacked the government's demand for a jail sentence for his client, calling it "cold-blooded." The lawyer insisted that government prosecutors did not understand what it would do to his client, "this fine man," to be put "behind bars" with "common criminals who have been convicted of embezzlement and other serious crimes."[3]

From Marshall B. Clinard and Richard Quinney (eds.), *Criminal Behavior Systems: A Typology,* pp. 140–51. Copyright © 1967 by Holt, Rinehart and Winston. Reprinted by permission.

1. Judge J. Cullen Ganey in "Application of the State of California," *Federal Supplement,* 195 (Eastern District, Pennsylvania, 1961), p. 39.

2. *New York Times,* February 7, 1961.

3. *New York Times,* February 7, 1961.

The difficulty of defense counsel in considering antitrust violations "serious crimes," crimes at least equivalent to embezzling, indicates in part why the 1961 prosecutions provide such fascinating material for criminological study. Edwin H. Sutherland, who originated the term "white collar crime" to categorize offenders such as antitrust violators, had lamented that his pioneering work was handicapped by the absence of adequate case histories of corporate offenders. "No firsthand research from this point of view has even been reported,"[4] Sutherland noted and, lacking such data, he proceeded to employ rather prosaic stories of derelictions by rather unimportant persons in small enterprises upon which to build an interpretative and theoretical structure for white collar crime.

To explain corporate offenses and offenders, Sutherland had to rely primarily upon the criminal biographies of various large companies, as these were disclosed in the annals of trial courts and administrative agencies. In the absence of information about human offenders, the legal fiction of corporate humanity, a kind of economic anthropomorphism, found its way into criminological literature. Factual gaps were filled by shrewd guesses, definitional and semantic strategies, and a good deal of extrapolation. It was as if an attempt were being made to explain murder by reference only to the listed rap sheet offenses of a murderer and the life stories and identification data of several lesser offenders.[5]

Sutherland was writing, of course, before the antitrust violations in the heavy electrical equipment industry became part of the public record. Though much of the data regarding them is tantalizingly incomplete, unresponsive to fine points of particular criminological concern, the antitrust offenses nonetheless represent extraordinary case studies of white-collar crime, that designation which, according to Sutherland, applies to behavior by "a person of high socioeconomic status who violates the laws designed to regulate his

---

4. Edwin H. Sutherland, *White Collar Crime.* New York: Holt, Rinehart and Winston, Inc., 1949, p. 240. Note: "Private enterprise remains extraordinarily private. . . . We know more about the motives, habits, and most intimate arcana of primitive peoples in New Guinea . . . than we do of the denizens of executive suites in Unilever House, Citroen, or General Electric (at least until a recent Congressional investigation)."—Roy Lewis and Rosemary Stewart, *The Managers.* New York: New American Library, 1961, pp. 111–112.

5. For an elaboration of this point, see Gilbert Geis, "Toward a Delineation of White-Collar Offenses," *Sociological Inquiry,* 32 (Spring 1962), pp. 160–171.

occupational activities"[6] and "principally refers to business managers and executives."[7] In particular, the antitrust cases provide the researcher with a mass of raw data against which to test and to refine earlier hunches and hypotheses regarding white-collar crime.

Facts of the Antitrust Violations

The most notable characteristic of the 1961 antitrust conspiracy was its willful and blatant nature. These were not complex acts only doubtfully in violation of a highly complicated statute. They were flagrant criminal offenses, patently in contradiction to the letter and the spirit of the Sherman Antitrust Act of 1890, which forbade price-fixing arrangements as restraints upon free trade.[8]

The details of the conspiracy must be drawn together from diverse secondhand sources because the grand jury hearings upon which the criminal indictments were based were not made public. The decision to keep the records closed was reached on the ground that the traditional secrecy of grand jury proceedings took precedence over public interest in obtaining information about the conspiracy and over the interest of different purchasers in acquiring background data upon which to base civil suits against the offending corporations for allegedly fraudulent sales.[9]

The federal government had initiated the grand jury probes in mid-1959, apparently after receiving complaints from officials of the Tennessee Valley Authority concerning identical bids they were getting from manufacturers of highly technical electrical equipment,

6. Edwin H. Sutherland in Vernon C. Branham and Samuel B. Kutash, *Encyclopedia of Criminology.* New York: Philosophical Library, Inc., 1949, p. 511.

7. Sutherland, *White Collar Crime,* p. 9, fn. 7.

8. *United States Statutes,* 26 (1890), p. 209; *United States Code,* 15 (1958), pp. 1, 2. See also William L. Letwin, "Congress and the Sherman Antitrust Law, 1887–1890," *University of Chicago Law Review,* 23 (Winter 1956), pp. 221–258, and Paul E. Hadlick, *Criminal Prosecutions under the Sherman Anti-Trust Act,* Washington, D.C.: Ransdell, 1939. The best interpretation of American antitrust law is A. D. Neale, *Antitrust Laws of the United States,* New York: Cambridge University Press, 1960.

9. Note, "Release of the Grand Jury Minutes to the National Deposition Program of the Electrical Equipment Cases," *University of Pennsylvania Law Review,* 112 (June 1964), pp. 1133–1145.

even though the bids were submitted in sealed envelopes.[10] Four grand juries were ultimately convened and subpoenaed 196 persons, some of whom obviously revealed the intimate details of the price-fixing procedures. A package of twenty indictments was handed down, involving 45 individual defendants and 29 corporations. Almost all of the corporate defendants pleaded guilty; the company officials tended to enter pleas of nolo contendere (no contest) which, in this case, might reasonably be taken to indicate that they did not see much likelihood of escaping conviction.

The pleas negated the necessity for a public trial and for public knowledge of the precise machinations involved in the offenses. At the sentencing hearing, fines amounting to $1,924,500 were levied against the defendants, $1,787,000 falling upon the corporations and $137,000 upon different individuals. The major fines were set against General Electric ($437,500) and Westinghouse ($372,500). Much more eye-catching were the jail terms of thirty days imposed upon seven defendants, of whom four were vice-presidents, two were division managers, and one was a sales manager.

The defendants sentenced to jail were handled essentially the same as other offenders with similar dispositions. They were handcuffed in pairs in the back seat of an automobile on their way to the Montgomery County Jail in Norristown, Pennsylvania, fingerprinted on entry, and dressed in the standard blue denim uniforms. During their stay, they were described as "model prisoners," and several were transferred to the prison farm. The remainder, working an eight-hour day for 30 cents, earned recognition from the warden as "the most intelligent prisoners" he had had during the year on a project concerned with organizing prison records. None of the seven men had visitors during the Wednesday and Saturday periods reserved for visiting; all indicated a desire not to be seen by their families or friends.[11]

Good behavior earned the men a five-day reduction in their sentence. Toward the end of the year, the remaining defendants, who had been placed on probation, were released from that status,

10. John Herling, *The Great Price Conspiracy*, Washington, D.C.: Robert B. Luce, 1962, pp. 1–12; John G. Fuller, *The Gentleman Conspirators*, New York: Grove Press, Inc., 1962, pp. 7–11. See also Myron W. Watkins, "Electrical Equipment Antitrust Cases—Their Implications for Government and Business," *University of Chicago Law Review*, 29 (August 1961) pp. 97–110.

11. United Press International, February 16, 1961; *New York Times*, February 25, 1961.

despite the strong protests of government officials. The judge, the same man who had imposed the original sentences, explained his action by noting that he "didn't think that this was the type of offense that probation lent itself readily to or was designed for." Supervision was seen as meaningless for men with such past records and such little likelihood of recidivism, particularly since the probation office was already "clogged to the gunwales" with cases.[12]

The major economic consequences to the corporations arose from civil suits for treble damages filed against them as provided in the antitrust laws. The original fines were, of course, negligible: For General Electric, a half-million dollar loss was no more unsettling than a $3 parking fine would be to a man with an income of $175,000 a year. Throughout the early stages of negotiations over the damage suits, General Electric maintained that it would resist such actions on grounds which are noteworthy as an indication of the source and the content of the rationale that underlay the self-justification of individual participants in the price-fixing conspiracy:

> We believe that the purchasers of electrical apparatus have received fair value by any reasonable standard. The prices which they have paid during the past years were appropriate to value received and reasonable as compared with the general trends of prices in the economy, the price trends for similar equipment and the price trends for materials, salaries, and wages. The foresight of the electrical utilities and the design and manufacturing skills of companies such as General Electric have kept electricity one of today's greatest bargains.[13]

By 1962, General Electric was granting that settlements totaling between $45 and $50 million would have to be arranged to satisfy claimants.[14] Municipalities and other purchasers of heavy electrical equipment were taking the period of lowest prices, when they assumed the price-rigging was least effective, using these prices as "legitimate," and calculating higher payments as products of the price conspiracy.[15] The initial G.E. estimate soon proved as untenable as its original thesis regarding value received. A mid-1964 calculation showed that 90

---

12. Telephone interview with Judge Ganey, Philadelphia, August 31, 1964; *New York Times*, December 20, 1961.

13. *New York Times*, February 7, 1961.

14. *New York Times*, July 27, 1962.

15. *New York Times*, March 14, 1961.

percent of some 1800 claims had been settled for a total of $160 million,[16] but General Electric could derive some solace from the fact that most of these payments would be tax-deductible.[17]

Techniques of the Conspiracy

The modus operandi for the antitrust violations shows clearly the awareness of the participants that their behavior was such that it had better be carried on as secretly as possible. Some comparison might be made between the antitrust offenses and other forms of fraud occurring in lower economic classes. It was one of Sutherland's most telling contentions that neither the method by which a crime is committed nor the manner in which it is handled by public agencies alters the essential criminal nature of the act and the criminal status of the perpetrator.[18] Selling faucet water on a street corner to a blind man who is led to believe that the product is specially prepared to relieve his ailment is seen as no different from selling a $50 million turbine to a city which is laboring under the misapprehension that it is purchasing the product at the best price possible from closed competitive bidding. The same may be said in regard to methods of treatment. Tuberculosis, for example, remains tuberculosis and its victim a tubercular whether the condition is treated in a sanitarium or whether it is ignored or even condoned by public authorities. So too with crime. As Miss Stein might have said: A crime is a crime is a crime.

Like most reasonably adept and optimistic criminals, the antitrust violators had hoped to escape apprehension: "I didn't expect to get caught and I went to great lengths to conceal my activities so that I wouldn't get caught," one of them said.[19] Another went into some

16. *New York Times,* April 29, 1964. Regarding Westinghouse, see *Wall Street Journal,* September 3, 1964.

17. *Wall Street Journal,* July 27, 1964.

18. Edwin H. Sutherland, "While-Collar Criminality," *American Sociological Review,* 5 (February 1940), pp. 1–12.

19. Senate Committee on the Judiciary, Subcommittee on Antitrust and Monopoly, 87th Cong., 2d Sess., 1961. "Administered Prices," *Hearings,* Pts. 27 and 28. Unless otherwise indicated, subsequent data and quotations are taken from these documents. Space considerations do not permit citation to the precise pages.

detail concerning the techniques of concealment: "it was considered discreet to not be too obvious and to minimize telephone calls, to use plain envelopes if mailing material to each other, not to be seen together on traveling, and so forth, ... not to leave wastepaper, of which there was a lot, strewn around a room when leaving." The plans themselves, while there were some slight variations over time and in terms of different participants, were essentially similar. The offenders hid behind a camouflage of fictitious names and conspiratorial codes. The attendance roster for the meetings was known as the "Christmas card list" and the gatherings, interestingly enough, as "choir practice."[20] The offenders used public telephones for much of their communication, and they met either at trade association conventions, where their relationship would appear reasonable, or at sites selected for their anonymity. It is quite noteworthy, in this respect, that while some of the men filed false claims, so as to mislead their superiors regarding the city they had visited, they never asked for expense money to places more distant than those they had actually gone to—on the theory, apparently, that whatever else was occurring, it would not do to cheat the company.

At the meetings, negotiations centered about the establishment of a "reasonable" division of the market for the various products. Generally participating companies were allocated essentially that part of the market which they had previously garnered. If Company A, for instance, had under competitive conditions secured 20 percent of the available business, then agreement might be reached that it would be given the opportunity to submit the lowest bid on 20 percent of the new contracts. A low price would be established, and the remainder of the companies would bid at approximately equivalent, though higher, levels. It sometimes happened, however, that because of things such as company reputation, or available servicing arrangements, the final contract was awarded to a firm which had not submitted the lowest bid. For this, among other reasons, debate among the conspirators was often acrimonious about the proper division of spoils, about alleged failures to observe previous agreements, and about other intramural matters. Sometimes, depending upon the contract, the conspirators would draw

20. The quotation is from an excellent two-part article by Richard Austin Smith. "The Incredible Electrical Conspiracy," *Fortune*, 63 (April 1961), pp. 132–137, and 63 (May 1961), 161–164, which is reproduced in *Hearings*, Pt. 27, pp. 17094–17105 and 17172–17182.

lots to determine who would submit the lowest bid; at other times the appropriate arrangement would be determined under a rotating system conspiratorially referred to as the "phase of the moon."

Explanations of the Conspiracy

Attempts to understand the reasons for and the general significance of the price-fixing conspiracy have been numerous. They include re-examinations of the antitrust laws[21] as well as denunciations of the corporate ethos and the general pattern of American life and American values. For example, "This is the challenge of the grim outcome in Philadelphia. Can corporations outgrow the idea that employees must produce, whatever the moral cost, or lose their perquisites? Is it possible to create a business ethic favoring honesty even at the expense of profit? Can our society get away from its pervasive attitude that a little cheating is harmless? The electrical cases raise those questions not only in the antitrust field, but in others, especially taxation. And they are questions not only for large corporations and not only for business but for all of us."[22]

A not inconsiderable number of the defendants took the line that their behavior, while technically criminal, had really served a worthwhile purpose by "stabilizing prices" (a much-favored phrase of the conspirators). This altruistic interpretation almost invariably was combined with an attempted distinction among illegal, criminal, and immoral acts, with the offender expressing the view that what he had done might have been designated by the statutes as criminal, but either he was unaware of such a designation or he thought it unreasonable that acts with admirable consequences should be considered criminal. The testimony of a Westinghouse executive during hearings by the Senate Subcommittee on Antitrust and Monopoly clearly illustrates this point of view:

Committee Attorney: Did you know that these meetings with competitors were illegal?

21. See, for instance, Leland Hazard, "Are Big Businessmen Crooks?" *Atlantic,* 208 (November 1961), pp. 57–61.

22. Anthony Lewis, *New York Times,* February 12, 1961.

Witness: Illegal? Yes, but not criminal. I didn't find that out until I read the indictment. . . . I assumed that criminal action meant damaging someone, and we did not do that. . . . I thought that we were more or less working on a survival basis in order to try to make enough to keep our plant and our employees.

This theme was repeated in essentially similar language by a number of witnesses. "It is against the law," an official of the Ingersoll-Rand Corporation granted, but he added: "I do not know that it is against public welfare because I am not certain that the consumer was actually injured by this operation." A Carrier Corporation executive testified that he was "reasonably in doubt" that the price-fixing meetings violated the antitrust law. "Certainly, we were in a gray area. I think the degree of violation, if you can speak of it that way, is what was in doubt." Another offender said: "We were not meeting for the purpose of getting the most that traffic could bear. It was to get a value for our product." Some of these views are gathered together in a statement by a former sales manager of the I-T-E Circuit Breaker Company:

One faces a decision, I guess, at such times, about how far to go with company instructions, and since the spirit of such meetings only appeared to be correcting a horrible price level situation, that there was not an attempt to actually damage customers, charge excessive prices, there was no personal gain in it for me, the company did not seem actually to be defrauding. Corporate statements can evidence the fact that there have been poor profits during all these years. . . . So I guess morally it did not seem quite so bad as might be inferred by the definition of the activity itself.

For the most part, personal explanations for the acts were sought in the structure of corporate pressures rather than in the avarice or lack of law-abiding character of the men involved. The defendants almost invariably testified that they came new to a job, found price-fixing an established way of life, and simply entered into it as they did into other aspects of their job. The explanatory scheme fit into a pattern that Senator Philip A. Hart of Michigan during the subcommittee hearings labeled *imbued fraud.*[23]

There was considerable agreement concerning the precise method

23. Analysis of the relationship between occupational norms and legal violations could represent a fruitful line of inquiry. See Richard Quinney, "The Study of White Collar Crime: Toward a Reorientation in Theory and Research," *Journal of Criminal Law, Criminology and Police Science,* 55 (June 1964), pp. 208–214.

in which the man initially became involved in price-fixing. "My first actual experience was back in the 1930's," a General Electric official said. "I was taken there by my boss . . . to sit down and price a job." An Ingersoll-Rand executive said: "[My superior] took me to a meeting to introduce me to some of our competitors, none of whom I had met before, and at that meeting pricing of condensers was discussed with the competitors." Essentially the same comment is repeated by witness after witness. "I found it this way when I was introduced to competitive discussion and just drifted into it," a Carrier Corporation man noted. A General Electric officer echoed this point: "Every direct supervisor that I had directed me to meet with competition. . . . It had become so common and gone on for so many years that I think we lost sight of the fact that it was illegal." Price-fixing, whether or not recognized as illegal by the offenders, was clearly an integral part of their jobs. "Meeting with competitors was just one of the many facets of responsibility that was delegated to me," one witness testified, while an Allis-Chalmers executive responded to the question "Why did you go to the meetings?" with the observation: "I thought it was part of my duty to do so."

What might have happened to the men if, for reasons of conscience or perhaps through a fear of the possible consequences, they had objected to the "duty" to participate in price-fixing schemes? This point was raised only by the General Electric employees, perhaps because they alone had some actual evidence upon which to base their speculations. In 1946, General Electric had first issued a directive, number 20.5, which spelled out the company's policy against price-fixing, in terms stronger than those found in the antitrust laws. A considerable number of the executives believed, in the words of one, that the directive was only for "public consumption," and not to be taken seriously. One man, however, refused to engage in price-fixing after he had initialed the document forbidding it. A witness explained to the Senate subcommittee what followed: "[My superior] told me, 'This fellow is a fine fellow, he is capable in every respect except he was not broad enough for his job, that he was so religious that he thought in spite of what his superiors said, he thought having signed that, that he should not do any of this and he is getting us in trouble with competition.'"

The man who succeeded the troublesome official, one of the defendants in the Philadelphia hearing, said that he had been told that he "would be expected to do otherwise" and that this "was why I was offered that promotion to Philadelphia because this man would not do it." At the same time, however, the General Electric witnesses specified clearly that it was not their jobs with the company that would be in jeopardy if they failed to price-fix, but rather the particular assignment they had. "If I didn't do it, I felt that somebody else would," said one, with an obvious note of self-justification. "I would be removed and somebody else would do it."

Westinghouse and General Electric differed considerably in their reactions to the exposure of the offenses, with Westinghouse electing to retain in its employ persons involved in the conspiracy, and General Electric deciding to dismiss the employees who had been before the court. The reasoning of the companies throws light both on the case and on the relationship between antitrust offenses and the more traditionally viewed forms of criminal behavior.

Westinghouse put forward four justifications for its retention decision. First, it declared, the men involved had not sought personal aggrandizement: "While their actions cannot in any way be condoned, these men did not act for personal gain, but in the belief, misguided though it may have been, that they were furthering the company's interest." Second, "the punishment incurred by them already was harsh" and "no further penalties would serve any useful purpose." Third, "each of these individuals is in every sense a reputable citizen, a respected and valuable member of the community and of high moral character." Fourth, there was virtually no likelihood that the individuals would repeat their offense.[24]

General Electric's punitive line toward its employees was justified on the ground that the men had violated not only federal law but also a basic company policy, and that they therefore deserved severe punishment. The company's action met with something less than wholehearted acclaim; rather, it was often interpreted as an attempt to scapegoat particular individuals for what was essentially the responsibility of the corporate enterprise and its top executives. "I do not understand the holier-than-thou attitude in GE when your directions came from very high at the top," Senator Kefauver said during his committee's hearings, while Senator John A. Carroll of Colorado expressed his view through a leading question: "Do you

24. Sharon (Pa.) *Herald*, February 6, 1961.

think you were thrown to the wolves to ease the public relations situation . . . that has developed since these indictments?" he asked a discharged General Electric employee. The witness thought that he had.

Perhaps most striking is the fact that though many offenders quite clearly stressed the likely consequences for them if they failed to conform to price-fixing expectations, not one hinted at the benefits he might expect, the personal and professional rewards, from participation in the criminal conspiracy. It remained for the sentencing judge and two top General Electric executives to deliver the harshest denunciations of the personal motives and qualities of the conspirators to be put forth during the case.

The statement of Judge J. Cullen Ganey, read prior to imposing sentence, received widespread attention. In it he sharply criticized the corporations as the major culprits, but he also pictured the defendants in a light other than that they chose to shed upon themselves in their subsequent discussions of the offenses: "they were torn between conscience and an approved corporate policy, with the rewarding objective of promotion, comfortable security, and large salaries. They were the organization or company man, the conformist who goes along with his superiors and finds balm for his conscience in additional comforts and security of his place in the corporate set-up."[25]

The repeated emphasis on "comfort" and "security" constitutes the basic element of Judge Ganey's view of the motivations of the offenders. Stress on passive acquiescence occurs in remarks by two General Electric executives viewing the derelictions of their subordinates. Robert Paxton, the retired company president, called antitrust agreements "monkey business" and denounced in vitriolic terms one of his former superiors who, when Paxton first joined General Electric, had put him to work attempting to secure a bid on a contract that had already been prearranged by a price-fixing agreement. Ralph Cordiner, the president and board chairman of General Electric, thought that the antitrust offenses were motivated by drives for easily acquired power. Cordiner's statement is noteworthy for its dismissal of the explanations of the offenders as "rationalizations": "One reason for the offenses was a desire to be

25. *New York Times*, February 7, 1961.

'Mr. Transformer' or 'Mr. Switchgear'* . . . and to have influence over a larger segment of the industry. . . . The second was that it was an indolent, lazy way to do business. When you get all through with the rationalizations, you have to come back to one or the other of these conclusions."

There were other explanations as well. One truculent offender, the 68-year-old president of a smaller company who had been spared a jail sentence only because of his age and the illness of his wife, categorically denied the illegality of his behavior. "We did not fix prices," he said. "I can't agree with you. I am telling you that all we did was recover costs." Some persons blamed the system of decentralization in the larger companies, which they said placed a heavy burden to produce profit on each of the relatively autono- mous divisions, particularly when bonuses—"incentive compensa- tion"—were at stake, while others maintained that the "dog-eat-dog" business conditions in the heavy electrical equipment industry were responsible for the violations, Perhaps the simplest explanation came from a General Electric executive. "I think," he said, "the boys could resist everything but temptation."

Portrait of an Offender

The highest paid executive to be given a jail sentence was a Gen- eral Electric vice-president, earning $135,000 a year—about $2600 every week. The details of his career and his participation in the conspiracy provide additional insight into the operations of white collar crime and white collar criminals.

The General Electric vice-president was one of the dispropor- tionate number of Southerners involved in the antitrust violations. He had been born in Atlanta and was 46 years old at the time he was sentenced to jail. He had graduated with a degree in electrical engineering from Georgia Tech, and received an honorary doctor- ate degree from Sienna College in 1958, was married, and the father of three children. He had served in the Navy during the Second

---

*Earlier, a witness had quoted his superior as saying: "I have the industry under my thumb. They will do just about as I ask them." This man, the witness said, "was known as Mr. Switchgear in the industry."

World War, rising to the rank of lieutenant commander, was a director of the Schenectady Boy's Club, on the board of trustees of Miss Hall's School, and, not without some irony, was a member of Governor Rockefeller's Temporary State Committee on Economic Expansion.[26]

Almost immediately after his sentencing, he issued a statement to the press, noting that he was to serve a jail term "for conduct which has been interpreted as being in conflict with the complex antitrust laws." He commented that "General Electric, Schenectady, and its people have undergone many ordeals together and we have not only survived them, but have come out stronger, more vigorous, more alive than ever. We shall again." Then he voiced his appreciation for "the letters and calls from people all over the country, the community, the shops, and the offices . . . expressing confidence and support."[27]

The vice-president was neither so sentimental about his company nor so certain about the complexity of the antitrust regulations when he appeared before the Kefauver committee five months later. "I don't get mad, Senator," he said at one point, referring to his behavior during a meeting with competitors, but he took another line when he attempted to explain why he was no longer associated with General Electric: ". . . when I got out of being a guest of the government for 30 days, I had found out that we were not to be paid while we were there,* and I got, frankly, madder than hell."

Previously, he had been mentioned as a possible president of General Electric, described by the then president, as "an exceptionally eager and promising individual." Employed by the company shortly after graduation from college, he had risen dramatically through the managerial ranks, and passed that point, described by a higher executive, "where the man, if his work has been sufficiently promising, has an opportunity to step across the barrier out of his function into the field of general management." In 1946, he had his first contact with price-fixing, being introduced to competitors by his superior and told that he "should be the one to contact them as far as power transformers were concerned in the future."

---

26. *New York Times*, February 7, 1961.
27. *Schenectady Union-Star*, February 10, 1961.
*A matter of some $11,000 for the jail term.

The meetings that he attended ran a rather erratic course, with numerous squabbles between the participants. Continual efforts had to be made to keep knowledge of the meetings from "the manufacturing people, the engineers, and especially the lawyers," but this was achieved, the witness tried to convince the Kefauver committee, because commercial transactions remained unquestioned by managerial personnel so long as they showed a reasonable profit. The price-fixing meetings continued from 1946 until 1949. At that time, a federal investigation of licensing and cross-patent activities in the transformer industry sent the conspirators scurrying for shelter. "The iron curtain was completely down" for a year, and sales people at General Electric were forbidden to attend gatherings of the National Electrical Manufacturers' Association, where they had traditionally connived with competitors.

Meetings resumed, however, when the witness's superior, described by him as "a great communicator, a great philosopher, and, frankly, a great believer in stabilities of prices," decided that "the market was getting in chaotic condition" and that they "had better go out and see what could be done about it." He was told to keep knowledge of the meetings from Robert Paxton, "an Adam Smith Advocate," then the plant works manager, because Paxton "don't understand these things."

Promoted to general manager in 1954, the witness was called to New York by the president of General Electric and told specifically, possibly in part because he had a reputation of being "a bad boy," to comply with the company policy and with the antitrust laws, and to see that his subordinates did so too. This instruction lasted as long as it took him to get from New York back to Massachusetts, where his superior there told him: "Now, keep on doing the way that you have been doing but just . . . be sensible about it and use your head on the subject." The price-fixing meetings therefore continued unabated, particularly as market conditions were aggravated by overproduction which had taken place during the Korean War. In the late 1950s foreign competition entered the picture, and lower bids from abroad often forced the American firms to give up on particular price-fixing attempts.

In 1957, the witness was promoted to vice-president, and again brought to New York for a lecture from the company president on the evils of price-fixing. This time, his "air cover gone"—he now had to report directly to top management—he decided to abandon altogether his involvement in price-fixing. He returned to his plant and issued stringent orders to his subordinates that they were no longer to attend meetings with competitors. Not surprisingly, since he himself had rarely obeyed such injunctions, neither did the sales persons in his division.

The witness was interrogated closely about his moral feelings regarding criminal behavior. He fumbled most of the questions, avoiding answering them directly, but ultimately came to the point of saying that the consequences visited upon him represented the major reason for a re-evaluation of his actions. He would not behave in the same manner again because of what "I have been through and what I have done to my family." He was also vexed with the treatment he had received from the newspapers: "They have never laid off a second. They have used some terms which I don't think are necessary—they don't use the term price fixing. It is always price rigging or trying to make it as sensational as possible."[28] The taint of a jail sentence, he said, had the effect of making people "start looking at the moral values a little bit." Senator Hart drew the following conclusions from the witness's comments:

> *Hart:* This was what I was wondering about, whether absent the introduction of this element of fear, there would have been any re-examination of the moral implications.
> *Witness:* I wonder, Senator. That is a pretty tough one to answer.
> *Hart:* If I understand you correctly, you have already answered it.
> . . . After the fear, there came the moral re-evaluation.

Nevertheless, the former General Electric vice-president viewed his situation rather philosophically. Regarding his resignation from the company, it was "the way the ball has bounced." He hoped that he would have "the opportunity to continue in American industry and do a job," and he wished some of the other men who had been dismissed a lot of good luck. "I want to leave the company with no bitterness and go out and see if I can't start a new venture along the right lines." Eight days later, he accepted a job as assistant to the

---

28. A contrary view is expressed in Note, "Increasing Community Control over Corporate Crime—A Problem in the Law of Sanctions," *Yale Law Journal,* 71 (December 1961), footnoted material pp. 287–289. It has been pointed out that *Time* magazine (February 17, 1961, pp. 64ff) reported the conspiracy in its "Business" section, whereas it normally presents crime news under a special heading of its own—Donald R. Taft and Ralph W. England, Jr., *Criminology,* 4th ed., New York: The Macmillan Company, 1964, p. 203.

president in charge of product research in a large corporation located outside Philadelphia.[29] Slightly more than a month after that, he was named president of the company, at a salary reported to be somewhat less than the $74,000 yearly received by his predecessor.[30]

A Summing Up

The antitrust violations in the heavy electrical industry permit a reevaluation of many of the earlier speculations about white collar crime. The price-fixing behavior, flagrant in nature, was clearly in violation of the criminal provisions of the Sherman Act of 1890, which had been aimed at furthering "industrial liberty." Rather, the price-fixing arrangements represented attempts at "corporate socialism," and in the words of Senator Kefauver to a subcommittee witness: "It makes a complete mockery not only of how we have always lived and what we have believed in and have laws to protect, but what you were doing was to make a complete mockery of the carefully worded laws of the government of the United States, ordinances of the cities, rules of the REA's [Rural Electrification Administration], with reference to sealed secret bids in order to get competition."

The facts of the antitrust conspiracy would seem clearly to resolve in the affirmative debate concerning the criminal nature and the relevance for criminological study of such forms of white collar crime,[31] though warnings regarding an indefinite and unwarranted extension of the designation "crime" to all acts abhorrent to academic criminologists must remain in force.[32] Many of

---

29. *New York Times,* May 12, 1961.

30. *New York Times,* June 23, 1961.

31. See Edwin H. Sutherland, "Is 'White Collar Crime' Crime?" *American Sociological Review,* 10 (April 1945), pp. 132–139. Note: "It may be hoped that the Philadelphia electric cases have helped to dispel this misapprehension. . . . It should now be clear that a deliberate or conscious violation of the antitrust laws . . . is a serious offense against society which is as criminal as any other act that injures many in order to profit a few. Conspiracy to violate the antitrust laws is economic racketeering. Those who are apprehended in such acts are, and will be treated as criminals."—Lee Loevinger, "Recent Developments in Antitrust Enforcement," Antitrust Section, American Bar Association, 18 (1961), p. 102.

32. Paul W. Tappan, "Who Is the Criminal?" *American Sociological Review,* 12 (February 1947), pp. 96–102.

Sutherland's ideas concerning the behavior of corporate offenders also receive substantiation. His stress on learning and associational patterns as important elements in the genesis of the violations receives strong support.[33] So too does his emphasis on national trade conventions as the sites of corporate criminal conspiracies.[34]

Others of Sutherland's views appear to require overhaul. His belief, for example, that "those who are responsible for the system of criminal justice are afraid to antagonize businessmen"[35] seems less than totally true in terms of the electrical industry prosecutions. Sutherland's thesis that "the customary pleas of the executives of the corporation . . . that they were ignorant of and not responsible for the action of the special department . . . is akin to the alibi of the ordinary criminal and need not be taken seriously"[36] also seems to be a rather injudicious blanket condemnation, The accuracy of the statement for the antitrust conspiracy must remain moot, but it would seem important that traditional safeguards concerning guilty knowledge as a basic ingredient in criminal responsibility be accorded great respect.[37] Nor, in terms of the antitrust data, does Sutherland appear altogether correct in his view that "the public agencies of communication, which continually define ordinary violations of the criminal code in a very critical manner, do not make similar definitions of white collar crime."[38]

Various analytical schemes and theoretical statements in criminology and related fields provide some insight into elements of the price-fixing conspiracy. Galbraith's caustic observation regarding the traditional academic view of corporate price-fixing arrangements represents a worthwhile point of departure: "Restraints on competition and the free movement of prices, the principal source of uncertainty to business firms, have been principally deplored by

33. Sutherland, *White Collar Crime*, pp. 234–57.

34. Ibid., p. 70.

35. Ibid., p. 10.

36. Ibid., p. 54.

37. For an excellent presentation, see Sanford H. Kadish, "Some Observations on the Use of Criminal Sanctions in Enforcing Economic Regulations," *University of Chicago Law Review*, 30 (Spring 1963), pp. 423–449. See also Richard A. Whiting, "Antitrust and the Corporate Executive," *Virginia Law Review*, 47 (October 1961), pp. 929–987.

38. Sutherland, *White Collar Crime*, p. 247.

university professors on lifelong appointments. Such security of tenure is deemed essential for fruitful and unremitting thought."[39]

It seems apparent, looking at the antitrust offenses in this light, that the attractiveness of a secure market arrangement represented a major ingredient drawing corporate officers to the price-fixing violations. The elimination of competition meant the avoidance of uncertainty, the formalization and predictability of outcome, the minimization of risks. It is, of course, this incentive which accounts for much of human activity, be it deviant or "normal," and this tendency that Weber found so pronounced in bureaucracies in their move from vital but erratic beginnings to more staid and more comfortable middle and old age.[40]

For the conspirators there had necessarily to be a conjunction of factors before they could participate in the violations. First, of course, they had to perceive that there would be gains accruing from their behavior. Such gains might be personal and professional, in terms of corporate advancement toward prestige and power, and they might be vocational, in terms of a more expedient and secure method of carrying out assigned tasks. The offenders also apparently had to be able to neutralize or rationalize their behavior in a manner in keeping with their image of themselves as law-abiding, decent, and respectable persons.[41] The ebb and flow of the price-fixing conspiracy also clearly indicates the relationship, often overlooked in explanations of criminal behavior, between extrinsic conditions and illegal acts. When the market behaved in a manner the executives thought satisfactory, or when enforcement agencies seemed particularly threatening, the conspiracy desisted. When market conditions deteriorated, while corporate pressures for achieving attractive profit-and-loss statements remained constant, and enforcement activity abated, the price-fixing agreements flourished.

39. John Kenneth Galbraith, *The Affluent Society*, Boston: Houghton Mifflin Co., 1958, p. 84. See also Richard Hofstadter, "Antitrust in America," *Commentary*, 38 (August 1964), pp. 47–53. An executive of one corporation is said lo have remarked regarding the collusive antitrust arrangements: "It is the only way business can be run. It's free enterprise." Quoted by Mr. Justice Clark to Antitrust Section, American Bar Association, St Louis, August 8, 1961, p. 4.

40. Max Weber, *The Theory of Social and Economic Organization*, translated by A. M. Henderson and Talcott Parsons. New York: Oxford University Press, 1947, pp. 367–373.

41. See Donald R. Cressey, *Other People's Money*. New York: The Free Press of Glencoe, 1953; Gresham M. Sykes and David Matza, "Techniques of Neutralization: A Theory of Delinquency," *American Sociological Review*, 22 (December 1957), pp. 664–670.

More than anything else, however, a plunge into the elaborate documentation of the antitrust cases of 1961, as well as an attempt to relate them to other segments of criminological work, points up the considerable need for more and better monographic field studies of law violators and of systems of criminal behavior, these to be followed by attempts to establish theoretical guidelines and to review and refine current interpretative viewpoints. There have probably been no more than a dozen, if that many, full-length studies of types of criminal (not delinquent) behavior in the past decade. The need for such work seems overriding, and the 1961 antitrust cases represent but one of a number of instances, whether in the field of white collar crime, organized crime, sex offenses, personal or property crimes, or similar areas of concern, where we are still faced with a less than adequate supply of basic and comparative material upon which to base valid and useful theoretical statements.

6
Why Should My Conscience Bother Me?
Hiding Aircraft Brake Hazards
Kermit Vandivier

The B. F. Goodrich Co. is what business magazines like to speak of as "a major American corporation." It has operations in a dozen states and as many foreign countries, and of these far-flung facilities, the Goodrich plant at Troy, Ohio, is not the most imposing. It is a small, one-story building, once used to manufacture airplanes. Set in the grassy flatlands of west-central Ohio, it employs only about six hundred people. Nevertheless, it is one of the three largest manufacturers of aircraft wheels and brakes, a leader in a most profitable industry. Goodrich wheels and brakes support such well-known planes as the F111, the C5A, the Boeing 727, the XB70 and many others. Its customers include almost every aircraft manufacturer in the world.

Contracts for aircraft wheels and brakes often run into millions of dollars, and ordinarily a contract with a total value of less than 570,000, though welcome, would not create any special stir of joy in the hearts of Goodrich sales personnel. But purchase order P-23718, issued on June 18, 1967, by the LTV Aerospace Corporation, and ordering 202 brake assemblies for a new Air Force plane at a total price of $69,417, was received by Goodrich with considerable glee. And there was good reason. Some ten years previously, Goodrich had built a brake for LTV that was, to say the least, considerably less than a rousing success. The brake had not lived up to Goodrich's promises, and after experiencing considerable difficulty, LTV had written off Goodrich as a source of brakes. Since that time, Goodrich salesmen had been unable to sell so much as a shot of brake fluid to LTV. So in 1967, when LTV requested bids on wheels and brakes for the new A7D light attack aircraft it proposed to build for the Air Force, Goodrich submitted a bid that was absurdly low, so low that LTV could not, in all prudence, turn it down.

Goodrich had, in industry parlance, "bought into the business." Not only did the company not expect to make a profit on the deal; it was prepared, if necessary, to lose money. For aircraft brakes are not something that can be ordered off the shelf. They are designed for a particular aircraft, and once an aircraft manufacturer buys a brake, he is forced to purchase all replacement parts from the brake manufacturer. The $70,000 that Goodrich would get for making the brake would be a drop in the bucket when compared with the cost of the linings and other parts the Air Force would have to buy from Goodrich during the lifetime of the aircraft. Furthermore, the company which manufactures brakes for one particular model of an aircraft quite naturally has the inside track to supply other brakes when the planes are updated and improved.

Thus, that first contract, regardless of the money involved, is very important, and Goodrich, when it learned that it had been awarded the A7D contract, was determined that while it may have slammed the door on its own foot ten years before, this time, the second time around. things would be different. The word was soon circulated throughout the plant: "We can't bungle it this time. We've got to give them a good brake, regardless of the cost."

There was another factor which had undoubtedly influenced LTV. All aircraft brakes made today are of the disk type, and the bid submitted by Goodrich called for a relatively small brake, one containing four disks and weighing only 106 pounds. The weight of any aircraft part is extremely important. The lighter a part is, the heavier the plane's payload can be. The four-rotor, 106-pound brake promised by Goodrich was about as light as could be expected, and this undoubtedly had helped move LTV to award the contract to Goodrich.

The brake was designed by one of Goodrich's most capable engineers, John Warren. A tall, lanky blond and a graduate of Purdue, Warren had come from the Chrysler Corporation seven years before and had become adept at aircraft brake design. The happy-go-lucky manner he usually maintained belied a temper which exploded whenever anyone ventured to offer any criticism of his work, no matter how small. On these occasions, Warren would turn red in the face, often throwing or slamming something and then stalking from the scene. As his co-workers learned the consequences of criticizing him, they did so less and less readily, and when he submitted his preliminary design for the A7D brake, it was accepted without question.

Warren was named project engineer for the A7D, and he, in turn, assigned the task of producing the final production design to a newcomer to the Goodrich engineering stable, Searle Lawson. Just turned twenty-six, Lawson had been out of the Northrup Institute of Technology only one year when he came to Goodrich in January 1967. Like Warren, he had worked for a while in the automotive industry, but his engineering degree was in aeronautical and astronautical sciences, and when the opportunity came to enter his special field, via Goodrich, he took it. At the Troy plant, Lawson had been assigned to various "paper projects" to break him in, and after several months spent reviewing statistics and old brake designs, he was beginning to fret at the lack of challenge. When told he was being assigned to his first "real" project, he was elated and immediately plunged into his work.

The major portion of the design had already been completed by Warren, and major assemblies for the brake had already been ordered from Goodrich suppliers. Naturally, however, before Goodrich could start making the brakes on a production basis, much testing would have to be done. Lawson would have to determine the best materials to use for the linings and discover what minor adjustments in the design would have to be made.

Then, after the preliminary testing and after the brake was judged ready for production, one whole brake assembly would undergo a series of grueling. simulated braking stops and other severe trials called qualification tests. These tests are required by the military, which gives very detailed specifications on how they are to be conducted, the criteria for failure, and so on. They are performed in the Goodrich plant's test laboratory, where huge machines called dynamometers can simulate the weight and speed of almost any aircraft. After the brakes pass the laboratory tests, they are approved for production, but before the brakes are accepted for use in military service, they must undergo further extensive flight tests.

Searle Lawson was well aware that much work had to be done before the A7D brake could go into production, and he knew that LTV had set the last two weeks in June, 1968, as the starting dates for flight tests. So he decided to begin testing immediately. Goodrich's suppliers had not yet delivered the brake housing and other parts, but the brake disks had arrived, and using the housing from a brake similar in size and weight to the A7D brake, Lawson built a prototype. The prototype was installed in a test wheel and placed on one of the big dynamometers in the plant's test laboratory. The dynamometers was adjusted to simulate the weight of the A7D and Lawson began a series of tests, "landing" the wheel and brake at the A7D's landing speed, and braking it to a stop. The main purpose of these preliminary tests was to learn what temperatures would develop within the brake during the simulated stops and to evaluate the lining materials tentatively selected for use.

During a normal aircraft landing the temperatures inside the brake may reach 1000 degrees, and occasionally a bit higher. During Lawson's first simulated landings, the temperature of his prototype brake reached 1500 degrees. The brake glowed a bright cherry-red and threw off incandescent particles of metal and lining material as the temperature reached its peak. After a few such stops, the brake was dismantled and the linings were found to be almost completely disintegrated. Lawson chalked this first failure up to chance and, ordering new lining materials, tried again.

The second attempt was a repeat of the first. The brake became extremely hot, causing the lining materials to crumble into dust.

After the third such failure, Lawson, inexperienced though he was, knew that the fault lay not in defective parts or unsuitable lining material but in the basic design of the brake itself. Ignoring Warren's original computations, Lawson made his own, and it didn't take him long to discover where the trouble lay—the brake was too small. There simply was not enough surface area on the disks to stop the aircraft without generating the excessive heat that caused the linings to fail.

The answer to the problem was obvious but far from simple—the four-disk brake would have to be scrapped, and a new design, using five disks, would have to be developed. The implications were not lost on Lawson. Such a step would require the junking of all the four-disk-brake subassemblies, many of which had now begun to arrive from the various suppliers. It would also mean several weeks of preliminary design and testing and many more weeks of waiting while the suppliers made and delivered the new subassemblies.

Yet, several weeks had already gone by since LTV's order had arrived, and the date for delivery of the first production brakes for flight testing was only a few months away.

Although project engineer John Warren had more or less turned the A7D over to Lawson, he knew of the difficulties Lawson had been experiencing. He had assured the young engineer that the problem revolved around getting the right kind of lining material. Once that was found, he said, the difficulties would end.

Despite the evidence of the abortive tests and Lawson's careful computations, Warren rejected the suggestion that the four-disk brake was too light for the job. Warren knew that his superior had already told LTV, in rather glowing terms, that the preliminary tests on the A7D brake were very successful. Indeed, Warren's superiors weren't aware at this time of the troubles on the brake. It would have been difficult for Warren to admit not only that he had made a serious error in his calculations and original design but that his mistakes had been caught by a green kid, barely out of college.

Warren's reaction to a five-disk brake was not unexpected by Lawson, and, seeing that the four-disk brake was not to be abandoned so easily, he took his calculations and dismal test results one step up the corporate ladder.

At Goodrich, the man who supervises the engineers working on projects slated for production is called, predictably, the projects manager. The job was held by a short, chubby and bald man named Robert Sink. A man truly devoted to his work, Sink was as likely to be found at his desk at ten o'clock on Sunday night as ten o'clock on Monday morning. His outside interests consisted mainly of tinkering on a Model-A Ford and an occasional game of golf. Some fifteen years before, Sink had begun working at Goodrich as a lowly draftsman. Slowly, he worked his way up. Despite his geniality, Sink was neither respected nor liked by the majority of the engineers, and his appointment as their supervisor did not improve their feelings about him. They thought he had only gone to high school. It quite naturally rankled those who had gone through years of college and acquired impressive specialties such as thermodynamics and astronautics to be commanded by a man whom they considered their intellectual inferior. But, though Sink had no college training, he had something even more useful: a fine working knowledge of company politics.

Puffing upon a Meerschaum pipe, Sink listened gravely as young Lawson confided his fears about the four-disk brake. Then he examined Lawson's calculations and the results of the abortive tests. Despite the fact that he was not a qualified engineer, in the strictest sense of the word, it must certainly have been obvious to Sink that Lawson's calculations were correct and that a four-disk brake would never have worked on the A7D.

But other things of equal importance were also obvious. First, to concede that Lawson's calculations were correct would also mean conceding that Warren's calculations were incorrect. As projects manager, he not only was responsible for Warren's activities but, in admitting that Warren had erred, he would have to admit that he had erred in trusting Warren's judgment. It also meant that, as projects manager, it would be he who would have to explain the whole messy situation to the Goodrich hierarchy, not only at Troy but possibly on the corporate level at Goodrich's Akron offices. And, having taken Warren's judgment of the four-disk brake at face value (he was forced to do this since, not being an engineer, he was unable to exercise any engineering judgment of his own), he had assured LTV, not once but several times, that about all there was left to do on the brake was pack it in a crate and ship it out the back door.

There's really no problem at all, he told Lawson. After all, Warren was an experienced engineer, and if he said the brake would work, it would work. Just keep on testing and probably, maybe even on the very next try, it'll work out just fine.

Lawson was far from convinced. but without the support of his superiors there was little he could do except keep on testing. By now, housings for the four-disk brake had begun to arrive at the plant, and Lawson was able to build up a production model of the brake and begin the formal qualification tests demanded by the military.

The first qualification attempts went exactly as the tests on the prototype had. Terrific heat developed within the brakes and, after a few, short, simulated stops, the linings crumbled. A new type of lining material was ordered and once again an attempt to qualify the brake was made. Again, failure.

Experts were called in from lining manufacturers, and new lining "mixes" were tried, always with the same result. Failure.

It was now the last week in March 1968, and flight tests were scheduled to begin in seventy days. Twelve separate attempts had been made to formally qualify the brake, and all had failed. It was no longer possible for anyone to ignore the glaring truth that the brake was a dismal failure and that nothing short of a major design change could ever make it work.

In the engineering department, panic set in. A glum-faced Lawson prowled the test laboratory dejectedly. Occasionally, Warren would witness some simulated stop on the brake and, after it was completed, troop silently back to his desk. Sink, too, showed an unusual interest in the trials, and he and Warren would converse in low tones while poring over the results of the latest tests. Even the most inexperienced of the lab technicians and the men who operated the testing equipment knew they had a "bad" brake on their hands, and there was some grumbling about "wasting time on a brake that won't work."

New menaces appeared. An engineering team from LTV arrived at the plant to get a good look at the brake in action. Luckily, they stayed only a few days, and Goodrich engineers managed to cover the true situation without too much difficulty.

On April 4, the thirteenth attempt at qualification was begun. This time no attempt was made to conduct the tests by the methods and techniques spelled out in the military specifications. Regardless of how it had to be done, the brake was to be "nursed" through the required fifty simulated stops.

Fans were set up to provide special cooling. Instead of maintaining pressure on the brake until the test wheel had come to a complete stop, the pressure was reduced when the wheel had decelerated to around 15 mph, allowing it to "coast" to a stop. After each stop, the brake was disassembled and carefully cleaned, and after some of the stops, internal brake parts were machined in order to remove warp and other disfigurations caused by the high heat.

By these and other methods, all clearly contrary to the techniques established by the military specifications, the brake was coaxed through the fifty stops. But even using these methods, the brake could not meet all the requirements. On one stop the wheel rolled for a distance of 16,000 feet, nearly three miles, before the brake could bring it to a stop. The normal distance required for such a stop was around 3500 feet.

On April 11, the day the thirteenth test was completed, I became personally involved in the A7D situation.

I had worked in the Goodrich test laboratory for five years, starting first as an instrumentation engineer, then later becoming a data analyst and technical writer. As part of my duties, I analyzed the reams and reams of instrumentation data that came from the many testing machines in the laboratory, then transcribed it to a more usable form for the engineering department. And when a new-type brake had successfully completed the required qualification tests, I would issue a formal qualification report.

Qualification reports were an accumulation of all the data and test logs compiled by the test technicians during the qualification tests, and were documentary proof that a brake had met all the requirements established by the military specifications and was therefore presumed safe for flight testing. Before actual flight tests were conducted on a brake, qualification reports had to be delivered to the customer and to various government officials.

On April 11, I was looking over the data from the latest A7D test, and I noticed that many irregularities in testing methods had been noted on the test logs.

Technically, of course, there was nothing wrong with conducting tests in any manner desired, so long as the test was for research purposes only. But qualification test methods are clearly delineated by the military, and I knew that this test had been a formal qualification attempt. One particular notation on the test logs caught my eye. For some of the stops, the instrument which recorded the brake pressure had been deliberately miscalibrated so that, while the brake pressure used during the stops was recorded as 1000 psi (the maximum pressure that would be available on the A7D aircraft), the pressure had actually been 1100 psi!

I showed the test logs to the test lab supervisor, Ralph Gretzinger, who said he had learned from the technician who had miscalibrated the instrument that he had been asked to do so by Lawson. Lawson, said Gretzinger, readily admitted asking for the miscalibration, saying he had been told to do so by Sink.

I asked Gretzinger why anyone would want to miscalibrate the data-recording instruments.

"Why? I'll tell you why," he snorted. "That brake is a failure. It's way too small for the job, and they're not ever going to get it to work. They're getting desperate, and instead of scrapping the damned thing and starting over, they figure they can horse around down here in the lab and qualify it that way."

An expert engineer, Gretzinger had been responsible for several innovations in brake design. It was he who had invented the unique brake system used on the famous XB70. A graduate of Georgia Tech, he was a stickler for detail and he had some very firm ideas about honesty and ethics. "If you want to find out what's going on," said Gretzinger, "ask Lawson, he'll tell you."

Curious, I did ask Lawson the next time he came into the lab. He seemed eager to discuss the A7D and gave me the history of his months of frustrating efforts to get Warren and Sink to change the brake design. "I just can't believe this is really happening," said Lawson, shaking his head slowly. "This isn't engineering, at least not what I thought it would be. Back in school, I thought that when you were an engineer, you tried to do your best, no matter what it cost. But this is something else."

He sat across the desk from me, his chin propped in his hand. "Just wait," he warned. "You'll get a chance to see what I'm talking about. You're going to get in the act too, because I've already had the word that we're going to make one more attempt to qualify the brake, and that's it. Win or lose, we're going to issue a qualification report!"

I reminded him that a qualification report could only be issued after a brake had successfully met all military requirements, and therefore, unless the next qualification attempt was a success, no report would be issued.

"You'll find out," retorted Lawson. "I was already told that regardless of what the brake does on test, it's going to be qualified." He said he had been told in those exact words at a conference with Sink and Russell Van Horn.

This was the first indication that Sink had brought his boss, Van Horn, into the mess. Although Van Horn, as manager of the design engineering section, was responsible for the entire department, he was not necessarily familiar with all phases of every project, and it was not uncommon for those under him to exercise the what-he-doesn't-know-won't-hurt-him philosophy. If he was aware of the full extent of the A7D situation, it meant that matters had truly reached a desperate stage—that Sink had decided not only to call for help but was looking toward that moment when blame must be borne and, if possible, shared.

Also, if Van Horn had said, "regardless what the brake does on test, it's going to be qualified," then it could only mean that, if necessary, a false qualification report would be issued! I discussed this possibility with Gretzinger, and he assured me that under no circumstances would such a report ever be issued.

"If they want a qualification report, we'll write them one, but we'll tell it just like it is," he declared emphatically. "No false data or false reports are going to come out of this lab."

On May 2, 1968, the fourteenth and final attempt to qualify the brake was begun. Although the same improper methods used to nurse the brake through the previous tests were employed, it soon became obvious that this too would end in failure.

When the tests were about half completed, Lawson asked if I would start preparing the various engineering curves and graphic displays which were normally incorporated in a qualification report. "It looks as though you'll be writing a qualification report shortly," he said.

I flatly refused to have anything to do with the matter and immediately told Gretzinger what I had been asked to do. He was furious and repeated his previous declaration that under no circumstances would any false data or other matter be issued from the lab.

"I'm going to get this settled right now, once and for all," he declared. "I'm going to see Line [Russell Line, manager of the Goodrich Technical Services Section, of which the test lab was a part] and find out just how far this thing is going to go!" He stormed out of the room.

In about an hour, he returned and called me to his desk. He sat silently for a few moments, then muttered, half to himself, "I wonder what the hell they'd do if I just quit?" I didn't answer and I didn't ask him what he meant. I knew. He had been beaten down. He had reached the point when the decision had to be made. Defy them now while there was still time—or knuckle under, sell out.

"You know," he went on uncertainly, looking down at his desk, "I've been an engineer for a long time, and I've always believed that ethics and integrity were every bit as important as theorems and formulas, and never once has anything happened to change my beliefs. Now this. . . . Hell, I've got two sons I've got to put through school and I just . . ." His voice trailed off.

He sat for a few more minutes, then, looking over the top of his glasses, said hoarsely, "Well, it looks like we're licked. The way it stands now, we're to go ahead and prepare the data and other things for the graphic presentation in the report, and when we're finished, someone upstairs will actually write the report."

"After all," he continued, "we're just drawing some curves, and what happens to them after they leave here, well, we're not responsible for that."

He was trying to persuade himself that as long as we were concerned with only one part of the puzzle and didn't see the completed picture, we really weren't doing anything wrong. He didn't believe what he was saying, and he knew I didn't believe it either. It was an embarrassing and shameful moment for both of us.

I wasn't at all satisfied with the situation and decided that I too would discuss the matter with Russell Line, the senior executive in our section.

Tall, powerfully built, his teeth flashing white, his face tanned *to* a coffee-brown by a daily stint with a sun lamp, Line looked and acted every inch the executive. He was a crossword-puzzle enthusiast and an ardent golfer, and though he had lived in Troy only a short time, he had been accepted into the Troy Country Club and made an official of the golf committee. He had been transferred from the Akron offices some two years previously, and an air of mystery surrounded him. Some office gossips figured he had been sent to Troy as the result of some sort of demotion. Others speculated that since the present general manager of the Troy plant was due shortly for retirement, Line had been transferred to Troy to assume that job and was merely occupying his present position to "get the feel of things." Whatever the case, he commanded great respect and had come to be well liked by those of us who worked under him.

He listened sympathetically while I explained how I felt about the A7D situation, and when I had finished, he asked me what I wanted him to do about it. I said that as employees of the Goodrich Company we had a responsibility to protect the company and its reputation if at all possible. I said I was certain that officers on the corporate level would never knowingly allow such tactics as had been employed on the A7D.

"I agree with you," he remarked, "but I still want to know what you want me to do about it."

I suggested that in all probability the chief engineer at the Troy plant, H. C. "Bud" Sunderman, was unaware of the A7D problem and that he, Line, should tell him what was going on.

Line laughed, good-humoredly. "Sure, I could, but I'm not going to. Bud probably already knows about this thing anyway, and if he doesn't, I'm sure not going to be the one to tell him."

"But why?"

"Because it's none of my business, and it's none of yours. I learned a long time ago not to worry about things over which I had no control. I have no control over this."

I wasn't satisfied with this answer, and I asked him if his conscience wouldn't bother him if, say, during flight tests on the brake, something should happen resulting in death or injury to the test pilot.

"Look," he said, becoming somewhat exasperated, "I just told you I have no control over this thing. Why should my conscience bother me?"

His voice took on a quiet, soothing tone as he continued. "You're just getting all upset over this thing for nothing. I just do as I'm told, and I'd advise you to do the same."

He had made his decision, and now I had to make mine.

I made no attempt to rationalize what I had been asked to do. It made no difference who would falsify which part of the report or whether the actual falsification would be by misleading numbers or misleading words. Whether by acts of commission or omission, all of us who contributed to the fraud would be guilty. The only question left for me to decide was whether or not I would become a party to the fraud.

Before coming to Goodrich in 1963, I had held a variety of jobs, each a little more pleasant, a little more rewarding than the last. At forty-two, with seven children, I had decided that the Goodrich Company would probably be my "home" for the rest of my working life. The job paid well, it was pleasant and challenging, and the future looked reasonably bright. My wife and I had bought a home and we were ready to settle down into a comfortable, middle-age, middle-class rut. If I refused to take part in the A7D fraud, I would have to either resign or be fired. The report would be written by someone anyway, but I would have the satisfaction of knowing I had had no part in the matter. But bills aren't paid with personal satisfaction, nor house payments with ethical principles. I made my decision. The next morning, I telephoned Lawson and told him I was ready to begin on the qualification report.

In a few minutes, he was at my desk, ready to begin. Before we started, I asked him, "Do you realize what we are going to do?"

"Yeah," he replied bitterly, "we're going to screw LTV. And speaking of screwing," he continued, "I know now how a whore feels, because that's exactly what I've become, an engineering whore. I've sold myself. It's all I can do to look at myself in the mirror when I shave. I make me sick."

I was surprised at his vehemence. It was obvious that he too had done his share of soul-searching and didn't like what he had found. Somehow, though, the air seemed clearer after his out-burst, and we began working on the report.

I had written dozens of qualification reports, and I knew what a "good" one looked like. Resorting to the actual test data only on occasion, Lawson and I proceeded to prepare page after page of elaborate, detailed engineering curves, charts, and test logs, which purported to show what had happened during the formal qualification tests. Where temperatures were too high, we deliberately chopped them down a few hundred degrees, and where they were too low, we raised them to a value that would appear reasonable to the LTV and military engineers. Brake pressure, torque values, distances, times, everything of consequence was tailored to fit the occasion.

Occasionally, we would find that some test either hadn't been performed at all or had been conducted improperly. On those occasions, we "conducted" the test—successfully, of course—on paper.

For nearly a month we worked on the graphic presentation that would be part of the report. Meanwhile, the fourteenth and final qualification attempt had been completed, and the brake, not unexpectedly, had failed again.

During that month, Lawson and I talked of little else except the enormity of what we were doing. The more involved we became in our work, the more apparent became our own culpability. We discussed such things as the Nuremberg trials and how they related to our guilt and complicity in the A7D situation. Lawson often expressed his opinion that the brake was downright dangerous and that, once on flight tests, "anything is liable to happen."

I saw his boss, John Warren, at least twice during that month and needled him about what we were doing. He didn't take the jibes too kindly but managed to laugh the situation off as "one of those things." One day I remarked that what we were doing amounted to fraud, and he pulled out an engineering handbook and turned to a section on laws as they related to the engineering profession.

He read the definition of fraud aloud, then said, "Well, technically I don't think what we're doing can be called fraud. I'll admit it's not right, but it's just one of those things. We're just kinda caught in the middle. About all I can tell you is, do like I'm doing. Make copies of everything and put them in your SYA file."

"What's an 'SYA' file?" I asked.

"That's a 'save your ass' file." He laughed.

Although I hadn't known it was called that, I had been keeping an SYA file since the beginning of the A7D fiasco. I had made a copy of every scrap of paper connected even remotely with the A7D and had even had copies of 16 mm movies that had been made during some of the simulated stops. Lawson, too, had an SYA file, and we both maintained them for one reason: Should the true state of events on the A7D ever be questioned, we wanted to have access to a complete set of factual data. We were afraid that should the question ever come up, the test data might accidentally be "lost."

We finished our work on the graphic portion of the report around the first of June. Altogether, we had prepared nearly two hundred pages of data, containing dozens of deliberate falsifications and misrepresentations. I delivered the data to Gretzinger, who said he had been instructed to deliver it personally to the chief engineer, Bud Sunderman, who in turn would assign some one in the engineering department to complete the written portion of the report. He gathered the bundle of data and left the office. Within minutes, he was back with the data, his face white with anger.

"That damned Sink's beat me to it," he said furiously. "He's already talked to Bud about this, and now Sunderman says no one in the engineering department has time to write the report. He wants us to do it, and I told him we couldn't."

The words had barely left his mouth when Russell Line burst in the door. "What the hell's all the fuss about this damned report?" he demanded loudly.

Patiently, Gretzinger explained. "There's no fuss. Sunderman just told me that we'd have to write the report down here, and I said we couldn't. Russ," he went on, "I've told you before that we weren't going to write the report. I made my position clear on that a long time ago."

Line shut him up with a wave of his hand and, turning to me, bellowed, "I'm getting sick and tired of hearing about this damned report. Now, write the goddam thing and shut up about it!" He slammed out of the office.

Gretzinger and I just sat for a few seconds looking at each other. Then he spoke.

"Well, I guess he's made it pretty clear, hasn't he? We can either write the thing or quit. You know, what we should have done was quit a long time ago. Now, it's too late."

Somehow, I wasn't at all surprised at this turn of events, and it didn't really make that much difference. As far as I was concerned, we were all up to our necks in the thing anyway, and writing the narrative portion of the report couldn't make me any more guilty than I already felt myself to be.

Still, Line's order came as something of a shock. All the time Lawson and I were working on the report, I felt, deep down, that somewhere, somehow, something would come along and the whole thing would blow over. But Russell Line had crushed that hope. The report was actually going to be issued. Intelligent, law-abiding officials of B. F. Goodrich, one of the oldest and most respected of American corporations, were actually going to deliver to a customer a product that was known to be defective and dangerous and which could very possibly cause death or serious injury.

Within two days, I had completed the narrative, or written portion of the report. As a final sop to my own self-respect, in the conclusion of the report I wrote, "The B. F. Goodrich P/N 2-1162-3 brake assembly does not meet the intent or the requirements of the applicable specification documents and therefore is not qualified."

This was a meaningless gesture, since I knew that this would certainly be changed when the report went through the final typing process. Sure enough, when the report was published, the negative conclusion had been made positive.

One final and significant incident occurred just before publication.

Qualification reports always bear the signature of the person who has prepared them. I refused to sign the report, as did Lawson. Warren was later asked to sign the report. He replied that he would "when I receive a signed statement from Bob Sink ordering me to sign it."

The engineering secretary who was delegated the responsibility of "dogging" the report through publication, told me later that after I, Lawson, and Warren had all refused to sign the report, she had asked Sink if he would sign. He replied, "On something of this nature, I don't think a signature is really needed."

On June 5, 1968, the report was officially published and copies were delivered in person to the Air Force and LTV. Within a week, flight tests were begun at Edwards Air Force Base in California. Searle Lawson was sent to California as Goodrich's representative. Within approximately two weeks, he returned because some rather unusual incidents during the tests had caused them to be canceled.

His face was grim as he related stories of several near crashes during landings—caused by brake troubles. He told me about one incident in which, upon landing, one brake was literally welded together by the intense heat developed during the test stop. The wheel locked, and the plane skidded for nearly 1500 feet before coming to a halt. The plane was jacked up and the wheel removed. The fused parts within the brake had to be pried apart.

Lawson had returned to Troy from California that same day, and that evening, he and others of the Goodrich engineering department left for Dallas for a high-level conference with LTV.

That evening I left work early and went to see my attorney. After I told him the story, he advised that, while I was probably not actually guilty of fraud, I was certainly part of a conspiracy to defraud. He advised me to go to the Federal Bureau of Investigation and offered to arrange an appointment. The following week he took me to the Dayton office of the FBI, and after I had been warned that I would not be immune from prosecution, I disclosed the A7D matter to one of the agents. The agent told me to say nothing about the episode to anyone and to report any further incident to him. He said he would forward the story to his superiors in Washington.

A few days later, Lawson returned from the conference in Dallas and said that the Air Force, which had previously approved the qualification report, had suddenly rescinded that approval and was demanding to see some of the raw test data taken during the tests. I gathered that the FBI had passed the word.

Omitting any reference to the FBI, I told Lawson I had been to an attorney and that we were probably guilty of conspiracy.

"Can you get me an appointment with your attorney?" he asked. Within a week, he had been to the FBI and told them of his part in the mess. He too was advised to say nothing but to keep on the job reporting any new development.

Naturally, with the rescinding of Air Force approval and the demand to see raw test data, Goodrich officials were in a panic. A conference was called for July 27, a Saturday morning affair at which Lawson, Sink, Warren and myself were present. We met in a tiny conference room in the deserted engineering department. Lawson and I, by now openly hostile to Warren and Sink, ranged ourselves on one side of the conference table while Warren sat on the other side. Sink, chairing the meeting, paced slowly in front of a blackboard, puffing furiously on a pipe.

The meeting was called, Sink began, "to see where we stand on the A7D." What we were going to do, he said, was to "level" with LTV and tell them the "whole truth" about the A7D. "After all," he said, "they're in this thing with us, and they have the right to know how matters stand."

"In other words," I asked, "we're going to tell them the truth?"

"That's right," he replied. "We're going to level with them and let them handle the ball from there."

"There's one thing I don't quite understand," I interjected. "Isn't it going to be pretty hard for us to admit to them that we've lied?"

"Now, wait a minute," he said angrily. "Let's don't go off halfcocked on this thing. It's not a matter of lying. We've just interpreted the information the way we felt it should be."

"I don't know what you call it," I replied, "but to me it's lying, and it's going to be damned hard to confess to them that we've been lying all along."

He became very agitated at this and repeated his "We're not lying," adding, "I don't like this sort of talk."

I dropped the matter at this point, and he began discussing the various discrepancies in the report.

We broke for lunch, and afterward, I came back to the plant to find Sink sitting alone at his desk, waiting to resume the meeting. He called me over and said he wanted to apologize for his outburst that morning. "This thing has kind of gotten me down," he confessed, "and I think you've got the wrong picture. I don't think you really understand everything about this."

Perhaps so, I conceded, but it seemed to me that if we had already told LTV one thing and then had to tell them another, changing our story completely, we would have to admit we were lying.

"No," he explained patiently, "we're not really lying. All we were doing was interpreting the figures the way we knew they should be. We were just exercising engineering license."

During the afternoon session, we marked some forty-three discrepant points in the report: forty-three points that LTV would surely spot as occasions where we had exercised "engineering license."

After Sink listed those points on the blackboard, we discussed each one individually. As each point came up, Sink would explain that it was probably "too minor to bother about," or that perhaps it "wouldn't be wise to open that can of worms," or that maybe this was a point that "LTV just wouldn't understand." When the meeting was over, it had been decided that only three points were "worth mentioning."

Similar conferences were held during August and September, and the summer was punctuated with frequent treks between Dallas and Troy, and demands by the Air Force to see the raw test data. Tempers were short and matters seemed to grow worse.

Finally, early in October 1968, Lawson submitted his resignation, to take effect on October 25. On October 18, I submitted my own resignation, to take effect on November 1. In my resignation, addressed to Russell Line, I cited the A7D report and stated: "As you are aware, this report contained numerous deliberate and willful misrepresentations which, according to legal counsel, constitute fraud and expose both myself and others to criminal charges of conspiracy to defraud. . . . The events of the past seven months have created an atmosphere of deceit and distrust in which it is impossible to work. . . ."

On October 25, I received a sharp summons to the office of Bud Sunderman. As chief engineer at the Troy plant, Sunderman was responsible for the entire engineering division. Tall and graying, impeccably dressed at all times, he was capable of producing a dazzling smile or a hearty chuckle or immobilizing his face into marble hardness, as the occasion required.

I faced the marble hardness when I reached his office. He motioned me to a chair. "I have your resignation here," he snapped, "and I must say you have made some rather shocking, I might even say irresponsible, charges. This is very serious."

Before I could reply, he was demanding an explanation. "I want to know exactly what the fraud is in connection with the A7D and how you can dare accuse this company of such a thing!"

I started to tell some of the things that had happened during the testing, but he shut me off saying, "There's nothing wrong with anything we've done here. You aren't aware of all the things that have been going on behind the scenes. If you had known the true situation, you would never have made these charges." He said that in view of my apparent "disloyalty" he had decided to accept my resignation "right now," and said it would be better for all concerned if I left the plant immediately. As I got up to leave he asked me if I intended to "carry this thing further."

I answered simply, "Yes," to which he replied, "Suit yourself." Within twenty minutes, I had cleaned out my desk and left. Forty-eight hours later, the B. F. Goodrich Company recalled the qualification report and the four-disk brake, announcing that it would replace the brake with a new, improved, five-disk brake at no cost to LTV.

Ten months later, on August 13, 1969, I was the chief government witness at a hearing conducted before Senator William Proxmire's Economy in Government Subcommittee of the Congress's Joint Economic Committee. I related the A7D story to the committee, and my testimony was supported by Searle Lawson, who followed me to the witness stand. Air Force officers also testified, as well as a four-man team from the General Accounting Office, which had conducted an investigation of the A7D brake at the request of Senator Proxmire. Both Air Force and GAO investigators declared that the brake was dangerous and had not been tested properly.

Testifying for Goodrich was R. G. Jeter, vice-president and general counsel of the company, from the Akron headquarters. Representing the Troy plant was Robert Sink. These two denied any wrongdoing on the part of the Goodrich Company, despite expert testimony to the contrary by Air Force and GAO officials. Sink was quick to deny any connection with the writing of the report or of directing any falsifications, claiming to be on the West Coast at the time. John Warren was the man who supervised its writing, said Sink.

As for me, I was dismissed as a high-school graduate with no technical training, while Sink testified that Lawson was a young, inexperienced engineer. "We tried to give him guidance," Sink testified, "but he preferred to have his own convictions."

About changing the data and figures in the report, Sink said: "When you take data from several different sources, you have to rationalize among those data what is the true story. This is part of your engineering know-how." He admitted that changes had been made in the data, "but only to make them more consistent with the over-all picture of the data that is available."

Jeter pooh-poohed the suggestion that anything improper occurred, saying: "We have thirty-odd engineers at this plant . . . and I say to you that it is incredible that these men would stand idly by and see reports changed or falsified. . . . I mean you just do not have to do that working for anybody. . . . Just nobody does that."

The four-hour hearing adjourned with no real conclusion reached by the committee. But, the following day the Department of Defense made sweeping changes in its inspection, testing and reporting procedures. A spokesman for the DOD said that changes were a result of the Goodrich episode.

The A7D is now in service, sporting a Goodrich-made five-disk brake, a brake that works very well, I'm told. Business at the Goodrich plant is good. Lawson is now an engineer for LTV and has been assigned to the A7D project. And I am now a newspaper reporter.

At this writing [1972], those remaining at Goodrich are still secure in the same positions, all except Russell Line and Robert Sink. Line has been rewarded with a promotion to production superintendent, a large step upward on the corporate ladder. As for Sink, he moved up into Line's old job.

Editors' Postscript

In the years since he wrote about his experiences at Goodrich, Mr. Vandivier has been a newspaper reporter. He retired from the *Troy Daily News* (Troy, Ohio) in 1993 but still submits a column.

Mr. Vandivier reports that he has met occasionally with all of the principals involved in the aircraft brake episode. There do not seem to be any hard feelings, and their relationships with him have been consistently "cordial." All are gone from Goodrich themselves, in many cases the victims of corporate downsizing, what Mr. Vandivier terms "the corporate deviance of the 90s."

If he had to do it all over again, Mr. Vandivier says he would, because "it had to be done." He wishes the whole thing had never happened, though, and notes that Goodrich was an exciting company involved in his main line of interest, which was electronics.

7

Why I Didn't Recognize Pinto Fire Hazards
How Organizational Scripts Channel Managers'
Thoughts and Actions

Dennis A. Gioia

In the summer of 1972 I made one of those important transitions
in life, the significance of which becomes obvious only in retrospect.
I left academe with a BS in Engineering Science and an MBA to
enter the world of big business. I joined Ford Motor Company
at World Headquarters in Dearborn, Michigan, fulfilling a long-
standing dream to work in the heart of the auto industry. I felt confident that I was in the right place at the right time to make a difference. My initial job title was "Problem Analyst"—a catchall label
that superficially described what I would be thinking about and
doing in the coming years. On some deeper level, however, the title
paradoxically came to connote the many critical things that I would
not be thinking about and acting upon.

By that summer of 1972 I was very full of myself. I had met my
life's goals to that point with some notable success. I had virtually
everything I wanted, including a strongly held value system that had
led me to question many of the perspectives and practices I observed
in the world around me. Not the least of these was a profound distaste for the Vietnam war, a distaste that had found me participating
in various demonstrations against its conduct and speaking as a part
of a collective voice on the moral and ethical failure of a democratic
government that would attempt to justify it. I also found myself in
MBA classes railing against the conduct of businesses of the era,
whose actions struck me as ranging from inconsiderate to indiffer-
ent to simply unethical. To me the typical stance of business seemed
to be one of disdain for, rather than responsibility toward, the

From "Pinto Fires and Personal Ethics: A Script Analysis of Missed Opportunities," *Journal of Business Ethics*, Vol. 11, pp. 379–89. Copyright © 1992 by Kluwer
Academic Publishers. Reprinted by permission.

society of which they were prominent members. I wanted something to change. Accordingly, I cultivated my social awareness; I held my principles high; I espoused my intention to help a troubled world; and I wore my hair long. By any measure I was a prototypical "child of the '60s."

Therefore, it struck quite a few of my friends in the MBA program as rather strange that I was in the program at all. ("If you are so disappointed in business, why study business?") Subsequently, they were practically dumbstruck when I accepted the job offer from Ford, apparently one of the great purveyors of the very actions I reviled. I countered that it was an ideal strategy, arguing that I would have a greater chance of influencing social change in business if I worked behind the scenes on the inside, rather than as a strident voice on the outside. It was clear to me that somebody needed to prod these staid companies into socially responsible action. I certainly aimed to do my part. Besides, I liked cars.

Into the Fray: Setting the Personal Stage

Predictably enough, I found myself on the fast track at Ford, participating in a "tournament" type of socialization (Van Maanen, 1978), engaged in a competition for recognition with other MBA's who had recently joined the company. And I quickly became caught up in the game. The company itself was dynamic; the environment of business, especially the auto industry, was intriguing; the job was challenging and the pay was great. The psychic rewards of working and succeeding in a major corporation proved unexpectedly seductive. I really became involved in the job.

Market forces (international competition) and government regulation (vehicle safety and emissions) were affecting the auto industry in disruptive ways that only later would be common to the wider business and social arena. They also produced an industry and a company that felt buffeted, beleaguered, and threatened by the changes. The threats were mostly external, of course, and led to a strong feeling of we-versus-them, where we (Ford members) needed to defend ourselves against them (all the outside parties and voices demanding that we change our ways). Even at this time, an intriguing question for me was whether I was a "we" or a "them." It was becoming apparent to me that my perspective was changing. I had long since cut my hair.

By the summer of 1973 I was pitched into the thick of the battle. I became Ford's Field Recall Coordinator—not a position that was particularly high in the hierarchy, but one that wielded influence far beyond its level. I was in charge of the operational coordination of all of the recall campaigns currently underway and also in charge of tracking incoming information to identify developing problems. Therefore, I was in a position to make initial recommendations about possible future recalls. The most critical type of recalls were labeled "safety campaigns"—those that dealt with the possibility of customer injury or death. These ranged from straightforward occurrences such as brake failure and wheels falling off vehicles, to more exotic and faintly humorous failure modes such as detaching axles that announced their presence by spinning forward and slamming into the startled driver's door and speed control units that locked on, and refused to disengage, as the car accelerated wildly while the spooked driver futilely tried to shut it off. Safety recall campaigns, however, also encompassed the more sobering possibility of on-board gasoline fires and explosions.

The Pinto Case: Setting the Corporate Stage

In 1970 Ford introduced the Pinto, a small car that was intended to compete with the then current challenge from European cars and the ominous presence on the horizon of Japanese manufacturers. The Pinto was brought from inception to production in the record time of approximately 25 months (compared to the industry average of 43 months), a time frame that suggested the necessity for doing things expediently. In addition to the time pressure, the engineering and development teams were required to adhere to the production "limits of 2,000" for the diminutive car: it was not to exceed either $2,000 in cost or 2,000 pounds in weight. Any decisions that threatened these targets or the timing of the car's introduction were discouraged. Under normal conditions design, styling, product planning, engineering, etc., were completed prior to production tooling. Because of the foreshortened time frame, however, some of these usually sequential processes were executed in parallel.

As a consequence, tooling was already well under way (thus "freezing" the basic design) when routine crash testing revealed that the Pinto's fuel tank often ruptured when struck from the rear at a relatively low speed (31 mph in crash tests). Reports (revealed much later) showed that the fuel tank failures were the result of some rather marginal design features. The tank was positioned between the rear bumper and the rear axle (a standard industry practice for the time). During impact, however, several studs protruding from the rear of the axle housing would puncture holes in the tank; the fuel filler neck also was likely to rip away. Spilled gasoline then could be ignited by sparks. Ford had in fact crash-tested 11 vehicles; 8 of these cars suffered potentially catastrophic gas tank ruptures. The only 3 cars that survived intact had each been modified in some way to protect the tank.

These crash tests, however, were conducted under the guidelines of Federal Motor Vehicle Safety Standard 301 which had been proposed in 1968 and strenuously opposed by the auto industry. FMVSS 301 was not actually adopted until 1976; thus, at the time of the tests, Ford was not in violation of the law. There were several possibilities for fixing the problem, including the option of redesigning the tank and its location, which would have produced tank integrity in a high-speed crash. That solution, however, was not only time-consuming and expensive, but also usurped trunk space, which was seen as a critical competitive sales factor. One of the production modifications to the tank, however, would have cost only $11 to install, but given the tight margins and restrictions of the "limits of 2,000," there was reluctance to make even this relatively minor change. There were other reasons for not approving the change, as well, including a widespread industry belief that all small cars were inherently unsafe solely because of their size and weight. Another more prominent reason was a corporate belief that "safety doesn't sell." This observation was attributed to Lee Iacocca and stemmed from Ford's earlier attempt to make safety a sales theme, an attempt that failed rather dismally in the marketplace.

Perhaps the most controversial reason for rejecting the production change to the gas tank, however, was Ford's use of cost-benefit analysis to justify the decision. The National Highway Traffic Safety Association (NHTSA, a federal agency) had approved the use of cost-benefit analysis as an appropriate means for establishing automotive safety design standards. The controversial aspect in making such calculations was that they required the assignment of some specific value for a human life. In 1970, that value was deemed to be approximately $200,000 as a "cost to society" for each fatality. Ford used NHTSA's figures in estimating the costs and benefits of altering the tank production design. An internal memo, later revealed in court, indicates the following tabulations concerning potential fires (Dowie, 1977):

Costs: *$137,000,000*

Estimated as the costs of a production fix to all similarly designed cars and trucks with the gas tank aft of the axle (12,500,000 vehicles × $11/vehicle)

Benefits: *$49,530,000*

Estimated as the savings from preventing (180 projected deaths × $200,000/death) ÷ (180 projected burn injuries × $67,000/injury) ÷ (2,100 burned cars × $700/car)

The cost-benefit decision was then construed as straightforward: No production fix would be undertaken. The philosophical and ethical implications of assigning a financial value for human life or disfigurement do not seem to have been a major consideration in reaching this decision.

Pintos and Personal Experience

When I took over the Recall Coordinator's job in 1973 I inherited the oversight of about 100 active recall campaigns, more than half of which were safety-related. These ranged from minimal in size (replacing front wheels that were likely to break on 12 heavy trucks) to maximal (repairing the power steering pump on millions of cars). In addition, there were quite a number of safety problems that were under consideration as candidates for addition to the recall list. (Actually, "problem" was a word whose public use was forbidden by the legal office at the time, even in service bulletins, because it suggested corporate admission of culpability. "Condition" was the sanctioned catchword.) In addition to these potential recall candidates, there were many files containing field reports of alleged component failure (another forbidden word) that had led to accidents, and in some cases, passenger injury. Beyond these existing files, I began to construct my own files of incoming safety problems.

One of these new files concerned reports of Pintos "lighting up" (in the words of a field representative) in rear-end accidents. There were actually very few reports, perhaps because component failure was not initially assumed. These cars simply were consumed by fire after apparently very low-speed accidents. Was there a problem? Not as far as I was concerned. My cue for labeling a case as a problem either required high frequencies of occurrence or directly traceable causes. I had little time for speculative contemplation on potential problems that did not fit a pattern that suggested known courses of action leading to possible recall. I do, however, remember being disquieted by a field report accompanied by graphic, detailed photos of the remains of a burned-out Pinto in which several people had died. Although that report became part of my file, I did not flag it as any special case.

It is difficult to convey the overwhelming complexity and pace of the job of keeping track of so many active or potential recall campaigns. It remains the busiest, most information-filled job I have ever held or would want to hold. Each case required a myriad of information-gathering and execution stages. I distinctly remember that the information-processing demands led me to confuse the facts of one problem case with another on several occasions because the telltale signs of recall candidate cases were so similar. I thought of myself as a fireman—a fireman who perfectly fit the description by one of my colleagues: "In this office everything is a crisis. You only have time to put out the big fires and spit on the little ones." By those standards the Pinto problem was distinctly a little one.

It is also important to convey the muting of emotion involved in the Recall Coordinator's job. I remember contemplating the fact that my job literally involved life-and-death matters. I was sometimes responsible for finding and fixing cars NOW, because somebody's life might depend on it. I took it *very* seriously. Early in the job, I sometimes woke up at night wondering whether I had covered all the bases. Had I left some unknown person at risk because I had not thought of something? That soon faded, however, and of necessity the consideration of people's lives became a fairly removed, dispassionate process. To do the job "well" there was little room for emotion. Allowing it to surface was potentially paralyzing and prevented rational decisions about which cases to recommend for recall. On moral grounds I knew I could recommend most of the vehicles on my safety tracking list for recall (and risk earning the label of a "bleeding heart"). On practical grounds, I recognized that people implicitly accept risks in cars. We could not recall all cars with *potential* problems and stay in business. I learned to be responsive to those cases that suggested an imminent, dangerous problem.

I should also note that the country was in the midst of its first, and worst, oil crisis at this time. The effects of the crisis had cast a pall over Ford and the rest of the automobile industry. Ford's product line, with the perhaps notable exception of the Pinto and Maverick small cars, was not well-suited to dealing with the crisis. Layoffs were imminent for many people. Recalling the Pinto in this context would have damaged one of the few trump cards the company had (although, quite frankly, I do not remember overtly thinking about that issue).

Pinto reports continued to trickle in, but at such a slow rate that they really did not capture particular attention relative to other, more pressing safety problems. However, I later saw a crumpled, burned car at a Ford depot where alleged problem components and vehicles were delivered for inspection and analysis (a place known as the "Chamber of Horrors" by some of the people who worked there). The revulsion on seeing this incinerated hulk was immediate and profound. Soon afterwards, and despite the fact that the file was very sparse, I recommended the Pinto case for preliminary department-level review concerning possible recall. After the usual round of discussion about criteria and justification for recall, everyone voted against recommending recall—including me. It did not fit the pattern of recallable standards; the evidence was not overwhelming that the car was defective in some way, so the case was actually fairly straightforward. It was a good business decision, even if people might be dying. (We did not then know about the preproduction crash test data that suggested a high rate of tank failures in "normal" accidents (cf. Perrow, 1984) or an abnormal failure mode.)

Later, the existence of the crash test data did become known within Ford, which suggested that the Pinto might actually have a recallable problem. This information led to a reconsideration of the case within our office. The data, however, prompted a comparison of the Pinto's survivability in a rear-end accident with that of other competitors' small cars. These comparisons revealed that although many cars in this subcompact class suffered appalling deformation in relatively low-speed collisions, the Pinto was merely the worst of a bad lot. Furthermore, the gap between the Pinto and the competition was not dramatic in terms of the speed at which fuel tank rupture was likely to occur. On that basis it would be difficult to justify the recall of cars that were comparable with others on the market. In the face of even more compelling evidence that people were probably going to die in this car, I again included myself in a group of decision makers who voted not to recommend recall to the higher levels of the organization.

Coda to the Corporate Case

Subsequent to my departure from Ford in 1975, reports of Pinto fires escalated, attracting increasing media attention, almost all of it critical of Ford. Anderson and Whitten (1976) revealed the internal memos concerning the gas tank problem and questioned how the few dollars saved per car could be justified when human lives were at stake. Shortly thereafter, a scathing article by Dowie (1977) attacked not only the Pinto's design, but also accused Ford of gross negligence, stonewalling, and unethical corporate conduct by alleging that Ford knowingly sold "firetraps" after willfully calculating the cost of lives against profits (see also Gatewood and Carroll, 1983). Dowie's provocative quote speculating on "how long the Ford Motor Company would continue to market lethal cars were Henry Ford II and Lee Iacocca serving 20 year terms in Leavenworth for consumer homicide" (1977, p. 32) was particularly effective in focusing attention on the case. Public sentiment edged toward labeling Ford as socially deviant because management was seen as knowing that the ear was defective, choosing profit over lives, resisting demands to fix the car, and apparently showing no public remorse (Swigert and Farrell, 1980–81).

Shortly after Dowie's (1977) exposé, NHTSA initiated its own investigation. Then, early in 1978 a jury awarded a Pinto burn victim $125 million in punitive damages (later reduced to $6.6 million, a judgment upheld on an appeal that prompted the judge to assert that "Ford's institutional mentality was shown to be one of callous indifference to public safety" [quoted in Cullen et al., 1987, p. 164]). A siege atmosphere emerged at Ford. Insiders characterized the mounting media campaign as "hysterical" and "a crusade against us" (personal communications). The crisis deepened. In the summer of 1978 NHTSA issued a formal determination that the Pinto was defective. Ford then launched a reluctant recall of all 1971–1976 cars (those built for the 1977 model year were equipped with a production fix prompted by the adoption of the FMVSS 301 gas tank standard). Ford hoped that the issue would then recede, but worse was yet to come.

The culmination of the case and the demise of the Pinto itself began in Indiana on August 10, 1978, when three teenage girls died in a fire triggered after their 1973 Pinto was hit from behind by a van. A grand jury took the unheard-of step of indicting Ford on charges of reckless homicide (Cullen et al., 1987). Because of the precedent-setting possibilities for all manufacturing industries, Ford assembled a formidable legal team headed by Watergate prosecutor James Neal to defend itself at the trial. The trial was a media event; it was the first time that a corporation was tried for alleged *criminal* behavior. After a protracted, acrimonious courtroom battle that included vivid clashes among the opposing attorneys, surprise witnesses, etc., the jury ultimately found in favor of Ford. Ford had dodged a bullet in the form of a consequential legal precedent, but because of the negative publicity of the case and the charges of corporate crime and ethical deviance, the conduct of manufacturing businesses was altered, probably forever. As a relatively minor footnote to the case, Ford ceased production of the Pinto.

Coda to the Personal Case

In the intervening years since my early involvement with the Pinto fire case, I have given repeated consideration to my role in it. Although most of the ethically questionable actions that have been cited in the press are associated with Ford's intentional stonewalling after it was clear that the Pinto was defective (see Cullen et al., 1986; Dowie, 1977; Gatewood and Carroll 1983)—and thus postdate my involvement with the case and the company—I still nonetheless wonder about my own culpability. Why didn't I see the gravity of the problem and its ethical overtones? What happened to the value system I carried with me into Ford? Should I have acted differently, given what I knew then? The experience with myself has sometimes not been pleasant. Somehow, it seems I should have done *something* different that might have made a difference.

As a consequence of this line of thinking and feeling, some years ago I decided to construct a "living case" out of my experience with the Pinto fire problem for use in my MBA classes. The written case description contains many of the facts detailed above; the analytical task of the class is to ask appropriate questions of me as a figure in the case to reveal the central issues involved. It is somewhat of a trying experience to get through these classes. After getting to know me for most of the semester, and then finding out that I did *not* vote to recommend recall, students are often incredulous, even angry at me for apparently not having lived what I have been teaching. To be fair and evenhanded here, many students understand my actions in the context of the times and the attitudes prevalent then. Others, however, are very disappointed that I appear to have failed during a time of trial. Consequently, I am accused of being a charlatan and otherwise vilified by those who maintain that ethical and moral principles should have prevailed in this case no matter what the mitigating circumstances. Those are the ones that hurt.

Those are also the ones, however, that keep the case and its lessons alive in my mind and cause me to have an ongoing dialogue with myself about it. It is fascinating to me that for several years after I first conducted the living case with myself as the focus, I remained convinced that I had made the "right" decision in not recommending recall of the cars. In light of the times and the evidence available, I thought I had pursued a reasonable course of action. More recently, however, I have come to think that I really should have done everything I could to get those cars off the road.

In retrospect I know that in the context of the times my actions were *legal* (they were all well within the framework of the law); they probably also were *ethical* according to most prevailing definitions (they were in accord with accepted professional standards and codes of conduct); the major concern for me is whether they were *moral* (in the sense of adhering to some higher standards of inner conscience and conviction about the "right" actions to take). This simple typology implies that I had passed at least two hurdles on a personal continuum that ranged from more rigorous, but arguably less significant criteria, to less rigorous, but more personally, organizationally, and perhaps societally significant standards:

X	X	?
Legal	Ethical	Moral

It is that last criterion that remains troublesome.

Perhaps these reflections are all just personal revisionist history. After all, I am still stuck in my cognitive structures, as everyone is. I do not think these concerns are all retrospective reconstruction, however. Another telling piece of information is this: The entire time I was dealing with the Pinto fire problem, I owned a Pinto. I even sold it to my sister. What does that say?

What Happened Here?

I, of course, have some thoughts about my experience with this damningly visible case. At the risk of breaking some of the accepted rules of scholarly analysis, rather than engaging in the usual comprehensive, dense, arm's-length critique, I would instead like to offer a rather selective and subjective focus on certain characteristics of human information processing relevant to this kind of situation, of which I was my own unwitting victim. I make no claim that my analysis necessarily "explains more variance" than other possible explanations. I do think that this selective view is enlightening in that it offers an alternative explanation for some ethically questionable actions in business.

The subjective stance adopted in the analysis is intentional also. This case obviously stems from a series of personal experiences, accounts, and introspections. The analytical style is intended to be consistent with the self-based case example; therefore, it appears to be less "formal" than the typical objectivist mode of explanation. I suspect that my chosen focus will be fairly non-obvious to the reader familiar with the ethical literature (as it typically is to the ethical actor). Although this analysis might be judged as somewhat self-serving, I nonetheless believe that it provides an informative explanation for some of the ethical foibles we see enacted around us.

To me, there are two major issues to address. First, how could my value system apparently have flip-flopped in the relatively short space of 1–2 years? Secondly, how could I have failed to take action on a retrospectively obvious safety problem when I was in the perfect position to do so? To begin, I would like to consider several possible explanations for my thoughts and actions (or lack thereof) during the early stages of the Pinto fire case.

One explanation is that I was simply revealed as a phony when the chips were down; that my previous values were not strongly inculcated; that I was all bluster, not particularly ethical, and as a result acted expediently when confronted with a reality test of those values. In other words, I turned traitor to my own expressed values. Another explanation is that I was simply intimidated; in the face of strong pressure to heel to company preferences, I folded—put ethical concerns aside, or at least traded them for a monumental guilt trip and did what anybody would do to keep a good job. A third explanation is that I was following a strictly utilitarian set of decision criteria (Valasquez et al., 1983) and, predictably enough, opted for a personal form of Ford's own cost-benefit analysis, with similar disappointing results. Another explanation might suggest that the interaction of my stage of moral development (Kohlberg, 1969) and the culture and decision environment at Ford led me to think about and act upon an ethical dilemma in a fashion that reflected a lower level of actual moral development than I espoused for myself (Trevino, 1986). Yet another explanation is that I was co-opted; rather than working from the inside to change a lumbering system as I had intended, the tables were turned and the system beat me at my own game. More charitably, perhaps, it is possible that I simply was a good person making bad ethical choices because of the corporate milieu (Gellerman, 1986).

I doubt that this list is exhaustive. I am quite sure that cynics could match my own MBA students' labels, which in the worst case include phrases like "moral failure" and "doubly reprehensible because you were in a position to make a difference." I believe, however, on the basis of a number of years of work on social cognition in organizations that a viable explanation is one that is not quite so melodramatic. It is an explanation that rests on a recognition that even the best-intentioned organization members organize information into cognitive structures or schemas that serve as (fallible) mental templates for handling incoming information and as guides for acting upon it. Of the many schemas that have been hypothesized to exist, the one that is most relevant to my experience at Ford is the notion of a script (Abelson, 1976, 1981).

My central thesis is this: My own schematized (scripted) knowledge influenced me to perceive recall issues in terms of the prevailing decision environment and to unconsciously overlook key features of the Pinto case, mainly because they did not fit an existing script. Although the outcomes of the case carry retrospectively obvious ethical overtones, the schemas driving my perceptions and actions precluded consideration of the issues in ethical terms because the scripts did not include ethical dimensions.

Script Schemas

A *schema* is a cognitive framework that people use to impose structure upon information, situations, and expectations to facilitate understanding (Gioia and Poole, 1984; Taylor and Crocker, 1981). Schemas . . . preclude the necessity for further active cognition. As a consequence, such structured knowledge allows virtually effortless interpretation of information and events (cf. Canter and Mischel, 1979). A *script* is a specialized type of schema. . . . One of the most important characteristics of scripts is that they simultaneously provide a cognitive framework for *understanding* information and events as well as a guide to appropriate *behavior* to deal with the situation faced. They thus serve as linkages between cognition and action (Gioia and Manz, 1985). . . .

Given the complexity of the organizational world, it is obvious that the schematizing or scripting of knowledge implies a great information-processing advantage—a decision maker need not actively think about each new presentation of information, situations, or problems; the mode of handling such problems has already been worked out in advance and remanded to a working stock of knowledge held in individual (or organizational) memory. Scripted knowledge saves a significant amount of mental work, a savings that in fact prevents the cognitive paralysis that would inevitably come from trying to treat each specific instance of a class of problems as a unique case that requires contemplation. Scripted decision making is thus efficient decision making but not necessarily good decision making (Gioia and Poole, 1984).

Of course, every advantage comes with its own set of built-in disadvantages. There is a price to pay for scripted knowledge. On the one hand, existing scripts lead people to selectively perceive information that is consistent with a script and thus to ignore anomalous information. Conversely, if there is missing information, the gaps in knowledge are filled with expected features supplied by the script (Bower et al., 1979; Graesser et al., 1980). In some cases, a pattern that matches an existing script, except for some key differences, can be "tagged" as a distinctive case (Graesser et al., 1979) and thus be made more memorable. In the worst-case scenario, however, a situation that does not fit the characteristics of the scripted perspective for handling problem cases often is simply not noticed. Scripts thus offer a viable explanation for why experienced decision makers (perhaps *especially* experienced decision makers) tend to overlook what others would construe as obvious factors in making a decision. . . .

Pinto Problem Perception and Scripts

It is illustrative to consider my situation in handling the early stages of the Pinto fire case in light of script theory. When I was dealing with the first trickling-in of field reports that might have suggested a significant problem with the Pinto, the reports were essentially similar to many others that I was dealing with (and dismissing) all the time. The sort of information they contained, which did not convey enough prototypical features to capture my attention, never got past my screening script. I had seen this type of information pattern before (hundreds of times!); I was making this kind of decision automatically every day. I had trained myself to respond to prototypical cues, and these didn't fit the relevant prototype for crisis cases. (Yes, the Pinto reports fit a prototype—but it was a prototype for "normal accidents" that did not deviate significantly from expected problems). The frequency of the reports relative to other, more serious problems (i.e., those that displayed more characteristic features of safety problems) also did not pass my scripted criteria for singling out the Pinto case. Consequently, I looked right past them.

Overlooking uncharacteristic cues also was exacerbated by the nature of the job. The overwhelming information overload that characterized the role as well as its hectic pace actually forced a greater reliance on scripted responses. It was impossible to handle the job requirements *without* relying on some sort of automatic way of assessing whether a case deserved active attention. There was so much to do and so much information to attend to that the only way to deal with it was by means of schematic processing. In fact, the one anomaly in the case that might have cued me to the gravity of the problem (the field report accompanied by graphic photographs) still did nor distinguish the problem as one that was distinctive enough to snap me out of my standard response mode and tag it as a failure that deserved closer monitoring.

Even the presence of an emotional component that might have short-circuited standard script processing instead became part of the script itself. Months of squelching the disturbing emotions associated with serious safety problems soon made muffled emotions a standard (and not very salient) component of the script for handling *any* safety problem. . . . On the basis of my experience, I would argue that for organization members trained to control emotions to perform the job role (cf. Pitre, 1990), emotion is either not a part of the internalized script, or at best becomes a difficult-to-access part of any script for job performance.

The one instance of emotion penetrating the operating script was the revulsion that swept over me at the sight of the burned vehicle at the return depot. That event was so strong that it prompted me to put the case up for preliminary consideration (in theoretical terms, it prompted me cognitively to "tag" the Pinto case as a potentially distinctive one). I soon "came to my senses," however, when rational consideration of the problem characteristics suggested that they did not meet the scripted criteria that were consensually shared among members of the Field Recall Office. At the preliminary review other members of the decision team, enacting their own scripts in the absence of my emotional experience, wondered why I had even brought the case up. . . .

The recall coordinator's job was serious business. The scripts associated with it influenced me much more than I influenced it. Before I went to Ford I would have argued strongly that Ford had an ethical obligation to recall. After I left Ford I now argue and teach that Ford had an ethical obligation to recall. But, *while I was there*, I perceived no strong obligation to recall and I remember no strong *ethical* overtones to the case whatsoever. It was a very straightforward decision, driven by dominant scripts for the time, place, and context.

Whither Ethics and Scripts?

Most models of ethical decision making in organizations implicitly assume that people recognize and think about a moral or ethical dilemma when they are confronted with one (cf. Kohlberg, 1969). I call this seemingly fundamental assumption into question. The unexplored ethical issue for me is the arguably prevalent case where organizational representatives are not aware that they are dealing with a problem that might have ethical overtones. If the case involves a familiar class of problems or issues, it is likely to be handled via existing cognitive structures or scripts—*scripts that typically include no ethical component in their cognitive content.*

Although we might hope that people in charge of important decisions like vehicle safety recalls might engage in active, logical analysis and consider the subtleties in the many different situations they face, the context of the decisions and their necessary reliance on schematic processing tends to preclude such consideration (cf. Gioia, 1989). Accounting for the subtleties of ethical consideration in work situations that are typically handled by schema-based processing is very difficult indeed. Scripts are built out of situations that are normal, not those that are abnormal, ill-structured, or unusual (which often can characterize ethical domains). The ambiguities associated with most ethical dilemmas imply that such situations demand a "custom" decision, which means that the inclusion of an ethical dimension as a component of an evolving script is not easy to accomplish. . . .

The upshot of the scripted view of organizational understanding and behavior is both an encouragement and an indictment of people facing situations laced with ethical overtones. It is encouraging because it suggests that organizational decision makers are not necessarily lacking in ethical standards; they are simply fallible information processors who fail to notice the ethical implications of a usual way of handling issues. It is an indictment because ethical dimensions are not usually a central feature of the cognitive structures that drive decision making. Obviously, they should be, but it will take substantial concentration on the ethical dimension of the corporate culture, as well as overt attempts to emphasize ethics in education, training, and decision making before typical organizational scripts are likely to be modified to include the crucial ethical component.

References

Abelson, R. P.: 1976, "Script Processing in Attitude Formation and Decision-Making," in J. S. Carroll and J. W. Payne (eds.), *Cognition and Social Behavior* (Erlbaum, Hillsdale, NJ), pp. 33–45.

Abelson, R. P.: 1981, "Psychological Status of the Script Concept," *American Psychologist* 36, pp. 715–729.

Anderson, J. and Whitten, L.: 1976, "Auto Maker Shuns Safer Gas Tank," *Washington Post* (December 30), p. B-7.

Bower, G. H., Black. J. B. and Turner, T. J.: 1979, "Scripts in Memory for Text," *Cognitive Psychology* 11, pp. 177–220.

Cantor, N. and Mischel, W.: 1979, "Prototypes in Person Perception," in L. Berkowitz (ed.), *Advances in Experimental Social Psychology* 12 (Academic Press, New York), pp. 3–51.

Cullen, F. T., Maakestad, W. J. and Cavender, G.: 1987, *Corporate Crime Under Attack* (Anderson Publishing Co., Chicago).

Dowie, M.: 1977, "How Ford Put Two Million Firetraps on Wheels," *Business and Society Review* 23, pp. 46–55.

Gatewood, E. and Carroll, A. B.: 1983, "The Anatomy of Corporate Social Response: The Rely, Firestone 500, and Pinto Cases," *Business Horizons,* pp, 9–16.

Gellerman, S.: 1986, "Why 'Good,' Managers Make Bad Ethical Choices," *Harvard Business Review* (July–August), pp. 85–90.

Gioia, D. A.: 1989, "Self-Serving Bias as a Self-Sensemaking Strategy," in P. Rosenfeld, and R. Giacalone (eds.), *Impression Management in the Organization* (LEA, Hillsdale, NJ), pp. 219–234.

Gioia, D. A. and Manz, C. C.: 1985, "Linking Cognition and Behavior: A Script Processing Interpretation of Vicarious Learning," *Academy of Management Review* 10, pp. 527–539.

Gioia, D. A. and Poole, P. P.: 1984, "Scripts in Organizational Behavior," *Academy of Management Review* 9, pp. 449–459.

Graesser, A. C., Gordon, S. G. and Sawyer, J. D.: 1979, "Recognition Memory for Typical and Atypical Actions in Scripted Activities: Test of Script Pointer and Tag Hypothesis," *Journal of Verbal Learning and Verbal Behavior* 18, pp. 319–332.

Graesser, A. C., Woll, S. B., Kowalski, D. J. and Smith, D. A.: 1980, "Memory for Typical and Atypical Actions in Scripted Activities," *Journal of Experimental Psychology* 6, pp. 503–515.

Kohlberg, L.: 1969, "Stage and Sequence: The Cognitive-Development Approach to Socialization," in D. A. Goslin (ed.), *Handbook of Socialization," Theory and Research* (Rand-McNally, Chicago), pp. 347–480.

Perrow, C.: 1984, *Normal Accidents* (Basic Books, New York).

Pitre, E.: 1990, "Emotional Control," working paper, the Pennsylvania State University.

Swigert, V. L. and Farrell, R. A.: 1980–81, "Corporate Homicide: Definitional Processes in the Creation of Deviance," *Law and Society Review* 15, pp. 170–183.

Taylor, S. E. and Crocker, J.: 1981, "Schematic Bases of Social Information Processing," in E. T. Higgins, C. P. Herman, and M. P. Zanna (eds.), *Social Cognition* 1 (Erlbaum, Hillsdale, NJ), pp. 89–134.

Trevino, L.: 1986, "Ethical Decision Making in Organizations: A Person-Situation Interactionist Model," *Academy of Management Review* 11, pp. 601–617.

Trevino, L.: 1992, "Moral Reasoning and Business Ethics: Implications for Research, Education and Management," *Journal of Business Ethics* 11, 445–459.

Valasquez, M., Moberg, D. J. and Cavanaugh, G. F.: 1983, "Organizational Statesmanship and Dirty Politics: Ethical Guidelines for the Organizational Politician," *Organizational Dynamics* (Autumn), pp. 65–80.

Van Maanen, J.: 1978, "People Processing: Strategies of Organizational Socialization," *Organizational Dynamics* (Summer), pp. 19–36.

8

The Nazi Holocaust
Using Bureaucracies, Overcoming Psychological Barriers to Genocide

Raul Hilberg

[During the 12 years of Nazi rule,] the Germans killed five million Jews. The onslaught did not come from the void; it was brought into being because it had meaning to its perpetrators. It was not a narrow strategy for the attainment of some ulterior goal, but an undertaking for its own sake, an event experienced as *Erlebnis*–lived and lived through by its participants.

The German bureaucrats who contributed their skills to the destruction of the Jews all shared in this experience, some in the technical work of drafting a decree or dispatching a train, others starkly at the door of a gas chamber. They could sense the enormity of the operation from its smallest fragments. At every stage they displayed a striking pathfinding ability in the absence of directives, a congruity of activities without jurisdictional guidelines, a fundamental comprehension of the task even when there were no explicit communications. One has the feeling that when Reinhard Heydrich and the ministerial *Staatssekretäre* met on the morning of January 20, 1942 to discuss the "Final Solution of the Jewish Question in Europe," they understood each other.

In retrospect it may be possible to view the entire design as a mosaic of small pieces, each commonplace and lusterless by itself. Yet this progression of everyday activities, these file notes, memoranda, and telegrams, embedded in habit, routine, and tradition, were fashioned into a massive destruction process. Ordinary men were to perform extraordinary tasks. A phalanx of functionaries in public offices and private enterprises was reaching for the ultimate. . . .

The Destructive Expansion

. . . The destruction of the Jews was a total process, comparable in its diversity to a modern war, a mobilization, or a national reconstruction. . . .

An administrative process of such range cannot be carried out by a single agency, even if it is a trained and specialized body like the Gestapo or a commissariat for Jewish affairs, for when a process cuts into every phase of human life, it must ultimately feed upon the resources of the entire organized community. That is why we find among the perpetrators the highly differentiated technicians of the armament inspectorates, the remote officials of the Postal Ministry, and—in the all-important operation of furnishing records for determination of descent—the membership of an aloof and withdrawn Christian clergy. The machinery of destruction, then, was structurally no different from organized German society as a whole; the difference was only one of function. The machinery of destruction *was* the organized community in one of its special roles.

Established agencies rely on existing procedures. In his daily work the bureaucrat made use of tried techniques and tested formulas with which he was familiar and which he knew to be acceptable to his superiors, colleagues, and subordinates. The usual practices were applied also in unusual situations. The Finance Ministry went through condemnation proceedings to set up the Auschwitz complex, and the German railroads billed the Security Police for the transport of the Jews, calculating the one-way fare for each deportee by the track kilometer. Swift operations precipitated greater complications and necessitated more elaborate adjustments. In the course of the roundup of the Warsaw Jews during the summer of 1942, the ghetto inhabitants left behind their unpaid gas and electricity bills, and as a consequence the German offices responsible for public utilities and finance in the city had to marshal all their expertise to restore an administrative equilibrium. . . .

Oral orders were given at every level. Höss was told to build his death camp at Auschwitz in a conversation with Himmler. Stangl received instructions about Sobibór from Globocnik on a park bench in Lublin. A railroad man in Kraków, responsible for scheduling death trains, recalls that he was told by his immediate supervisor to run the transports whenever they were requested by the SS.

In essence, then, there was an atrophy of laws and a corresponding multiplication of measures for which the sources of authority
were more and more ethereal. Valves were being opened for a
decision flow. The experienced functionary was coming into his
own. A middle-ranking bureaucrat, no less than his highest superior, was aware of currents and possibilities. In small ways as well
as large, he recognized what was ripe for the time. Most often it
was he who initiated action.

Thousands of proposals were introduced in memoranda, presented at conferences, and discussed in letters. The subject matter ranged from dissolution of mixed marriages to the deportation of the Jews of Liechtenstein or the construction of some
"quick-working" device for the annihilation of Jewish women and
children at Łódź and the surrounding towns of the Warthegau.
At times it was assumed that the moment had come, even if there
was no definite word from above. Hans Globke wrote anti-Jewish
provisions in a decree on personal names in December 1932,
before there was a Nazi regime or a Führer. The Trusteeship
Office in Warsaw began to seize Jewish real property "in expectation" of a "lawful regulation," meanwhile performing the "indispensable" preparatory work.

. . .

A destruction process has an inherent pattern. There is only one
way in which a scattered group can effectively be destroyed. Three
steps are organic in the operation:

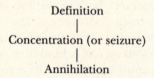

This is the invariant structure of the basic process, for no group
can be killed without a concentration or seizure of the victims, and
no victims can be segregated before the perpetrator knows who
belongs to the group.

There are additional steps in a modern destructive undertaking.
These measures are required not for the annihilation of the victim
but for the preservation of the economy. Basically, they are all

expropriations. In the destruction of the Jews, expropriatory decrees were introduced after every organic step. Dismissals and Aryanizations came after the definition, exploitation and starvation measures followed concentration, and the confiscation of personal belongings was incidental to the killing operation. In its completed form a destruction process in a modern society will thus be structured as shown in this chart:

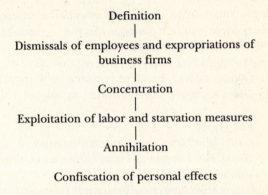

Definition
|
Dismissals of employees and expropriations of
business firms
|
Concentration
|
Exploitation of labor and starvation measures
|
Annihilation
|
Confiscation of personal effects

The sequence of steps in a destruction process is thus determined. If there is an attempt to inflict maximum injury upon a group of people, it is therefore inevitable that a bureaucracy—no matter how decentralized its apparatus or how unplanned its activities—should push its victims through these stages.

The expansion of destruction did not stop at this point. As the machine was thrown into high gear and as the process accelerated toward its goal, German hostility became more generalized. The Jewish target became too narrow; other targets were added. This development is of the utmost importance, for it casts a revealing light upon the perpetrators' fundamental aim.

If a group seeks merely the destruction of hostile institutions, the limit of its most drastic action would be drawn with the complete destruction of the bearers of the institution. The Germans, however, did not draw the line with the destruction of Jewry. They attacked still other victims, some of whom were thought to be like Jews, some of whom were quite unlike Jews, and some of whom were Germans. The Nazi destruction process was, in short, not aimed at institutions; it was targeted at people. The Jews were only the first victims of the German bureaucracy; they were only the first caught in its path. That they should have been chosen first is not accidental. Historical precedents, both administrative and conceptual, determined the selection of the people that for centuries had been the standby victim of recurring destructions. No other group could fill this role so well. None was so vulnerable. But the choice was not confined to the Jews. The following are three illustrations.

Example I.   The destruction process engulfed a group classified as a parasitic people leading a parasitic life: the Gypsies. There were 34,000 to 40,000 Gypsies in the Reich. In accordance with a Himmler directive, the Criminal Police was empowered to seize all persons who looked like Gypsies or who wandered around in "Gypsy-like" manner. Those who were seized were classified as follows:

Z	Full Gypsy
ZM+	Gypsy Mischling, predominantly Gypsy
ZM	Gypsy Mischling with equal Gypsy and German "bloodshares"
ZM–	Gypsy Mischling, predominantly German
NZ	Free of Gypsy blood

The victims in the first three categories were subjected to special wage regulations, taxes, and movement restrictions. Special provisions were made for "privileged Gypsy mixed marriages," and so on. In the 1940's the Germans went one step further. Mobile units of the Security Police in Russia killed roving Gypsies, the military commander in Serbia concentrated Gypsies and shot them, and the SS and Police rounded up Gypsies inside and outside the Reich for deportation to ghettos, concentration camps, and killing centers.

Example II.   The Poles in the territories incorporated by the Reich were in a rather precarious position. It had been planned to shove them into the Generalgouvernement, while the incorporated provinces to the west were to have become purely German. But that program, like the forced emigration of the Jews from Europe, collapsed. In the back of some people's minds, a "terrible solution" now loomed for these Poles. On May 27, 1941, an interministerial conference took place under the chairmanship of Staatssekretär

Conti of the Interior Ministry. The subject of discussion was the reduction of the Polish population in the incorporated territories. The following proposals were entertained: (1) no Pole to be allowed to marry before the age of twenty-five; (2) no permission to be granted unless the marriage was economically sound; (3) a tax on illegitimate births; (4) sterilization following illegitimate birth; (5) no tax exemptions for dependents; (6) permission to submit to abortion to be granted upon application of the expectant mother.

One year later, on May 1, 1942, Gauleiter Greiser of the incorporated Wartheland reported to Himmler that the "special treatment" of 100,000 Jews in his Gau would be completed in another two or three months. Greiser then proceeded in the same paragraph to request Himmler's permission for the use of the experienced Sonderkommando at Kulmhof in order to liberate the Gau from still another danger that threatened "with each passing week to assume catastrophic proportions." Greiser had in his province 35,000 tubercular Poles. He wanted to kill them. The suggestion was passed on to health expert Blome (Conti's deputy), who wanted to refer the matter to Hitler. Months passed without a decision. Finally, Greiser expressed his disappointment to Himmler in words that recall the analogy principle: "I for my person do not believe that the Führer has to be bothered with this question again, especially since he told me only during our last conversation, with reference to the Jews, that I may deal with those in any way I pleased."

Example III.   In consequence of an agreement between Himmler and Justice Minister Thierack, so-called asocials were transferred from prisons to concentration camps. On November 16, 1944, after the transfer of the "asocials" had largely been completed, the judiciary met to discuss a weird subject: ugliness. The phrase on the agenda was "gallery of outwardly asocial prisoners." The summary of that conference states:

> During various visits to the penitentiaries, prisoners have always been observed who—because of their bodily characteristics—hardly deserve the designation human: they look like miscarriages of hell. Such prisoners should be photographed. It is planned that they too shall be eliminated. Crime and sentence are irrelevant. Only such photographs should be submitted which clearly show the deformity.

The Obstacles

A destructive development unparalleled in history had surfaced in Nazi Germany. The bureaucratic network of an entire nation was involved in these operations, and its capabilities were being expanded by an atmosphere facilitating initiatives in offices at every level. Destruction was brought to its logical, final conclusion, and even as this fate overtook the Jews, a veritable target series was established to engulf yet other groups.

The German bureaucracy, however, did not always move with unencumbered ease. From time to time barriers appeared on the horizon and caused momentary pauses. Most of these stoppages were occasioned by those ordinary difficulties encountered by every bureaucracy in every administrative operation: procurement difficulties, shortages, mixups, misunderstandings, and all the other annoyances of the daily bureaucratic process. We shall not be concerned with these occurrences here. But some of the hesitations and interruptions were the products of extraordinary administrative and psychological obstacles. These blocks were peculiar to the destruction process alone, and they must therefore claim our special attention.

Administrative Problems

The destruction of the Jews was not a gainful operation. It imposed a strain upon the administrative machine and its facilities. In a wider sense, it became a burden that rested upon Germany as a whole.

One of the most striking facts about the German apparatus was the sparseness of its personnel, particularly in those regions outside the Reich where most of the victims had to be destroyed. Moreover, that limited manpower was preoccupied with a bewildering variety of administrative undertakings. Upon close examination, the machinery of destruction turns out to have been a loose organization of part-timers. There were at most a handful of bureaucrats who could devote all their time to anti-Jewish activities. There were the "experts" on Jewish affairs in the ministries, the mobile killing units of the Reich Security Main Office, the commanders of the killing centers. But even an expert like Eichmann had two jobs: the deportation of Jews and the resettlement of ethnic Germans. The mobile killing units had to shoot Jews, Gypsies, commissars, and partisans alike, while a camp commander like Höss was host to an industrial complex next to his gas chambers.

In the totality of the administrative process, the destruction of the Jews presented itself as an additional task to a bureaucratic machine that was already straining to fulfill the requirements of the battlefronts. One need think only of the railroads, which served as the principal means for transporting troops, munitions, supplies, and raw materials. Every day, available rolling stock had to be allocated, and congested routes assigned for trains urgently requested by military and industrial users. Notwithstanding these priorities, no Jew was left alive for lack of transport to a killing center. The German bureaucracy was not deterred by problems, never resorting to pretense, like the Italians, or token measures, like the Hungarians, or procrastinations, like the Bulgarians. German administrators were driven to accomplishment. Unlike their collaborators, German decision makers never contented themselves with the minimum. They always did the maximum.

Indeed there were moments when an agency's eagerness to participate in the decision making led to bureaucratic competition and rivalry. Such a contest was in the offing when Unterstaatssekretär Luther concluded an agreement with the Reich Security Main Office to preserve the Foreign Office's power to negotiate with Axis satellites on Jewish matters. Again, within the SS itself, a jealous struggle was waged between two technocrats of destruction, Obersturmbannführer Höss and Kriminalkommissar Wirth, over the replacement of carbon monoxide with Zyklon B in the death camps. We have observed this bureaucratic warfare also in the attempt of the judiciary to conserve its jurisdiction in Jewish affairs. When that attempt was finally given up, Justice Minister Thierack wrote to his friend Bormann: "I intend to turn over criminal jurisdiction against Poles, Russians, Jews, and Gypsies to the Reichsführer-SS. In doing so, I base myself on the principle that the administration of justice can make only a small contribution to the extermination of these peoples." This letter reveals an almost melancholy tone. The judiciary had done its utmost; it was no longer needed. . . .

Psychological Problems

The most important problems of the destruction process were not administrative but psychological. The very conception of the drastic Final Solution was dependent on the ability of the perpetrators to cope with weighty psychological obstacles and impediments. The psychological blocks differed from the administrative difficulties in one important respect. An administrative problem could be solved and eliminated, but the psychological difficulties had to be dealt with continuously. They were held in check but never removed. Commanders in the field were ever watchful for symptoms of psychological disintegration. In the fall of 1941 Higher SS and Police Leader Russia Center von dem Bach shook Himmler with the remark: "Look at the eyes of the men of this Kommando, how deeply shaken they are. These men are finished for the rest of their lives. What kind of followers are we training here? Either neurotics or savages!" Von dem Bach was not only an important participant in killing operations. He was also an acute observer. With this remark he pointed to the basic psychological problem of the German bureaucracy, namely that the German administration had to make determined efforts to prevent the breakdown of its men into either "savages" or "neurotics." This was essentially a dual task—one part disciplinary, the other part moral.

The disciplinary problem was understood clearly. The bureaucrats were fully aware of the dangers of plundering, torture, orgies, and atrocities. Such behavior was first of all wasteful from an administrative point of view, for the destruction process was an organized undertaking which had room only for organized tasks. Moreover, "excesses" attracted attention to aspects of the destruction process that had to remain secret. Such were the activities of Brigadeführer Dirlewnager, whose rumored attempts to make human soap drew the attention of the public to the killing centers. Indeed, atrocities could bring the entire "noble" work into disrepute.

What was wasteful administratively was dangerous psychologically. Loose behavior was an abuse of the machine, and a debauched administration could disintegrate. That was why the German administration had a certain preference for quick-blow-type action. Maximum destructive effect was to be achieved with minimum destructive effort. The personnel of the machinery of destruction were not supposed to look to the right or to the left. They were not allowed to have either personal motives or personal gains. An elaborate discipline was introduced into the machine of destruction.

The first and most important rule of conduct of this discipline was that all Jewish property belonged to the Reich. So far as Himmler was concerned, the enforcement of this rule was a success. In 1943 he told his Gruppenführer:

> The riches which they [the Jews] owned we have taken from them. I have given strict orders, which Obergruppenführer Pohl has carried out, that this wealth should naturally be delivered to the Reich. We have taken nothing. Individuals who have transgressed are being punished in accordance with an order which I gave in the beginning and which threatened that anyone who takes just one mark is a condemned man. A number of SS men—not many—have transgressed against that order, and they will be condemned to death mercilessly. We had the moral right vis-à-vis OUR people to annihilate THIS people which wanted to annihilate us. But we have no right to take a single fur, a single watch, a single mark, a single cigarette, or anything whatever. We don't want in the end, just because we have exterminated a germ, to be infected by that germ and die from it. I will not stand by while a slight infection forms. Whenever such an infected spot appears, we will burn it out. But on the whole we can say that we have fulfilled this heavy task with love for our people, and we have not been damaged in the innermost of our being, our soul, our character.

There is, of course, considerable evidence that more than a few individuals "transgressed" against the discipline of the destruction process. No estimate can be formed of the extent to which transport Kommandos, killing units, the ghetto and killing center personnel, and even Kommando 1005—the grave destruction Kommando—filled their pockets with the belongings of the dead. Moreover, we should note that Himmler's rule dealt only with *unauthorized* takings by participating personnel in the field. It did not deal with *authorized* distributions to the participants.

The essence of corruption is to reward people on the basis of their proximity to the loot—in a corrupt system the tax collectors become rich. In the course of the destruction process, many distributions were made to the closest participants. We need remind ourselves only of the Finance Ministry's appropriation of fine furniture during the deportation of Jews from Germany; the distribution of better apartments to civil servants; the cuts taken by the railways, SS and Police, and postal service in the allocation of the furniture of the Dutch, Belgian, and French Jews; the "gifts" of watches and "Christmas presents" to SS men and their families. The destruction process had its own built-in corruption. Only unauthorized corruption was forbidden.

The second way in which the Germans sought to avoid damage to "the soul" was in the prohibition of unauthorized killings. A sharp line was drawn between killings pursuant to order and killings induced by desire. In the former case a man was thought to have overcome the "weaknesses" of "Christian morality"; in the latter case he was overcome by his own baseness. That was why in the occupied USSR both the army and the civil administration sought to restrain their personnel from joining the shooting parties at the killing sites.

Perhaps the best illustration of the official attitude is to be found in an advisory opinion by a judge on Himmler's Personal Staff, Obersturmbannführer Bender. Bender dealt with procedure to be followed in the case of unauthorized killings of Jews by SS personnel. He concluded that if purely political motives prompted the killing, if the act was an expression of idealism, no punishment was necessary unless the maintenance of order required disciplinary action or prosecution. However, if selfish, sadistic, or sexual motives were found, punishment was to be imposed for murder or for manslaughter, in accordance with the facts.

The German disciplinary system is most discernible in the mode of the killing operation. At the conclusion of the destruction process, Hitler remarked in his testament that the Jewish "criminals" had "atoned" for their "guilt" by "humane means." The "humaneness" of the destruction process was an important factor in its success. It must be emphasized, of course, that this "humaneness" was evolved not for the benefit of the victims but for the welfare of its perpetrators. Time and again, attempts were made to reduce opportunities for "excesses" of all sorts. Much research was expended for the development of devices and methods that arrested propensities for uncontrolled behavior and at the same time lightened the crushing psychological burden on the killers. The construction of gas vans and gas chambers, the employment of Ukranian, Lithuanian, and Latvian auxiliaries to kill Jewish women and children, the use of Jews for the burial and burning of bodies—all these were efforts in the same direction. Efficiency was the real aim of all that "humaneness."

So far as Himmler was concerned, his SS and Police had weathered the destruction process. In October 1943, when he addressed his top commanders, he said to them:

> Most of you know what it means when 100 corpses lie there, or 500 lie there, or 1000 lie there. To have gone through this and—apart from the exceptions caused by human weakness—to have remained decent, that has hardened us. That is a page of glory in our history never written and never to be written.

However, the descent into savagery was not nearly so important a factor in the destruction process as the feeling of growing uneasiness that pervaded the bureaucracy from the lowest strata to the highest. That uneasiness was the product of moral scruples—the lingering effect of two thousand years of Western morality and ethics. A Western bureaucracy had never before faced such a chasm between moral precepts and administrative action; an administrative machine had never been burdened with such a drastic task. In a sense the task of destroying the Jews put the German bureaucracy to a supreme test. The German technocrats solved also that problem and passed also this test.

To grasp the full significance of what these men did we have to understand that we are not dealing with individuals who had their own separate moral standards. The bureaucrats who were drawn into the destruction process were not different in their moral makeup from the rest of the population. The German perpetrator was not a special kind of German. What we have to say here about his morality applies not to him specially but to Germany as a whole. How do we know this?

We know that the very nature of administrative planning, of the jurisdictional structure, and of the budgetary system precluded the special training of personnel. Any member of the Order Police could be a guard at a ghetto or on a train. Every lawyer in the Reich Security Main Office was presumed to be suitable for leadership in the mobile killing units; every finance expert to the Economic-Administrative Main Office was considered a natural choice for service in a death camp. In other words, all necessary operations were accomplished with whatever personnel were at hand. However one may wish to draw the line of active participation, the machinery of destruction was a remarkable cross-section of the German population. Every profession, every skill, and every social status was represented in it. We know that in a totalitarian state the formation of an opposition movement outside the bureaucracy is next to impossible. However, if there is very serious opposition in the population, if there are insurmountable psychological obstacles to a course of action, such impediments reveal themselves *within* the bureaucratic apparatus. We know what such barriers will do, for they emerged clearly in the Italian Fascist state. Again and again the Italian generals and consuls, prefects and police inspectors refused to cooperate in the deportations. The destruction process in Italy and the Italian-controlled areas was carried out against unremitting Italian opposition. No such opposition is to be found in the German area. No obstruction stopped the German machine of destruction. No moral problem proved insurmountable. When all participating personnel were put to the test, there were very few lingerers and almost no deserters. The old moral order did not break through anywhere along the line. This is a phenomenon of the greatest magnitude.

How did the German bureaucrat cope with his moral inhibitions? He did so in an inner struggle, recognizing the basic truth that he had a choice. He knew that at crucial junctures every individual makes decisions, and that every decision is individual. He knew this fact as he faced his own involvement and while he went on and on. At the same time he was not psychically unarmed. When he wrestled with himself, he had at his disposal the most complex psychological tools fashioned during centuries of German cultural development. Fundamentally, this arsenal of defenses consisted of two parts: a mechanism of repressions and a system of rationalizations.

First of all, the bureaucracy wanted to hide its deeds. It wanted to conceal the destructive process not only from all outsiders but also from the censuring gaze of its own conscience. The repression proceeded through five stages.

As we might expect, every effort was made to hide the ultimate aim of the destruction process from Axis partners and from the Jews. Inquiries such as Hungarian Prime Minister Kállay put to the Foreign Office about the disappearance of European Jewry or questions that foreign journalists in Kiev asked army authorities about mass shootings could obviously not be answered. Rumors, which could spread like wildfire, had to be smothered. "Plastic" evidence, such as "souvenir" photographs of killings, mass graves, and the wounded Jews who had risen from their graves, had to be destroyed. . . .

[T]he first stage in the repression was to shut off the supply of information from all those who did not have to know it. Whoever did not participate was not supposed to know.

The second stage was to make sure that whoever knew would participate. There was nothing so irksome as the realization that someone was watching over one's shoulder, that someone would be free to talk and accuse because he was not himself involved. This fear was the origin of what Leo Alexander called the "blood kit," the irresistible force that drew every official "observer" into the destruction process. The "blood kit" explains why so many office chiefs of the Reich Security Main Office were assigned to mobile killing units and why staff officers with killing units were ordered to participate in the killing operations. The "blood kit" also explains why Unterstaatssekretär Luther of the Foreign Office's Abteilung Deugschland insisted that the Political Division countersign all instructions to embassies and legations for the deportation of Jews. Finally, the "blood kit" explains the significant words spoken by Generalgouverneur Frank at the conclusion of a police conference in Kraków: "We want to remember that we are, all of us assembled here, on Mr. Roosevelt's war-criminals list. I have the honor of occupying first place on that list. We are therefore, so to speak, accomplices in a world-historical sense."

The third stage in the process of repression was the prohibition of criticism. Public protests by outsiders were extremely rare. The criticisms were expressed, if at all, in mutterings on the rumor circuit. It is sometimes hard even to distinguish between expressions of sensationalism and real criticism, for often the two were mixed. One example of such mixed reactions is to be found in the circulation of rumours in Germany about the mobile killing operations in Russia. The Party Chancellery, in confidential instructions to its regional machinery, attempted to combat these rumors. Most of the reports, the chancellery stated, were "distorted" and "exaggerated." "It is conceivable," the circular continued, "that not all of our people—especially people who have no conception of the Bolshevik terror—can understand sufficiently the necessity for these measures." In their very nature, "these problems," which were sometimes "very difficult," could be solved "in the interest of the security of our people" only with "ruthless severity.". . .

In its fourth stage the repressive mechanism eliminated the destruction process as a subject of social conversation. Among the closest participants, it was considered bad form to talk about the killings. This is what Himmler had to say on the subject in his speech of October 4, 1943:

> I want to mention here very candidly a particularly difficult chapter. Among us it should be mentioned once, quite openly, but in public we will never talk about it. Just as little as we hesitated on June 30, 1934, to do our duty and to put comrades who had transgressed [the brownshirts] to the wall, so little have we talked about it and will ever talk about it. It was with us, thank God, an inborn gift of tactfulness, that we have never conversed about this matter, never spoken about it. Every one of us was horrified, and yet every one of us knew that we would do it again if it were ordered and if it were necessary. I am referring to the evacuation of the Jews, to the extermination of the Jewish people.

This then was the reason why that particular "page of glory" was never to be written. There are some things that can be done only so long as they are not discussed, for once they are discussed they can no longer be done. . . .

The fifth and final stage in the process of repression was to omit mention of "killings" or "killing installations" even in the secret correspondence in which such operations had to be reported. The reader of these reports is immediately struck by their camouflaged vocabulary: *Endlösung der Judenfrage* ("final solution of the Jewish question"), *Lösungsmöglichkeiten* ("solution possibilities"), *Sonderbehandlung* or *SB* ("special treatment"), *Evakuierung* ("evacuation"), *Aussiedlung* (same), *Umsiedlung* (same), *Spezialeinrichtungen* ("special installations"), *durchgeschleusst* ("dragged through"), and many others.

There is one report that contains a crude cover story. In 1943 the Foreign Office inquired whether it would be possible to exchange 30,000 Baltic and White Russian Jews for Reich Germans in Allied countries. The Foreign Office representative in Riga replied that he had discussed the matter with the Security Police commander in charge. The Commander of Security Police had felt that the "interned" Jews could not be sent away for "weighty Security Police reasons." As was known, a large number of Jews had been "done away with" in "spontaneous actions." In some places these actions had resulted in "almost total extermination." A removal of the remaining Jews would therefore give rise to "anti-German atrocity propaganda.". . .

The process of repression was continuous, but it was never completed. The killing of the Jews could not be hidden completely, either from the outside world or from the inner self. Therefore the bureaucracy was not spared an open encounter with its conscience. It had to pit argument against argument and philosophy against philosophy. Laboriously, and with great effort, the bureaucracy had to justify its activities. . . .

[Rationalization]

Psychological justification is called rationalization. The Germans employed two kinds of rationalizations. The first was an attempt to justify the destruction process as a whole. It was designed to explain why the Jews had to be destroyed. It was focused on the Jew. The other explanations served only to justify individual participation in the destruction process—a signature on a piece of paper or the squeeze of a trigger. They were focused entirely on the perpetrator. Let us consider first the broad rationalizations that encompassed the whole destruction process. In the formation of these justifications, old conceptions about the Jew, reinforced and expanded by new propaganda, played an important role. Precisely how did German propaganda function in this process?

The Germans had two kinds of propaganda. One was designed to produce action. It exhorted people to come to a mass meeting, to boycott Jewish goods, or to kill Jews. This type of propaganda does not concern us here since it was confined, on the whole, to the incitement of demonstrations and pogroms, the so-called *Einzelaktionen*. But the Germans also engaged in a campaign that consisted of a series of statements implying that the Jew was evil. This propaganda had a very important place in the arsenal of psychological defense mechanisms.

Repeated propagandistic allegations may be stored and drawn upon according to need. The statement "The Jew is evil" is taken from the storehouse and is converted in the perpetrator's mind into a complete rationalization: "I kill the Jew because the Jew is evil." To understand the function of such formulations is to realize why they were being constructed until the very end of the war. Propaganda was needed to combat doubts and guilt feelings wherever they arose, whether inside or outside the bureaucracy, and whenever they surfaced, before or after the perpetration of the acts.

In fact, we find that in April 1943, after the deportations of the Jews from the Reich had largely been completed, the press was ordered to deal with the Jewish question continuously and without letup. In order to build up a storehouse, the propaganda had to be turned out on a huge scale. "Research institutes" were formed, doctoral dissertations were written, and volumes of propaganda literature were printed by every conceivable agency. Sometimes a scholarly investigation was conducted too assiduously. One economic study, rich in the common jargon but uncommonly balanced in content, appeared in Vienna with the notation "Not in the book trade"—the author had discovered that the zenith of Jewish financial power had been reached in 1913.

. . .

What did all this propaganda accomplish? How was the Jew portrayed in this unending flow of leaflets and pamphlets, books, and speeches? How did the propaganda image of the Jew serve to justify the destruction process?

First of all, the Germans drew a picture of an international Jewry ruling the world and plotting the destruction of Germany and German life. "If international-finance Jewry," said Adolf Hitler in 1939, "inside and outside of Europe should succeed in plunging the nations into another world war, then the result will not be the Bolshevization of the earth and with it the victory of the Jews, but the annihilation of the Jewish race in Europe." In 1944 Himmler said to his commanders: "This was the most frightening order which an organization could receive—the order to solve the Jewish question," but if the Jews had still been in the rear, the front line could not have been held, and if any of the commanders were moved to pity, they had only to think of the bombing terror, "which after all is organized in the last analysis by the Jews."

The theory of world Jewish rule and of the incessant Jewish plot against the German people penetrated into all offices. It became interwoven with foreign policy and sometimes led to preposterous results. Thus the conviction grew that foreign statesmen who were not very friendly toward Germany were Jews, part-Jews, married to Jews, or somehow dominated by Jews. Streicher did not hesitate to state publicly that he had it on good Italian authority that the Pope had Jewish blood. Similarly, Staatssekretär Weizsäcker of the Foreign Office once questioned the British chargé d'affaires about the percentage of "Aryan" blood in Mr. Rublee, an American on a mission in behalf of refugees. . . .

However, the Jews were portrayed not only as a world conspiracy but also as a criminal people. This is the definition of the Jews as furnished in instructions to the German press:

> *Stress:* In the case of the Jews there are not merely a few criminals (as in every other people), but all of Jewry rose from criminal roots, and in its very nature it is criminal. The Jews are no people like other people, but a pseudo-people welded together by hereditary criminality. . . . The annihilation of Jewry is no loss to humanity, but just as useful as capital punishment or protective custody against other criminals.

And this is what Streicher had to say: "Look at the path which the Jewish people has traversed for millenia: Everywhere murder; everywhere mass murder!"

A Nazi researcher, Helmut Schramm, collected all the legends of Jewish ritual murder. The book was an immediate success with Himmler. "Of the book *The Jewish Ritual Murders*," he wrote to Kaltenbrunner, "I have ordered a large number. I am distributing it down to Standartenführer [SS colonel]. I am sending you several hundred copies so that you can distribute them to your Einsatzkommandos, and above all to the men who are busy with the Jewish question." *The Ritual Murders* was a collection of stories about alleged tortures of Christian children. Actually, hundreds of thousands of Jewish children were being killed in the destruction process. Perhaps that is why *The Ritual Murders* became so important. In fact, Himmler was so enthusiastic about the book that he ordered Kaltenbrunner to start investigations of "ritual murders" in Romania, Hungary, and Bulgaria. He also suggested that Security Police people be put to work tracing British court records and police descriptions of missing children, "so that we can report in our radio broadcasts to England that in the town of XY a child is missing and that it is probably another case of Jewish ritual murder.". . . .

A third rationalization that focused on the Jew was the conception of Jewry as a lower form of life. Generalgouverneur Frank was given to the use of such phrases as "Jews and lice." In a speech delivered on December 19, 1940, he pointed out that relatives of military personnel surely were sympathizing with men stationed in Poland, a country "which is so full of lice and Jews." But the situation was not so bad, he continued, though of course he could not rid the country of lice and Jews in a year. On July 19, 1943, the chief of the Generalgouvernement Health Division reported during a meeting that the typhus epidemic was subsiding. Frank remarked in this connection that the "removal" of the "Jewish element" had undoubtedly contributed to better health in Europe. He meant this not only in the literal sense but also politically: the reestablishment of sound living conditions on the European continent. In a similar vein, Foreign Office Press Chief Schmidt once declared during a visit to Slovakia, "The Jewish question is no question of humanity, and it is no question of religion; it is solely a question of political hygiene." . . .

[Individual Rationalizations]

In addition to the formulations that were used to justify the whole undertaking as a war against "international Jewry," as a judicial proceeding against "Jewish criminality," or simply as a "hygienic" process against "Jewish vermin," there were also rationalizations fashioned in order to enable the individual bureaucrat to justify his individual task in the destruction process. It must be kept in mind that most of the participants did not fire rifles at Jewish children or pour gas into gas chambers. A good many, of course, also had to perform these very "hard" tasks, but most of the administrators and most of the clerks did not see the final, drastic link in these measures of destruction.

Most bureaucrats composed memoranda, drew up blueprints, signed correspondence, talked on the telephone, and participated in conferences. They could destroy a whole people by sitting at their desks. Except for inspection tours, which were not obligatory, they never had to see "100 bodies lie there, or 500, or 1,000." However, these men were not naive. They realized the connection between their paperwork and the heaps of corpses in the East, and they also realized the shortcomings of arguments that placed all evil on the Jew and all good on the German. That was why they were compelled to justify their individual activities. The justifications contain the implicit admission that the paperwork was to go on regardless of the actual plans of world Jewry and regardless of the actual behavior of the Jews who were about to be killed. . . .

The oldest, the simplest, and therefore the most effective rationalization was the doctrine of superior orders. First and foremost there was discipline. First and foremost there was duty. No matter what objections there might be, orders were given to be obeyed. A clear order was like absolution. Armed with such an order, a perpetrator felt that he could pass his responsibility and his conscience upward. When Himmler addressed a killing party in Minsk, he told his men that they need not worry. Their conscience was in no way impaired, for they were soldiers who had to carry out every order unconditionally.

Every bureaucrat knows, of course, that open defiance of orders is serious business, but he also knows that there are many ingenious ways of evading orders. In fact, the opportunities for evading them increase as one ascends in the hierarchy. Even in Nazi Germany orders were disobeyed, and they were disobeyed even in Jewish matters. We have mentioned the statement of Reichsbankdirektor Wilhelm, who would not participate in the distribution of "second-hand goods." Nothing happened to him. A member of the Reich Security Main Office, Sturmbannführer Hartl, simply refused to take over an Einsatzkommando in Russia. Nothing happened to this man, either. Even Generalkommissar Kube, who had actually frustrated a killing operation in Minsk and who had otherwise expressed himself in strong language, was only warned.

The bureaucrat clung to his orders not so much because he feared his superior (with whom he was often on good terms) but because he feared his own conscience. The many requests for "authorization," whether for permission to mark Jews with a star or to kill them, demonstrate the true nature of these orders. When they did not exist the bureaucrats had to invent them.

The second rationalization was the administrator's insistence that he did not act out of personal vindictiveness. In the mind of the bureaucrat, duty was an assigned path; it was his "fate." The German bureaucrat made a sharp distinction between duty and personal feelings. He insisted that he did not "hate" Jews, and sometimes he even went out of his way to perform "good deeds" for Jewish friends and acquaintances. When the trials of war criminals started, there was hardly a defendant who could not produce evidence that he had helped some half-Jewish physics professor, or that he had used his influence to permit a Jewish symphony conductor to conduct a little while longer, or that he had intervened on behalf of some couple in mixed marriage in connection with an apartment. While these courtesies were petty in comparison with the destructive conceptions that these men were implementing concurrently, the "good deeds" performed an important psychological function. They separated "duty" from personal feelings. They preserved a sense of "decency." The destroyer of the Jews was no "anti-Semite.". . .

The third justification was the rationalization that one's own activity was not criminal, that the next fellow's action was the criminal act. The Ministerialrat who was signing papers could console himself with the thought that he did not do the shooting. But that was not enough. He had to be sure that *if* he were ordered to shoot, he would not follow orders but would draw the line right then and there.

The following exchange took place during a war crimes trial. A Foreign Office official, Albrecht von Kessel, was asked by defense counsel (Dr. Becker) to explain the meaning of "final solution."

ANSWER: This expression "final solution" was used with various meanings. In 1936 "final solution" meant merely that all Jews should leave Germany. And, of course, it was true that they were to be robbed; that wasn't very nice, but it wasn't criminal.

JUDGE MAGUIRE: Was that an accurate translation?

DR. BECKER: I did not check on the translation. Please repeat the sentence.

ANSWER: I said it was not criminal; it was not nice, but it was not criminal. That is what I said. One didn't want to take their life; one merely wanted to take money away from them. That was all.

The most important characteristic of this dividing line was that it could be *shifted* when the need arose. . . .

There was a fourth rationalization that implicitly took cognizance of the fact that all shifting lines are unreal. It was a rationalization that was built on a simple premise: No man alone can build a bridge and no man alone can destroy the Jews. The participant in the destruction process was always in company. Among his superiors he could always find those who were doing more than he; among his subordinates he could always find those who were ready to take his place. No matter where he looked, he was one among thousands. His own importance was diminished, and he felt that he was replaceable, perhaps even dispensable. . . .

When Werner von Tippelskirch, a Foreign Office official, was interrogated after the war, he pointed out that he had never protested against the killing of Jews in Russia because he had been "powerless." His superiors, Erdmannsdorff, Wörmann, and Weizsäcker, had also been "powerless." All of them had waited for a "change of regime." Asked by Prosecutor Kempner whether it was right to wait for a change of regime "and in the meantime send thousands of people to their death," von Tippelskirch replied, "A difficult question." For Staatssekretär von Weizsäcker himself the question of what he could have done was circular. If he had had influence he would have stopped measures altogether. But the "if" presupposed a fairyland. In such a land he would not have had to use his influence.

9

The My Lai Massacre
Crimes of Obedience and Sanctioned Massacres
Herbert C. Kelman and V. Lee Hamilton

March 16, 1968, was a busy day in U.S. history. Stateside, Robert F. Kennedy announced his presidential candidacy, challenging a sitting president from his own party—in part out of opposition to an undeclared and disastrous war. In Vietnam, the war continued. In many ways, March 16 may have been a typical day in that war. We will probably never know. But we do know that on that day a typical company went on a mission—which may or may not have been typical—to a village called Son (or Song) My. Most of what is remembered from that mission occurred in the subhamlet known to Americans as My Lai 4.

The My Lai massacre was investigated and charges were brought in 1969 and 1970. Trials and disciplinary actions lasted into 1971. Entire books have been written about the army's year-long cover-up of the massacre (for example, Hersh, 1972), and the cover-up was a major focus of the army's own investigation of the incident. Our central concern here is the massacre itself—a crime of obedience— and public reactions to such crimes, rather than the lengths to which many went to deny the event. Therefore this account concentrates on one day: March 16, 1968.

Many verbal testimonials to the horrors that occurred at My Lai were available. More unusual was the fact that an army photographer, Ronald Haeberle, was assigned the task of documenting the anticipated military engagement at My Lai—and documented a massacre instead. Later, as the story of the massacre emerged, his photographs were widely distributed and seared the public conscience. What might have been dismissed as unreal or exaggerated was depicted in photographs of demonstrable authenticity. The dominant image appeared on the cover of *Life*: piles of bodies jumbled together in a ditch along a trail—the dead all apparently unarmed. All were Oriental, and all appeared to be children, women, or old men. Clearly there had been a mass execution, one whose image would not quickly fade.

So many bodies (over twenty in the cover photo alone) are hard to imagine as the handiwork of one killer. These were not. They were the product of what we call a crime of obedience. Crimes of obedience begin with orders. But orders are often vague and rarely survive with any clarity the transition from one authority down a chain of subordinates to the ultimate actors. The operation at Son My was no exception.

"Charlie" Company, Company C, under Lt. Col. Frank Barker's command, arrived in Vietnam in December of 1967. As the army's investigative unit, directed by Lt. Gen. William R. Peers, characterized the personnel, they "contained no significant deviation from the average" for the time. Seymour S. Hersh (1970) described the "average" more explicitly: "Most of the men in Charlie Company had volunteered for the draft; only a few had gone to college for even one year. Nearly half were black, with a few Mexican-Americans. Most were eighteen to twenty-two years old. The favorite reading matter of Charlie Company, like that of other line infantry units in Vietnam, was comic books" (p. 18). The action at My Lai, like that throughout Vietnam, was fought by a cross-section of those Americans who either believed in the war or lacked the social resources to avoid participating in it. Charlie Company was indeed average for that time, that place, and that war.

Two key figures in Charlie Company were more unusual. The company's commander, Capt. Ernest Medina, was an upwardly mobile Mexican-American who wanted to make the army his career, although he feared that he might never advance beyond captain because of his lack of formal education. His eagerness had earned him a nickname among his men: "Mad Dog Medina." One of his admirers was the platoon leader Second Lt. William L. Calley, Jr., an undistinguished, five-foot-three-inch junior-college dropout who had failed four of the seven courses in which he had enrolled his first year. Many viewed him as one of those "instant officers" made possible only by the army's then-desperate need for manpower. Whatever the cause, he was an insecure leader whose frequent claim was "I'm the boss." His nickname among some of the troops was "Surfside 5½," a reference to the swashbuckling heroes of a popular television show, "Surfside 6."

The Son My operation was planned by Lieutenant Colonel Barker and his staff as a search-and-destroy mission with the objective of rooting out the Forty-eighth Viet Cong Battalion from their base area of Son My village. Apparently no written orders were ever issued. Barker's superior, Col. Oran Henderson, arrived at the staging point the day before. Among the issues he reviewed with the assembled officers were some of the weaknesses of prior operations by their units, including their failure to be appropriately aggressive in pursuit of the enemy. Later briefings by Lieutenant Colonel Barker and his staff asserted that no one except Viet Cong was expected to be in the village after 7 A.M. on the following day. The "innocent" would all be at the market. Those present at the briefings gave conflicting accounts of Barker's exact orders, but he conveyed at least a strong suggestion that the Son My area was to be obliterated. As the army's inquiry reported: "While there is some conflict in the testimony as to whether LTC Barker ordered the destruction of houses, dwellings, livestock, and other foodstuffs in the Song My area, the preponderance of the evidence indicates that such destruction was implied, if not specifically directed, by his orders of 15 March" (Peers Report, in Goldstein et al., 1976, p. 94).

Evidence that Barker ordered the killing of civilians is even more murky. What does seem clear, however, is that—having asserted that civilians would be away at the market—he did not specify what was to be done with any who might nevertheless be found on the scene. The Peers Report therefore considered it "reasonable to conclude that LTC Barker's minimal or nonexistent instructions concerning the handling of noncombatants created the potential for grave misunderstandings as to his intentions and for interpretation of his orders as authority to fire, without restriction, on all persons found in target area" (Goldstein et al., 1976, p. 95). Since Barker was killed in action in June 1968, his own formal version of the truth was never available.

Charlie Company's Captain Medina was briefed for the operation by Barker and his staff. He then transmitted the already vague orders to his own men. Charlie Company was spoiling for a fight, having been totally frustrated during its months in Vietnam—first by waiting for battles that never came, then by incompetent forays led by inexperienced commanders, and finally by mines and booby traps. In fact, the emotion-laden funeral of a sergeant killed by a booby trap was held on March 15, the day before My Lai. Captain Medina gave the orders for the next day's action at the close of that funeral. Many were in a mood for revenge.

It is again unclear what was ordered. Although all participants were still alive by the time of the trials for the massacre, they were either on trial or probably felt under threat of trial. Memories are often flawed and self-serving at such times. It is apparent that Medina relayed to the men at least some of Barker's general message—to expect Viet Cong resistance, to burn, and to kill live-stock. It is not clear that he ordered the slaughter of the inhabit-ants, but some of the men who heard him thought he had. One of those who claimed to have heard such orders was Lt. William Calley.

As March 16 dawned, much was expected of the operation by those who had set it into motion. Therefore a full complement of "brass" was present in helicopters overhead, including Barker, Colonel Henderson, and their superior, Major General Koster (who went on to become commandant of West Point before the story of My Lai broke). On the ground, the troops were to carry with them one reporter and one photographer to immortalize the anticipated battle.

The action for Company C began at 7:30 as their first wave of helicopters touched down near the subhamlet of My Lai 4. By 7:47 all of Company C was present and set to fight. But instead of the Viet Cong Forty-eighth Battalion, My Lai was filled with the old men, women, and children who were supposed to have gone to market. By this time, in their version of the war, and with whatever orders they thought they had heard, the men from Company C were never-theless ready to find Viet Cong everywhere. By nightfall, the offi-cial tally was 128 VC killed and three weapons captured, although later unofficial body counts ran as high as 500. The operation at Son My was over. And by nightfall, as Hersh reported: "The Viet Cong were back in My Lai 4, helping the survivors bury the dead. It took five days. Most of the funeral speeches were made by the Communist guerrillas. Nguyen Bat was not a Communist at the time

of the massacre, but the incident changed his mind. 'After the shooting,' he said, 'all the villagers became Communists'" (1970, p. 74).
To this day, the memory of the massacre is kept alive by markers
and plaques designating the spots where groups of villagers were
killed, by a large statue, and by the My Lai Museum, established in
1975 (Williams, 1985).

But what could have happened to leave American troops reporting
a victory over Viet Cong when in fact they had killed hundreds of
noncombatants? It is not hard to explain the report of victory; that
is the essence of a cover-up. It is harder to understand how the
killings came to be committed in the first place, making a cover-up
necessary.

Mass Executions and the Defense of Superior Orders

Some of the atrocities on March 16, 1968, were evidently unofficial, spontaneous acts: rapes, tortures, killings. For example, Hersh
(1970) describes Charlie Company's Second Platoon as entering
"My Lai 4 with guns blazing" (p. 50); more graphically, Lieutenant
"Brooks and his men in the second platoon to the north had begun
to systematically ransack the hamlet and slaughter the people, kill
the livestock, and destroy the crops. Men poured rifle and machine-
gun fire into huts without knowing—or seemingly caring—who was
inside" (pp. 49–50).

Some atrocities toward the end of the action were part of an
almost casual "mopping-up," much of which was the responsibility
of Lieutenant LaCross's Third Platoon of Charlie Company. The
Peers Report states: "The entire 3rd Platoon then began moving
into the western edge of My Lai (4), for the mop-up operation. . . .
The squad . . . began to burn the houses in the southwestern portion of the hamlet" (Goldstein et al., 1976, p. 133). They became
mingled with other platoons during a series of rapes and killings
of survivors for which it was impossible to fix responsibility. Certainly
to a Vietnamese all GIs would by this point look alike: "Nineteen-
year-old Nguyen Thi Ngoc Tuyet watched a baby trying to open her
slain mother's blouse to nurse, A soldier shot the infant while it was
struggling with the blouse, and then slashed it with his bayonet."

Tuyet also said she saw another baby hacked to death by GIs wielding their bayonets. "Le Tong, a twenty-eight-year-old rice farmer, reported seeing one woman raped after GIs killed her children. Nguyen Khoa, a thirty-seven-year-old peasant, told of a thirteen-year-old girl who was raped before being killed. GIs then attacked Khoa's wife, tearing off her clothes. Before they could rape her, however, Khoa said, their six-year-old son, riddled with bullets, fell and saturated her with blood. The GIs left her alone" (Hersh, 1970, p. 72). All of Company C was implicated in a pattern of death and destruction throughout the hamlet, much of which seemingly lacked rhyme or reason.

But a substantial amount of the killing was *organized* and traceable to one authority: the First Platoon's Lt. William Calley. Calley was originally charged with 109 killings, almost all of them mass executions at the trail and other locations. He stood trial for 102 of these killings, was convicted of 22 in 1971, and at first received a life sentence. Though others—both superior and subordinate to Calley—were brought to trial, he was the only one convicted for the My Lai crimes. Thus, the only actions of My Lai for which *anyone* was ever convicted were mass executions, ordered and committed. We suspect that there are commonsense reasons why this one type of killing was singled out. In the midst of rapidly moving events with people running about, an execution of stationary targets is literally a still life that stands out and whose participants are clearly visible. It can be proven that specific people committed specific deeds. An execution, in contrast to the shooting of someone on the run, is also more likely to meet the legal definition of an act resulting from intent—with malice aforethought. Moreover, American military law specifically forbids the killing of unarmed civilians or military prisoners, as does the Geneva Convention between nations. Thus common sense, legal standards, and explicit doctrine all made such actions the likeliest target for prosecution.

When Lieutenant Calley was charged under military law it was for violation of the Uniform Code of Military Justice (UCMJ) Article 118 (murder). This article is similar to civilian codes in that it provides for conviction if an accused:

> without justification or excuse, unlawfully kills a human being, when he—
> 1. has a premeditated design to kill;

2. intends to kill or inflict great bodily harm;
3. is engaged in an act which is inherently dangerous to others and evinces a wanton disregard of human life; or
4. is engaged in the perpetration or attempted perpetration of burglary, sodomy, rape, robbery, or aggravated arson. (Goldstein et al., 1976, p. 507)

For a soldier, one legal justification for killing is warfare; but warfare is subject to many legal limits and restrictions, including, of course, the inadmissibility of killing unarmed noncombatants or prisoners whom one has disarmed. The pictures of the trail victims at My Lai certainly portrayed one or the other of these. Such an action would be illegal under military law; ordering another to commit such an action would be illegal; and following such an order would be illegal.

But following an order may provide a second and pivotal justification for an act that would be murder when committed by a civilian. . . . American military law assumes that the subordinate is inclined to follow orders, as that is the normal obligation of the role. Hence, legally, obedient subordinates are protected from unreasonable expectations regarding their capacity to evaluate those orders:

> An order requiring the performance of a military duty may be inferred to be legal. An act performed manifestly beyond the scope of authority, or pursuant to an order that a man of ordinary sense and understanding would know to be illegal, or in a wanton manner in the discharge of a lawful duty, is not excusable. (Par. 216, Subpar. d, Manual for Courts Martial, United States, 1969 Rev.)

Thus what *may* be excusable is the good-faith carrying out of an order, as long as that order appears to the ordinary soldier to be a legal one. In military law, invoking superior orders moves the question from one of the action's consequences—the body count—to one of evaluating the actor's motives and good sense.

In sum, if anyone is to be brought to justice for a massacre, common sense and legal codes decree that the most appropriate targets are those who make themselves executioners. This is the kind of target the government selected in prosecuting Lieutenant Calley with the greatest fervor. And in a military context, the most promising way in which one can redefine one's undeniable deeds into acceptability is to invoke superior orders. This is what Calley did in attempting to avoid conviction. Since the core legal issues involved points of mass execution—the ditches and trail where America's image of My Lai was formed—we review these events in greater detail.

The day's quiet beginning has already been noted. Troops landed and swept unopposed into the village. The three weapons eventually reported as the haul from the operation were picked up from three apparent Viet Cong who fled the village when the troops arrived and were pursued and killed by helicopter gunships. Obviously the Viet Cong did frequent the area. But it appears that by about 8:00 A.M. no one who met the troops was aggressive, and no one was armed. By the laws of war Charlie Company had no argument with such people.

As they moved into the village, the soldiers began to gather its inhabitants together. Shortly after 8:00 A.M. Lieutenant Calley told Pfc. Paul Meadlo that "you know what to do with" a group of villagers Meadlo was guarding. Estimates of the numbers in the group ranged as high as eighty women, children, and old men, and Meadlo's own estimate under oath was thirty to fifty people. As Meadlo later testified, Calley returned after ten to fifteen minutes: "He [Calley] said, 'How come they're not dead?' I said, 'I didn't know we were supposed to kill them.' He said, 'I want them dead.' He backed off twenty or thirty feet and started shooting into the people—the Viet Cong—shooting automatic. He was beside me. He burned four or five magazines. I burned off a few, about three. I helped shoot 'em" (Hammer, 1971, p. 155). Meadlo himself and others testified that Meadlo cried as he fired; others reported him later to be sobbing and "all broke up." It would appear that to Lieutenant Calley's subordinates something was unusual, and stressful, in these orders.

At the trial, the first specification in the murder charge against Calley was for this incident; he was accused of premeditated murder of "an unknown number, not less than 30, Oriental human beings, males and females of various ages, whose names are unknown, occupants of the village of My Lai 4, by means of shooting them with a rifle" (Goldstein et al., 1976, p. 497).

Among the helicopters flying reconnaissance above Son My was that of CWO Hugh Thompson. By 9:00 or soon after Thompson had noticed some horrifying events from his perch. As he spotted wounded civilians, he sent down smoke markers so that soldiers on the ground could treat them. They killed them instead. He reported to headquarters, trying to persuade someone to stop what was going on. Barker, hearing the message, called down to Captain Medina. Medina, in turn, later claimed to have told Calley that it was "enough for today." But it was not yet enough.

At Calley's orders, his men began gathering the remaining villagers—roughly seventy-five individuals, mostly women and children—and herding them toward a drainage ditch. Accompanied by three or four enlisted men, Lieutenant Calley executed several batches of civilians who had been gathered into ditches. Some of the details of the process were entered into testimony in such accounts as Pfc. Dennis Conti's: "A lot of them, the people, were trying to get up and mostly they were just screaming and pretty bad shot up. . . . I seen a woman tried to get up. I seen Lieutenant Calley fire. He hit the side of her head and blew it off" (Hammer, 1971, p. 125).

Testimony by other soldiers presented the shooting's aftermath. Specialist Four Charles Hall, asked by Prosecutor Aubrey Daniel how he knew the people in the ditch were dead, said: "There was blood coming from them. They were just scattered all over the ground in the ditch, some in piles and some scattered out 20, 25 meters perhaps by the ditch. . . . They were very old people, very young children, and mothers. . . . There was blood all over them" (Goldstein et al., 1976, pp. 501–02). And Pfc. Gregory Olsen corroborated the general picture of the victims: "They were—the majority were women and children, some babies. I distinctly remember one middle-aged Vietnamese male dressed in white right at my feet as I crossed. None of the bodies were mangled in any way. There was blood. Some appeared to be dead, others followed me with their eyes as I walked across the ditch" (Goldstein et al., 1976, p. 502).

The second specification in the murder charge stated that Calley did "with premeditation, murder an unknown number of Oriental human beings, not less than seventy, males and females of various ages, whose names are unknown, occupants of the village of My Lai 4, by means of shooting them with a rifle" (Goldstein et al., 1976, p. 497). Calley was also charged with and tried for shootings of individuals (an old man and a child); these charges were clearly supplemental to the main issue at trial—the mass killings and how they came about.

It is noteworthy that during these executions more than one enlisted man avoided carrying out Calley's orders, and more than one, by sworn oath, directly refused to obey them. For example, Pfc. James Joseph Dursi testified, when asked if he fired when Lieutenant Calley ordered him to: "No. I just stood there. Meadlo turned to me after a couple of minutes and said 'Shoot! Why don't you shoot! Why don't you fire!' He was crying and yelling. I said, 'I can't! I won't!' And the people were screaming and crying and yelling. They kept firing for a couple of minutes, mostly automatic and semi-automatic" (Hammer, 1971, p. 143).

Specialist Four Ronald Grzesik reported an even more direct confrontation with Calley, although under oath he hedged about its subject:

> GRZESIK: Well, Lieutenant Calley—I walked past the ditch. I was called back by someone, I don't recall who. I had a discussion with Lieutenant Calley. He said to take the fire team back into the village and help the second platoon search.
> DANIEL: Did Lieutenant Calley say anything before he gave you that order?
> GRZESIK: He said, "Finish them off." I refused.
> DANIEL: What did you refuse to do?
> GRZESIK: To finish them off.
> DANIEL: What did he mean? Who did he mean to finish off?
> GRZESIK: I don't know what he meant or who he meant by them.
> (Hammer, 1971, p. 150)

In preceding months, not under oath, Grzesik had indicated that he had a good idea what was meant but that he simply would not comply. It is likely that the jury at Calley's trial did not miss the point.

Disobedience of Lieutenant Calley's own orders to kill represented a serious legal and moral threat to a defense *based* on superior orders, such as Calley was attempting. This defense had to assert that the orders seemed reasonable enough to carry out, that they appeared to be legal orders. Even if the orders in question were not legal, the defense had to assert that an ordinary individual could not and should not be expected to see the distinction. In short, if what happened was "business as usual," even though it might be bad business, then the defendant stood a chance of acquittal. But under direct command from "Surfside 5½," some ordinary enlisted men managed to refuse, to avoid, or at least to stop doing what they were ordered to do. As "reasonable men" of "ordinary sense and understanding," they had apparently found something awry that morning; and it would have been hard for an officer to plead successfully that he was more ordinary than his men in his capacity to evaluate the reasonableness of orders.

Even those who obeyed Calley's orders showed great stress. For example, Meadlo eventually began to argue and cry directly in front of Calley. Pfc. Herbert Carter shot himself in the foot, possibly because he could no longer take what he was doing. We were not destined to hear a sworn version of the incident, since neither side at the Calley trial called him to testify.

The most unusual instance of resistance to authority came from the skies. CWO Hugh Thompson, who had protested the apparent carnage of civilians, was Calley's inferior in rank but was not in his line of command. He was also watching the ditch from his helicopter and noticed some people moving after the first round of slaughter—chiefly children who had been shielded by their mothers' bodies. Landing to rescue the wounded, he also found some villagers hiding in a nearby bunker. Protecting the Vietnamese with his own body, Thompson ordered his men to train their guns on the Americans and to open fire if the Americans fired on the Vietnamese. He then radioed for additional rescue helicopters and stood between the Vietnamese and the Americans under Calley's command until the Vietnamese could be evacuated. He later returned to the ditch to unearth a child buried, unharmed, beneath layers of bodies. In October 1969, Thompson was awarded the Distinguished Flying Cross for heroism at My Lai, specifically (albeit inaccurately) for the rescue of children hiding in a bunker "between Viet Cong forces and advancing friendly forces" and for the rescue of a wounded child "caught in the intense crossfire" (Hersh, 1970, p. 119). Four months earlier, at the Pentagon, Thompson had identified Calley as having been at the ditch.

By about 10:00 A.M., the massacre was winding down. The remaining actions consisted largely of isolated rapes and killings, "clean-up" shootings of the wounded, and the destruction of the village by fire. We have already seen some examples of these more indiscriminate and possibly less premeditated acts. By the 11:00 A.M. lunch break, when the exhausted men of Company C were relaxing, two young girls wandered back from a hiding place only to be invited to share lunch. This surrealist touch illustrates the extent to which the soldiers' action had become dissociated from its meaning. An hour earlier, some of these men were making sure that not even a child would escape the executioner's bullet. But now the job was done and it was time for lunch—and in this new context it seemed only natural to ask the children who had managed to escape execution to join them. The massacre had ended. It remained only for the Viet Cong to reap the political rewards among the survivors in hiding.

The army command in the area knew that something had gone wrong. Direct commanders, including Lieutenant Colonel Barker, had firsthand reports, such as Thompson's complaints. Others had such odd bits of evidence as the claim of 128 Viet Cong dead with a booty of only three weapons. But the cover-up of My Lai began at once. The operation was reported as a victory over a stronghold of the Viet Cong Forty-eighth.

My Lai might have remained a "victory" but for another odd twist. A soldier who had not even been at the massacre, Ronald Ridenhour, talked to several friends and acquaintances who had been. As he later wrote: "It was late in April 1968 that I first heard of 'Pinkville' [a nickname reflecting the villagers' reputed Communist sympathies] and what allegedly happened there. I received that first report with some skepticism, but in the following months I was to hear similar stories from such a wide variety of people that it became impossible for me to disbelieve that something rather dark and bloody did indeed occur sometime in March 1968 in a village called 'Pinkville' in the Republic of Viet Nam" (Goldstein et al., 1976, p. 34). Ridenhour's growing conviction that a massacre—or something close to it—had occurred was reinforced by his own travel over the area by helicopter soon after the event. My Lai was desolate. He gradually concluded that someone was covering up the incident within the army and that an independent investigation was needed.

At the end of March 1969, he finally wrote a letter detailing what he knew about "Pinkville." The letter, beginning with the paragraph quote above, was sent to thirty individuals—the president, Pentagon officials, and some members of the Senate and House. Ridenhour's congressman, fellow Arizonan Morris Udall, gave it particular heed. The slow unraveling of the cover-up began. During the following months, the army in fact initiated an investigation but carried it out in strict secrecy. Ridenhour, convinced that the cover-up was continuing, sought journalistic help and finally, by coincidence, connected with Seymour Hersh. Hersh followed up and broke the story, which eventually brought him a Pulitzer Prize and other awards for his investigative reporting. The cover-up collapsed, leaving only the question of the army's resolve to seek justice in the case: Against whom would it proceed, with how much speed and vigor, and with what end in mind?

William Calley was not the only man tried for the events at My Lai. The actions of over thirty soldiers and civilians were scrutinized by investigators; over half of these had to face charges or disciplinary action of some sort. Targets of investigation included Captain Medina, who was tried, and various higher-ups, including General Koster. But Lieutenant Calley was the only person convicted, the only person to serve time.

The core of Lieutenant Calley's defense was superior orders. What this meant to him—in contrast to what it meant to the judge and jury—can be gleaned from his responses to a series of questions from his defense attorney, George Latimer, in which Calley sketched out his understanding of the laws of war and the actions that constitute doing one's duty within those laws:

> LATIMER: Did you receive any training . . . which had to do with the obedience to orders?
> CALLEY: Yes, sir.
> LATIMER: . . . [W]hat were you informed [were] the principles involved in that field?
> CALLEY: That all orders were to be assumed legal, that the soldier's job was to carry out any order given him to the best of his ability.
> LATIMER: . . . . [W]hat might occur if you disobeyed an order by a senior officer?
> CALLEY: You could be court-martialed for refusing an order and refusing an order in the face of the enemy, you could be sent to death, sir.
> LATIMER: [I am asking] whether you were required in any way, shape or form to make a determination of the legality or illegality of an order?
> CALLEY: No, sir. I was never told that I had the choice, sir.
> LATIMER: If you had a doubt about the order, what were you supposed to do?
> CALLEY: . . . I was supposed to carry the order out and then come back and make my complaint. (Hammer, 1971, pp. 240–41)

Lieutenant Calley steadfastly maintained that his actions within My Lai had constituted, in his mind, carrying out orders from Captain Medina. Both his own actions and the orders he gave to others (such as the instruction to Meadlo to "waste 'em") were entirely in response to superior orders. He denied any intent to kill individuals and any but the most passing awareness of distinctions among the individuals: "I was ordered to go in there and destroy the enemy. That was my job on that day. That was the mission I was given. I did not sit down and think in terms of men, women, and children. They were all classified the same, and that was the classification that we dealt with, just as enemy soldiers." When Latimer asked if in his own opinion Calley had acted "rightly and according to your understanding of your directions and orders," Calley replied, "I felt then and I still do that I acted as I was directed, and I carried out the orders that I was given, and I do not feel wrong in doing so, sir" (Hammer, 1971, p. 257).

His court-martial did not accept Calley's defense of superior orders and clearly did not share his interpretation of his duty. The jury evidently reasoned that, even if there had been orders to destroy everything in sight and to "waste the Vietnamese," any reasonable person would have realized that such orders were illegal and should have refused to carry them out. The defense of superior orders under such conditions is inadmissible under international and military law. The U.S. Army's *Law of Land Warfare* (Dept. of the Army, 1956), for example, states that "the fact that the law of war has been violated pursuant to an order of a superior authority, whether military or civil, does not deprive the act in question of its character of a war crime, nor does it constitute a defense in the trial of an accused individual, unless he did not know and could not reasonably have been expected to know that the act was unlawful" and that "members of the armed forces are bound to obey only lawful orders" (in Falk et al., 1971, pp. 71–72).

The disagreement between Calley and the court-martial seems to have revolved around the definition of the responsibilities of a subordinate to obey, on the one hand, and to evaluate, on the other. This tension . . . runs through the analyses and empirical studies. . . . For now, it can best be captured via the charge to the jury in the Calley court-martial, made by the trial judge, Col. Reid Kennedy. The forty-one pages of the charge include the following:

> Both combatants captured by and noncombatants detained by the opposing force . . . have the right to be treated as prisoners. . . .

Summary execution of detainees or prisoners is forbidden by law.
. . . I therefore instruct you . . . that if unresisting human beings
were killed at My Lai (4) while within the effective custody and control of our military forces, their deaths cannot be considered justified. . . . Thus if you find that Lieutenant Calley received an order
directing him to kill unresisting Vietnamese within his control or
within the control of his troops, *that order would be an illegal order.*

A determination that an order is illegal does not, of itself, assign
criminal responsibility to the person following the order for acts
done in compliance with it. Soldiers are taught to follow orders,
and special attention is given to obedience of orders on the battle-
field. Military effectiveness depends on obedience to orders. On
the other hand, the obedience of a soldier is not the obedience of
an automaton. A soldier is a reasoning agent, obliged to respond,
not as a machine, but as a person. The law takes these factors into
account in assessing criminal responsibility for acts done in compliance with illegal orders.

The acts of a subordinate done in compliance with an unlawful
order given him by his superior are excused and impose no criminal liability upon him unless the superior's order is one which a man
of *ordinary sense and understanding* would, under the circumstances,
know to be unlawful, or if the order in question is actually known
to the accused to be unlawful. (Goldstein et al., 1976, pp. 525–526;
emphasis added)

By this definition, subordinates take part in a balancing act, one
tipped toward obedience but tempered by "ordinary sense and
understanding."

A jury of combat veterans proceeded to convict William Calley
of the premeditated murder of no less than twenty-two human
beings. (The army, realizing some unfortunate connotations in
referring to the victims as "Oriental human beings," eventually
referred to them as "human beings.") Regarding the first specification in the murder charge, the bodies on the trail, he was convicted of premeditated murder of not less than one person. (Medical testimony had been able to pinpoint only one person whose
wounds as revealed in Haeberle's photos were sure to be immediately fatal.) Regarding the second specification, the bodies in the
ditch, Calley was convicted of the premeditated murder of not less
than twenty human beings. Regarding additional specifications that
he had killed an old man and a child, Calley was convicted of premeditated murder in the first case and of assault with intent to
commit murder in the second.

Lieutenant Calley was initially sentenced to life imprisonment. That sentence was reduced: first to twenty years, eventually to ten (the latter by Secretary of Defense Callaway in 1974).[1] Calley served three years before being released on bond. The time was spent under house arrest in his apartment, where he was able to receive visits from his girlfriend. He was granted parole on September 10, 1975.

Sanctioned Massacres

The slaughter at My Lai is an instance of a class of violent acts that can be described as sanctioned massacres (Kelman, 1973): acts of indiscriminate, ruthless, and often systematic mass violence, carried out by military or paramilitary personnel while engaged in officially sanctioned campaigns, the victims of which are defenseless and unresisting civilians, including old men, women, and children. Sanctioned massacres have occurred throughout history. Within American history, My Lai had its precursors in the Philippine war around the turn of the century (Schirmer, 1971) and in the massacres of American Indians. Elsewhere in the world, one recalls the Nazis' "final solution" for European Jews, the massacres and deportations of Armenians by Turks, the liquidation of the kulaks and the great purges in the Soviet Union, and more recently the massacres in Indonesia and Bangladesh, in Biafra and Burundi, in South Africa and Mozambique, in Cambodia and Afghanistan, in Syria and Lebanon. Sanctioned massacres may vary on a number of dimensions. For present purposes, however, we want to focus on features they share. Two of these are the *context* and the *target* of the violence.

---

1. The involvement of President Nixon in the case may have had something to do with these steadily lower sentences. Immediately after the Calley conviction, Nixon issued two presidential edicts. The president first announced that Calley was to stay under house arrest until appeals were settled, rather than in the stockade. The subsequent announcement was that President Nixon would personally review the case. These edicts received wide popular support. The latter announcement in particular brought sharp criticism from Prosecutor Daniel and others, on grounds that Nixon was interfering inappropriately with the process of justice in the case. Nevertheless, the president's interest and intention to review the case could have colored the subsequent appeals process or the actions of the secretary of defense. By the time of Secretary Callaway's action, of course, the president was himself fighting to avoid impeachment.

Sanctioned massacres tend to occur in the context of an overall policy that is explicitly or implicitly genocidal: designed to destroy all or part of a category of people defined in ethnic, national, racial, religious, or other terms. Such a policy may be deliberately aimed at the systematic extermination of a population group as an end in itself, as was the case with the Holocaust during World War II. In the Nazis' "final solution" for European Jewry, a policy aimed at exterminating millions of people was consciously articulated and executed (see Levinson, 1973), and the extermination was accomplished on a mass-production basis through the literal establishment of a well-organized, efficient death industry. Alternatively, such a policy may be aimed at an objective other than extermination—such as the pacification of the rural population of South Vietnam, as was the case in U.S. policy for Indochina—but may include the deliberate decimation of large segments of a population as an acceptable means to that end.

We agree with Bedau's (1974) conclusion from his carefully reasoned argument that the charge of U.S. genocide in Vietnam has not been definitively proven, since such a charge requires evidence of a specific genocidal *intent*. Although the evidence suggests that the United States committed war crimes and crimes against humanity in Indochina (see Sheehan, 1971; Browning and Forman, 1972), it does not show that extermination was the conscious purpose of U.S. policy. The evidence reviewed by Bedau, however, suggests that the United States did commit genocidal acts in Vietnam as a means to other ends. Central to U.S. strategy in South Vietnam were such actions as unrestricted air and artillery bombardments of peasant hamlets, search-and-destroy missions by ground troops, crop destruction programs, and mass deportation of rural populations. These actions (and similar ones in Laos and Cambodia) were clearly and deliberately aimed at civilians and resulted in the death, injury, and/ or uprooting of large numbers of that population and in the destruction of their countryside, their source of livelihood, and their social structure. These consequences were anticipated by policymakers and indeed were intended as part of their pacification effort; the actions were designed to clear the countryside and deprive guerrillas of their base of operations, even if this meant destroying the civilian population. Massacres of the kind that occurred at My Lai were not deliberately planned, but they took place in an atmosphere in which the rural Vietnamese population was viewed as expendable and actions that resulted in the killing of large numbers of that population as strategic necessities.

A second feature of sanctioned massacres is that their targets have not themselves threatened or engaged in hostile actions toward the perpetrators of the violence. The victims of this class of violence are often defenseless civilians, including old men, women, and children. By all accounts, at least after the first moments at My Lai, the victims there fit this description, although in guerrilla warfare there always remains some ambiguity about the distinction between armed soldiers and unarmed civilians. As has often been noted, U.S. troops in Vietnam had to face the possibility that a woman or even a child might be concealing a hand grenade under clothing.

There are, of course, historical and situational reasons particular groups become victims of sanctioned massacres, but these do not include their own immediate harmfulness or violence toward the attackers. Rather, their selection as targets for massacre at a particular time can ultimately be traced to their relationship to the pursuit of larger policies. Their elimination may be seen as a useful tool or their continued existence as an irritating obstacle in the execution of policy.

The genocidal or near-genocidal context of this class of violence and the fact that it is directed at a target that—at least from an observer's perspective—did not provoke the violence through its own actions has some definite implications for the psychological environment within which sanctioned massacres occur. It is an environment almost totally devoid of the conditions that usually provide at least some degree of moral justification for violence. Neither the reason for the violence nor its purpose is of the kind that is normally considered justifiable. Although people may disagree about the precise point at which they would draw the line between justifiable and unjustifiable violence, most would agree that violence in self-defense or in response to oppression and other forms of strong provocation is at least within the realm of moral discourse. In contrast, the violence of sanctioned massacres falls outside that realm.

In searching for a psychological explanation for mass violence under these conditions, one's first inclination is to look for forces that might impel people toward such murderous acts. Can we identify, in massacre situations, psychological forces so powerful that they outweigh the moral restraints that would normally inhibit unjustifiable violence?

The most obvious approach—searching for psychological dispositions within those who perpetrate these acts—does not yield a satisfactory explanation of the phenomenon, although it may tell us something about the types of individuals most readily recruited for participation. For example, any explanation involving the attackers' strong sadistic impulses is inadequate. There is no evidence that the majority of those who participate in such killings are sadistically inclined. Indeed, speaking of the participants in the Nazi slaughters, Arendt (1964) points out that they "were not sadists or killers by nature; on the contrary, a systematic effort was made to weed out all those who derived physical pleasure from what they did" (p. 105). To be sure, some of the commanders and guards of concentration camps could clearly be described as sadists, but what has to be explained is the existence of concentration camps in which these individuals could give play to their sadistic fantasies. These opportunities were provided with the participation of large numbers of individuals to whom the label of sadist could not be applied.

A more sophisticated type of dispositional approach seeks to identify certain characterological themes that are dominant within a given culture. An early example of such an approach is Fromm's (1941) analysis of the appeals of Nazism in terms of the prevalence of sadomasochistic strivings, particularly among the German lower middle class. It would be important to explore whether similar kinds of characterological dispositions can be identified in the very wide range of cultural contexts in which sanctioned massacres have occurred. However general such dispositions turn out to be, it seems most likely that they represent states of readiness to participate in sanctioned massacres when the opportunity arises rather than major motivating forces in their own right. Similarly, high levels of frustration within a population are probably facilitators rather than instigators of sanctioned massacres, since there does not seem to be a clear relationship between the societal level of frustration and the occurrence of such violence. Such a view would be consistent with recent thinking about the relationship between frustration and aggression (see, for example, Bandura, 1973).

Could participation in sanctioned massacres be traced to an inordinately intense hatred toward those against whom the violence is directed? The evidence does not seem to support such an interpretation. Indications are that many of the active participants in the extermination of European Jews, such as Adolf Eichmann (Arendt, 1964), did not feel any passionate hatred of Jews. There is certainly no reason to believe that those who planned and executed American policy in Vietnam felt a profound hatred of the Vietnamese population, although deeply rooted racist attitudes may conceivably have played a role.

To be sure, hatred and rage *play a part* in sanctioned massacres. Typically, there is a long history of profound hatred against the groups targeted for violence—the Jews in Christian Europe, the Chinese in Southeast Asia, the Ibos in northern Nigeria—which helps establish them as suitable victims. Hostility also plays an important part at the point at which the killings are actually perpetrated, even if the official planning and the bureaucratic preparations that ultimately lead up to this point are carried out in a passionless and businesslike atmosphere. For example, Lifton's (1973) descriptions of My Lai, based on eyewitness reports, suggest that the killings were accompanied by generalized rage and by expressions of anger and revenge toward the victims. Hostility toward the target, however, does not seem to be the *instigator* of these violent actions. The expressions of anger in the situation itself can more properly be viewed as outcomes rather than causes of the violence. They serve to provide the perpetrators with an explanation and rationalization for their violent actions and appropriate labels for their emotional state. They also help reinforce, maintain, and intensify the violence, but the anger is not the primary source of the violence. Hostility toward the target, historically rooted or situationally induced, contributes heavily toward the violence, but it does so largely by dehumanizing the victims rather than by motivating violence against them in the first place.

In sum, the occurrence of sanctioned massacres cannot be adequately explained by the existence of psychological forces—whether these be characterological dispositions to engage in murderous violence or profound hostility against the target—so powerful that they must find expression in violent acts unhampered by moral restraints. Instead, the major instigators for this class of violence derive from the policy process. The question that really calls for psychological analysis is why so many people are willing to formulate, participate in, and condone policies that call for the mass killings of defenseless civilians. Thus it is more instructive to look not at the motives for violence but at the conditions under which the usual moral inhibitions against violence become weakened. Three social processes that tend to create such conditions can be identified: authorization, routinization, and dehumanization. Through authorization, the situation becomes so defined that the individual is absolved of the responsibility to make personal moral choices. Through routinization, the action becomes so organized that there is no opportunity for raising moral questions. Through dehumanization, the actors' attitudes toward the target and toward themselves become so structured that it is neither necessary nor possible for them to view the relationship in moral terms.

Authorization

Sanctioned massacres by definition occur in the context of an authority situation, a situation in which, at least for many of the participants, the moral principles that generally govern human relationships do not apply. Thus, when acts of violence are explicitly ordered, implicitly encouraged, tacitly approved, or at least permitted by legitimate authorities, people's readiness to commit or condone them is enhanced. That such acts are authorized seems to carry automatic justification for them. Behaviorally, authorization obviates the necessity of making judgments or choices. Not only do normal moral principles become inoperative, but—particularly when the actions are explicitly ordered—a different kind of morality, linked to the duty to obey superior orders, tends to take over.

In an authority situation, individuals characteristically feel obligated to obey the orders of the authorities, whether or not these correspond with their personal preferences. They see themselves as having no choice as long as they accept the legitimacy of the orders and of the authorities who give them. Individuals differ considerably in the degree to which—and the conditions under which—they are prepared to challenge the legitimacy of an order on the grounds that the order itself is illegal, or that those giving it have overstepped their authority, or that it stems from a policy that violates fundamental societal values. Regardless of such individual differences, however, the basic structure of a situation of legitimate authority requires subordinates to respond in terms of their role obligations rather than their personal preferences; they can openly disobey only by challenging the legitimacy of the authority. Often people obey without question even though the behavior they engage in may entail great personal sacrifice or great harm to others.

An important corollary of the basic structure of the authority situation is that actors often do not see themselves as personally responsible for the consequences of their actions. Again, there are individual differences, depending on actors' capacity and readiness to evaluate the legitimacy of orders received. Insofar as they see themselves as having had no choice in their actions, however, they do not feel personally responsible for them. They were not personal agents, but merely extensions of the authority. Thus, when their actions cause harm to others, they can feel relatively free of guilt. A similar mechanism operates when a person engages in antisocial behavior that was not ordered by the authorities but was tacitly encouraged and approved by them—even if only by making it clear that such behavior will not be punished. In this situation, behavior that was formerly illegitimate is legitimized by the authorities' acquiescence.

In the My Lai massacre, it is likely that the structure of the authority situation contributed to the massive violence in both ways—that is, by conveying the message that acts of violence against Vietnamese villagers were *required*, as well as the message that such acts, even if not ordered, were *permitted* by the authorities in charge. The actions at My Lai represented, at least in some respects, responses to explicit or implicit orders. Lieutenant Calley indicated, by orders and by example, that he wanted large numbers of villagers killed. Whether Calley himself had been ordered by his superiors to "waste" the whole area, as he claimed, remains a matter of controversy. Even if we assume, however, that he was not explicitly ordered to wipe out the village, he had reason to believe that such actions were expected by his superior officers. Indeed, the very nature of the war conveyed this expectation. The principal measure of military success was the "body count"—the number of enemy soldiers killed—and any Vietnamese killed by the U.S. military was commonly defined as a "Viet Cong." Thus, it was not totally bizarre for Calley to believe that what he was doing at My Lai was to increase his body count, as any good officer was expected to do.

Even to the extent that the actions at My Lai occurred spontaneously, without reference to superior orders, those committing them had reason to assume that such actions might be tacitly approved of by the military authorities. Not only had they failed to punish such acts in most cases, but the very strategies and tactics that the authorities consistently devised were based on the proposition that the civilian population of South Vietnam—whether "hostile" or "friendly"—was expendable. Such policies as search-and-destroy missions, the establishment of free-shooting zones, the use of antipersonnel weapons, the bombing of entire villages if they were suspected of harboring guerrillas, the forced migration of masses of the rural population, and the defoliation of vast forest areas helped legitimize acts of massive violence of the kind occurring at My Lai.

Some of the actions at My Lai suggest an orientation to authority based on unquestioning obedience to superior orders, no matter how destructive the actions these orders call for. Such obedience is specifically fostered in the course of military training and reinforced by the structure of the military authority situation. It also reflects, however, an ideological orientation that may be more widespread in the general population, as some of the data presented . . . demonstrate.

Routinization

Authorization processes create a situation in which people become involved in an action without considering its implications and without really making a decision. Once they have taken the initial step, they are in a new psychological and social situation in which the pressures to continue are powerful. As Lewin (1947) has pointed out, many forces that might originally have kept people out of a situation reverse direction once they have made a commitment (once they have gone through the "gate region") and now serve to keep them in the situation. For example, concern about the criminal nature of an action, which might originally have inhibited a person from becoming involved, may now lead to deeper involvement in efforts to justify the action and to avoid negative consequences.

Despite these forces, however, given the nature of the actions involved in sanctioned massacres, one might still expect moral scruples to intervene; but the likelihood of moral resistance is greatly reduced by transforming the action into routine, mechanical, highly programmed operations. Routinization fulfills two functions. First, it reduces the necessity of making decisions, thus minimizing the occasions in which moral questions may arise. Second, it makes it easier to avoid the implications of the action, since the actor focuses on the details of the job rather than on its meaning. The latter effect is more readily achieved among those who participate in sanctioned massacres from a distance—from their desks or even from the cockpits of their bombers.

Routinization operates both at the level of the individual actor and at the organizational level. Individual job performance is broken down into a series of discrete steps, most of them carried out in automatic, regularized fashion. It becomes easy to forget the nature of the product that emerges from this process. When Lieutenant Calley said of My Lai that it was "no great deal," he probably implied that it was all in a day's work. Organizationally, the task is divided among different offices, each of which has responsibility for a small portion of it. This arrangement diffuses responsibility and limits the amount and scope of decision making that is necessary. There is no expectation that the moral implications will be considered at any of these points, nor is there any opportunity to do so. The organizational processes also help further legitimize the actions of each participant. By proceeding in routine fashion—processing papers, exchanging memos, diligently carrying out their assigned tasks—the different units mutually reinforce each other in the view that what is going on must be perfectly normal, correct, and legitimate. The shared illusion that they are engaged in a legitimate enterprise helps the participants assimilate their activities to other purposes, such as the efficiency of their performance, the productivity of their unit, or the cohesiveness of their group (see Janis, 1972).

Normalization of atrocities is more difficult to the extent that there are constant reminders of the true meaning of the enterprise. Bureaucratic inventiveness in the use of language helps to cover up such meaning. For example, the SS had a set of *Sprachregelungen,* or "language rules," to govern descriptions of their extermination program. As Arendt (1964) points out, the term *language rule* in itself was "a code name; it meant what in ordinary language would be called a lie" (p. 85). The code names for killing and liquidation were "final solution," "evacuation," and "special treatment." The war in Indochina produced its own set of euphemisms, such as "protective reaction," "pacification," and "forced-draft urbanization and modernization." The use of euphemisms allows participants in sanctioned massacres to differentiate their actions from ordinary killing and destruction and thus to avoid confronting their true meaning.

Dehumanization

Authorization processes override standard moral considerations; routinization processes reduce the likelihood that such considerations will arise. Still, the inhibitions against murdering one's fellow human beings are generally so strong that the victims must also be stripped of their human status if they are to be subjected to systematic killing. Insofar as they are dehumanized, the usual principles of morality no longer apply to them.

Sanctioned massacres become possible to the extent that the victims are deprived in the perpetrators' eyes of the two qualities essential to being perceived as fully human and included in the moral compact that governs human relationships: *identity*—standing as independent, distinctive individuals, capable of making choices and entitled to live their own lives—and *community*—fellow membership in an interconnected network of individuals who care for each other and respect each other's individuality and rights (Kelman, 1973; see also Bakan, 1966, for a related distinction between "agency" and "communion"). Thus, when a group of people is defined entirely in terms of a category to which they belong, and when this category is excluded from the human family, moral restraints against killing them are more readily overcome.

Dehumanization of the enemy is a common phenomenon in any war situation. Sanctioned massacres, however, presuppose a more extreme degree of dehumanization, insofar as the killing is not in direct response to the target's threats or provocations. It is not what they have done that marks such victims for death but who they are—the category to which they happen to belong. They are the victims of policies that regard their systematic destruction as a desirable end or an acceptable means. Such extreme dehumanization becomes possible when the target group can readily be identified as a separate category of people who have historically been stigmatized and excluded by the victimizers: often the victims belong to a distinct racial, religious, ethnic, or political group regarded as inferior or sinister. The traditions, the habits, the images, and the vocabularies for dehumanizing such groups are already well established and can be drawn upon when the groups are selected for massacre. Labels help deprive the victims of identity and community, as in the epithet "gooks" that was commonly used to refer to Vietnamese and other Indochinese peoples.

The dynamics of the massacre process itself further increase the participants' tendency to dehumanize their victims. Those who participate as part of the bureaucratic apparatus increasingly come to see their victims as bodies to be counted and entered into their reports, as faceless figures that will determine their productivity rates and promotions. Those who participate in the massacre directly—in the field, as it were—are reinforced in their perception of the victims as less than human by observing their very victimization. The only way they can justify what is being done to these people—both by others and by themselves—and the only way they can extract some degree of meaning out of absurd events in which they find themselves participating (see Lifton, 1971, 1973) is by coming to believe that the victims are subhuman and deserve to be rooted out. And thus the process of dehumanization feeds on itself.

References

Arendt, H. 1964. *Eichmann in Jerusalem: A report on the banality of evil.* New York: Viking Press.

Bakan, D. 1966. *The duality of human existence.* Chicago: Rand McNally.

Bandura, A. 1973. Social learning theory of aggression. In J. F. Knutson (Ed.), *Control of aggression: Implications from basic research.* Chicago: Aldine-Atherton.

Bedau, H. A. 1974. Genocide in Vietnam. In V. Held, S. Morgenbesser, & T. Nagel (Eds.), *Philosophy, morality, and international affairs* (pp. 5–46). New York: Oxford University Press.

Browning, F., & Forman, D. (Eds.). 1972. *The wasted nations: Report of the International Commission of Enquiry into United States Crimes in Indochina, June 20–25, 1971.* New York: Harper & Row.

Department of the Army. 1956. *The law of land warfare* (Field Manual, No. 27-10). Washington, D.C.: U.S. Government Printing Office.

Falk, R. A.; Kolko, G.; & Lifton, R. J. (Eds.). 1971. *Crimes of war.* New York: Vintage Books.

Fromm, E. 1941. *Escape from freedom.* New York: Rinehart.

Goldstein, J.; Marshall, B.; & Schwartz, J. (Eds.). 1976. *The My Lai massacre and its cover-up: Beyond the reach of law?* (The Peers report with a supplement and introductory essay on the limits of law). New York: Free Press.

Hammer, R. 1971. *The court-martial of Lt. Calley.* New York: Coward, McCann, & Geoghegan.

Hersh, S. 1970. *My Lai 4: A report on the massacre and its aftermath.* New York: Vintage Books.

Hersh, S. 1972. *Cover-up.* New York: Random House.

Janis, I. L. 1972. *Victims of groupthink: A psychological study of foreign-policy decisions and fiascoes.* Boston: Houghton Mifflin.

Kelman, H. C. 1973. Violence without moral restraint: Reflections on the dehumanization of victims and victimizers. *Journal of Social Issues,* 29(4), 25–61.

Lewin, K. 1947. Group decision and social change. In T. M. Newcomb & E. L. Harley (Eds.), *Readings in social psychology.* New York: Holt.

Lifton, R. J. 1971. Existential evil. In N. Sanford, C. Comstock, & Associates, *Sanctions for evil: Sources of social destructiveness.* San Francisco: Jossey-Bass.

Lifton, R. J. 1973. *Home from the war—Vietnam veterans: Neither victims nor executioners.* New York: Simon & Schuster.

Schirmer, D. B. 1971, April 24. My Lai was not the first time. *New Republic,* pp. 18–21.

Sheehan, N. 1971, March 28. Should we have war crime trials? *The New York Times Book Review,* pp. 1–3, 30–34.

Williams, B. 1985, April 14–15. "I will never forgive," says My Lai survivor. *Jordan Times* (Amman), p. 4.

10

The *Challenger* Disaster
Organizational Demands and Personal Ethics

Russell Boisjoly, Ellen Foster Curtis, and Eugene Mellican

On January 28, 1986, the space shuttle *Challenger* exploded 73 seconds into its flight, killing the seven astronauts aboard. As the nation mourned the tragic loss of the crew members, the Rogers Commission was formed to investigate the causes of the disaster. The Commission concluded that the explosion occurred due to seal failure in one of the solid rocket booster joints. Testimony given by Roger Boisjoly, Senior Scientist and acknowledged rocket seal expert, indicated that top management at NASA and Morton Thiokol had been aware of problems with the O-ring seals, but agreed to launch against the recommendation of Boisjoly and other engineers. Boisjoly had alerted management to problems with the O-rings as early as January, 1985, yet several shuttle launches prior to the *Challenger* had been approved without correcting the hazards. This suggests that the management practice of NASA and Morton Thiokol had created an environment which altered the framework for decision making, leading to a breakdown in communication between technical experts and their supervisors, and top level management, and to the acceptance of risks that both organizations had historically viewed as unacceptable. With human lives and the national interest at stake, serious ethical concerns are embedded in this dramatic change in management practice.

In fact, one of the most important aspects of the *Challenger* disaster—both in terms of the causal sequence that led to it and the lessons to be learned from it—is its ethical dimension. Ethical

From "Roger Boisjoly and the Challenger Disaster: The Ethical Dimensions." *Journal of Business Ethics*, Vol. 8, pp. 217–30. Copyright © 1989 by Kluwer Academic Publishers. Reprinted by permission.

issues are woven throughout the tangled web of decisions, events, practices, and organizational structures that resulted in the loss of the *Challenger* and its seven astronauts. Therefore, an ethical analysis of this tragedy is essential for a full understanding of the event itself and for the implications it has for any endeavor where public policy, corporate practice, and individual decisions intersect.

The significance of an ethical analysis of the *Challenger* disaster is indicated by the fact that it immediately presents one of the most urgent, but difficult, issues in the examination of corporate and individual behavior today, i.e., whether existing ethical theories adequately address the problems posed by new technologies, new forms of organization, and evolving social systems. At the heart of this issue is the concept of responsibility. No ethical concept has been more affected by the impact of these changing realities. Modern technology has so transformed the context and scale of human action that not only do the traditional parameters of responsibility seem inadequate to contain the full range of human acts and their consequences, but even more fundamentally, it is no longer the individual that is the primary locus of power and responsibility, but public and private institutions. Thus, it would seem, it is no longer the character and virtues of individuals that determine the standards of moral conduct, it is the policies and structures of the institutional settings within which they live and work.

Many moral conflicts facing individuals within institutional settings do arise from matters pertaining to organizational structures or questions of public policy. As such, they are resolvable only at a level above the responsibilities of the individual. Therefore, some writers argue that the ethical responsibilities of the engineer or manager in a large corporation have as much to do with the organization as with the individual. Instead of expecting individual engineers or managers to be moral heroes, emphasis should be on the creation of organizational structures conducive to ethical behavior among all agents under their aegis. It would be futile to attempt to establish a sense of ethical responsibility in engineers and management personnel and ignore the fact that such persons work within a socio-technical environment which increasingly undermines the notion of individual, responsible moral agency (Boling and Dempsey, 1981; DeGeorge, 1981).

Yet, others argue that precisely because of these organizational realities individual accountability must be re-emphasized to counteract the diffusion of responsibility within large organizations and to prevent its evasion under the rubric of collective responsibility. Undoubtedly institutions do take on a kind of collective life of their own, but they do not exist, or act, independently of the individuals that constitute them, whatever the theoretical and practical complexities of delineating the precise relationships involved. Far from diminishing individuals' obligations, the reality of organizational life increases them because the consequences of decisions and acts are extended and amplified through the reach and power of that reality. Since there are pervasive and inexorable connections between ethical standards and behavior of individuals within an organization and its structure and operation, "the sensitizing of professionals to ethical considerations should be increased so that institutional structures will reflect enhanced ethical sensitivities as trained professionals move up the organizational ladder to positions of leadership" (Mankin, 1981, p. 17).

By reason of the courageous activities and testimony of individuals like Roger Boisjoly, the *Challenger* disaster provides a fascinating illustration of the dynamic tension between organizational and individual responsibility. By focusing on this central issue, this article seeks to accomplish two objectives: first, to demonstrate the extent to which the *Challenger* disaster not only gives concrete expression to the ethical ambiguity that permeates the relationship between organizational and individual responsibility, but also, in fact, is a result of it; second, to reclaim the meaning and importance of individual responsibility within the diluting context of large organizations.

In meeting these objectives, the article is divided into two parts: a case study of Roger Boisjoly's efforts to galvanize management support for effectively correcting the high risk O-ring problems, his attempt to prevent the launch, the scenario which resulted in the launch decision, and Boisjoly's quest to set the record straight despite enormous personal and professional consequences; and an ethical analysis of these events.

Preview for Disaster

On January 24, 1985, Roger Boisjoly, Senior Scientist at Morton Thiokol, watched the launch of Flight 51-C of the space shuttle program. He was at Cape Canaveral to inspect the solid rocket boosters from Flight 51-C following their recovery in the Atlantic Ocean and to conduct a training session at Kennedy Space Center (KSC) on the proper methods of inspecting the booster joints. While watching the launch, he noted that the temperature that day was much cooler than recorded at other launches, but was still much warmer than the 18 degree temperature encountered three days earlier when he arrived in Orlando. The unseasonably cold weather of the past several days had produced the worst citrus crop failures in Florida history.

When he inspected the solid rocket boosters several days later, Boisjoly discovered evidence that the primary O-ring seals on two field joints had been compromised by hot combustion gases (i.e., hot gas blow-by had occurred) which had also eroded part of the primary O-ring. This was the first time that a primary seal on a field joint had been penetrated. When he discovered the large amount of blackened grease between the primary and secondary seals, his concern heightened. The blackened grease was discovered over 80 degree and 110 degree arcs, respectively, on two of the seals, with the larger arc indicating greater hot gas blow-by. Postflight calculations indicated that the ambient temperature of the field joints at launch time was 53 degrees. This evidence, coupled with his recollection of the low temperature the day of the launch and the citrus crop damage caused by the cold spell, led to his conclusion that the severe hot gas blow-by may have been caused by, and related to, low temperature. After reporting these findings to his superiors, Boisjoly presented them to engineers and management at NASA's Marshall Space Flight Center (MSFC). As a result of his presentation at MSFC, Roger Boisjoly was asked to participate in the Flight Readiness Review (FRR) on February 12, 1985, for Flight 51-E which was scheduled for launch in April, 1985. This FRR represents the first association of low temperature with blow-by on a field joint, a condition that was considered an "acceptable risk" by Larry Mulloy, NASA's Manager for the Booster Project, and other NASA officials.

Roger Boisjoly had twenty-five years of experience as an engineer in the aerospace industry. Among his many notable assignments were the performance of stress and deflection analysis on the flight control equipment of the Advanced Minuteman Missile at Autonetics, and serving as a lead engineer on the lunar module of Apollo at Hamilton Standard. He moved to Utah in 1980 to take a position in the Applied Mechanics Department as a Staff Engineer at the Wasatch Division of Morton Thiokol. He was considered the leading expert in the United States on O-rings and rocket joint seals and received plaudits for his work on the joint seal problems from Joe C. Kilminster, Vice President of Space Booster Programs, Morton Thiokol (Kilminster, July, 1985). His commitment to the company and the community was further demonstrated by his service as Mayor of Willard, Utah, from 1982 to 1983.

The tough questioning he received at the February 12th FRR convinced Boisjoly of the need for further evidence linking low temperature and hot gas blow-by. He worked closely with Arnie Thompson, Supervisor of Rocket Motor Cases, who conducted subscale laboratory tests in March, 1985, to further test the effects of temperature on O-ring resiliency. The bench tests that were performed provided powerful evidence to support Boisjoly's and Thompson's theory: Low temperatures greatly and adversely affected the ability of O-rings to create a seal on solid rocket booster joints. If the temperature was too low (and they did not know what the threshold temperature would be), it was possible that neither the primary or secondary O-rings would seal!

One month later the post-flight inspection of Flight 51-B revealed that the primary seal of a booster nozzle joint did not make contact during its two minute flight. If this damage had occurred in a field joint, the secondary O-ring may have failed to seal, causing the loss of the flight. As a result, Boisjoly and his colleagues became increasingly concerned about shuttle safety. This evidence from the inspection of Flight 51-B was presented at the FRR for Flight 51-F on July 1, 1985; the key engineers and managers of NASA and Morton Thiokol were now aware of the critical O-ring problems and the influence of low temperature on the performance of the joint seals.

During July, 1985, Boisjoly and his associates voiced their desire to devote more effort and resources to solving the problems of

O-ring erosion. In his activity reports dated July 22 and 29, 1985, Boisjoly expressed considerable frustration with the lack of progress in this area, despite the fact that a Seal Erosion Task Force had been informally appointed on July 19. Finally, Boisjoly wrote the following memo, labelled "Company Private," to R. K. (Bob) Lund, Vice President of Engineering for Morton Thiokol, to express the extreme urgency of his concerns. Here are some excerpts from that memo:

> This letter is written to insure that management is fully aware of the seriousness of the current O-ring erosion problems. . . . The mistakenly accepted position on the joint problem was to fly without fear of failure . . . is now drastically changed as a result of the SRM 16A nozzle joint erosion which eroded a secondary O-ring with the primary O-ring never sealing. If the same scenario should occur in a field joint (and it could), then it is a jump ball as to the success or failure of the joint. . . . The result would be a catastrophe of the highest order—loss of human life. . . .
>
> It is my honest and real fear that if we do not take immediate action to dedicate a team to solve the problem, with the field joint having the number one priority, then we stand in jeopardy of losing a flight along with all the launch pad facilities (Boisjoly, July, 1985a).

On August 20, 1985, R. K. Lund formally announced the formation of the Seal Erosion Task Team. The team consisted of only five full-time engineers from the 2500 employed by Morton Thiokol on the Space Shuttle Program. The events of the next five months would demonstrate that management had not provided the resources necessary to carry out the enormous task of solving the seal erosion problem.

On October 3, 1985, the Seal Erosion Task Force met with Joe Kilminster to discuss the problems they were having in gaining organizational support necessary to solve the O-ring problems. Boisjoly later stated that Kilminster summarized the meeting as a "good bullshit session." Once again frustrated by bureaucratic inertia, Boisjoly wrote in his activity report dated October 4:

> NASA is sending an engineering representative to stay with us starting Oct. 14th. We feel that this is a direct result of their feeling that we (MTI) are not responding quickly enough to the seal problem. . . . [U]pper management apparently feels that the SRM program is ours for sure and the customer be damned (Boisjoly, October, 1985b).

Boisjoly was not alone in his expression of frustration. Bob Ebeling, Department Manager, Solid Rocket Motor Igniter and Final Assembly, and a member of the Seal Erosion Task Force, wrote in a memo to Allan McDonald, Manager of the Solid Rocket Motor Project, "HELP! The seal task force is constantly being delayed by every possible means. . . . We wish we could get action by verbal request, but such is not the case. This is a red flag" (McConnell, 1987).

At the Society of Automotive Engineers (SAE) conference on October 7, 1985, Boisjoly presented a six-page overview of the joints and the seal configuration to approximately 130 technical experts in hope of soliciting suggestions for remedying the O-ring problems. Although MSFC had requested the presentation, NASA gave strict instructions not to express the critical urgency of fixing the joints, but merely to ask for suggestions for improvement. Although no help was forthcoming, the conference was a milestone in that it was the first time that NASA allowed information on the O-ring difficulties to be expressed in a public forum. That NASA also recognized that the O-ring problems were not receiving appropriate attention and manpower considerations from Morton Thiokol management is further evidenced by Boisjoly's October 24 log entry, "Jerry Peoples (NASA) has informed his people that our group needs more authority and people to do the job. Jim Smith (NASA) will corner Al McDonald today to attempt to implement this direction."

The October 30 launch of Flight 61-A of the *Challenger* provided the most convincing, and yet to some the most contestable, evidence to date that low temperature was directly related to hot gas blow-by. The left booster experienced hot gas blow-by in the center and aft field joints without any seal erosion. The ambient temperature of the field joints was estimated to be 75 degrees at launch time based on post-flight calculations. Inspection of the booster joints revealed that the blow-by was less severe than that found on Flight 51-C because the seal grease was a grayish black color, rather than the jet black hue of Flight 51-C. The evidence was now consistent with the bench tests for joint resiliency conducted in March. That is, at 75 degrees the O-ring lost contact with its sealing surface for 2.4 seconds, whereas at 50 degrees the O-ring lost contact for 10 minutes. The actual flight data revealed greater hot gas blow-by for the O-rings on Flight 51-C which had an ambient temperature of 53 degrees than for Flight 61-A which had an ambient temperature of

75 degrees. Those who rejected this line of reasoning concluded that temperature must be irrelevant since hot gas blow-by had occurred even at room temperature (75 degrees). This difference in interpretation would receive further attention on January 27, 1986.

During the next two and one-half months, little progress was made in obtaining a solution to the O-ring problems. Roger Boisjoly made the following entry into his log on January 13, 1986, "O-ring resiliency tests that were requested on September 24, 1985, are now scheduled for January 15, 1986."

The Day Before the Disaster

At 10 A.M. on January 27, 1986, Arnie Thompson received a phone call from Boyd Brinton, Thiokol's Manager of Project Engineering at MSFC, relaying the concerns of NASA's Larry Wear, also at MSFC, about the 18 degree temperature forecast for the launch of Flight 51-L, the *Challenger,* scheduled for the next day. This phone call precipitated a series of meetings within Morton Thiokol, at the Marshall Space Flight Center, and at the Kennedy Space Center that culminated in a three-way telecon involving three teams of engineers and managers, that began at 8:15 P.M. E.S.T.

Joe Kilminster, Vice President, Space Booster Programs, of Morton Thiokol began the telecon by turning the presentation of the engineering charts over to Roger Boisjoly and Arnie Thompson. They presented thirteen charts which resulted in a recommendation against the launch of the *Challenger.* Boisjoly demonstrated their concerns with the performance of the O-rings in the field joints during the initial phases of *Challenger*'s flight with charts showing the effects of primary O-ring erosion, and its timing, on the ability to maintain a reliable secondary seal. The tremendous pressure and release of power from the rocket boosters create rotation in the joint such that the metal moves away from the O-rings so that they cannot maintain contact with the metal surfaces. If, at the same time, erosion occurs in the primary O-ring for any reason, then there is a reduced probability of maintaining a secondary seal. It is highly probable that as the ambient temperature drops, the primary O-ring will not seat; that there will be hot gas blow-by and erosion of the primary O-ring; and that a catastrophe will occur when the secondary O-ring fails to seal.

Bob Lund presented the final chart that included the Morton Thiokol recommendations that the ambient temperature including wind must be such that the seal temperature would be greater than 53 degrees to proceed with the launch. Since the overnight low was predicted to be 18 degrees, Bob Lund recommended against launch on January 28, 1986, or until the seal temperature exceeded 53 degrees.

NASA's Larry Mulloy bypassed Bob Lund and directly asked Joe Kilminster for his reaction. Kilminster stated that he supported the position of his engineers and he would not recommend launch below 53 degrees.

George Hardy, Deputy Director of Science and Engineering at MSFC, said he was "appalled at that recommendation," according to Allan McDonald's testimony before the Rogers Commission. Nevertheless, Hardy would not recommend to launch if the contractor was against it. After Hardy's reaction, Stanley Reinartz, Manager of Shuttle Project Office at MSFC, objected by pointing out that the solid rocket motors were qualified to operate between 40 and 90 degrees Fahrenheit.

Larry Mulloy, citing the data from Flight 61-A which indicated to him that temperature was not a factor, strenuously objected to Morton Thiokol's recommendation. He suggested that Thiokol was attempting to establish new Launch Commit Criteria at 53 degrees and that they couldn't do that the night before a launch. In exasperation Mulloy asked, "My God, Thiokol, when do you want me to launch? Next April?" (McConnell, 1987). Although other NASA officials also objected to the association of temperature with O-ring erosion and hot gas blow-by, Roger Boisjoly was able to hold his ground and demonstrate with the use of his charts and pictures that there was indeed a relationship: The lower the temperature, the higher the probability of erosion and blow-by and the greater the likelihood of an accident. Finally, Joe Kilminster asked for a five minute caucus off-net.

According to Boisjoly's testimony before the Rogers Commission, Jerry Mason, Senior Vice President of Wasatch Operations, began the caucus by saying that "a management decision was necessary." Sensing that an attempt would be made to overturn the no-launch decision, Boisjoly and Thompson attempted to re-review the material previously presented to NASA for the executives in the room. Thompson took a pad of paper and tried to sketch out the problem with the joint, while Boisjoly laid out the photos of the compromised joints from Flights 51-C and 61-A. When they became convinced that no one was listening, they ceased their efforts. As Boisjoly would later testify, "There was not one positive pro-launch statement ever made by anybody" (Report of the Presidential Commission, 1986, IV, p. 792, hereafter abbreviated as R.C.).

According to Boisjoly, after he and Thompson made their last attempts to stop the launch, Jerry Mason asked rhetorically, "Am I the only one who wants to fly?" Mason turned to Bob Lund and asked him to "take off his engineering hat and put on his management hat." The four managers held a brief discussion and voted unanimously to recommend *Challenger's* launch.

Exhibit 1 shows the revised recommendations that were presented that evening by Joe Kilminster after the caucus to support management's decision to launch. Only one of the rationales presented that evening supported the launch ("demonstrated sealing threshold is 3 times greater than 0.038" erosion experienced on SRM-15"). Even so, the issue at hand was sealability at low temperature, not erosion. While one other rationale could be considered a neutral statement of engineering fact ("O-ring pressure leak check places secondary seal in outboard position which minimizes sealing time"), the other seven rationales are negative, anti-launch, statements. After hearing Kilminster's presentation, which was accepted without a single probing question, George Hardy asked him to sign the chart and telefax it to Kennedy Space Center and Marshall Space Flight Center. At 11 P.M. E.S.T. the teleconference ended.

Aside from the four senior Morton Thiokol executives present at the teleconference, all others were excluded from the final decision. The process represented a radical shift from previous NASA policy. Until that moment, the burden of proof had always been on the engineers to prove beyond a doubt that it was safe to launch. NASA, with their objections to the original Thiokol recommendation against the launch, and Mason, with his request for a "management decision," shifted the burden of proof in the opposite direction. Morton Thiokol was expected to prove that launching *Challenger* would not be safe (R.C., IV, p. 793).

EXHIBIT 1
MTI Assessment of Temperature Concern on SRM-25 (51L) Launch

- Calculations show that SRM-25 O-rings will be 20°
  colder than SRM-15 O-rings
- Temperature data not conclusive on predicting primary O-ring blow-by
- Engineering assessment is that:
  - Colder O-rings will have increased effective durometer ("harder")
- "Harder" O-rings will take longer to "seat"
  - More gas may pass primary O-ring before the primary seal seats (relative to SRM-15)
  - Demonstrated sealing threshold is 3 times greater than 0.038" erosion experienced on SRM-15
- If the primary seal does not seat, the secondary seal will seat
  - Pressure will get to secondary seal before the metal parts rotate
  - O-ring pressure leak check places secondary seal in outboard position which minimizes sealing time
- MTI recommends STS-51L launch proceed on 28 January 1986
  - SRM-25 will not be significantly different from SRM-15

Joe C. Kilminster, Vice President Space Booster Programs.

The change in the decision so deeply upset Boisjoly that he returned to his office and made the following journal entry:

> I sincerely hope this launch does not result in a catastrophe. I personally do not agree with some of the statements made in Joe Kilminster's written summary stating that SRM-25 is okay to fly (Boisjoly, 1987).

The Disaster and Its Aftermath

On January 28, 1986, a reluctant Roger Boisjoly watched the launch of the *Challenger*. As the vehicle cleared the tower, Bob Ebeling whispered, "We've just dodged a bullet." (The engineers who opposed the launch assumed that O-ring failure would result in an explosion almost immediately after engine ignition.) To continue in Boisjoly's words, "At approximately T + 60 seconds Bob told me he had just completed a prayer of thanks to the Lord for a successful launch. Just thirteen seconds later we both saw the horror of the destruction as the vehicle exploded" (Boisjoly, 1987).

Morton Thiokol formed a failure investigation team on January 31, 1986, to study the *Challenger* explosion. Roger Boisjoly and Arnie

Thompson were part of the team that was sent to MSFC in Huntsville, Alabama. Boisjoly's first inkling of a division between himself and management came on February 13 when he was informed at the last minute that he was to testify before the Rogers Commission the next day. He had very little time to prepare for his testimony. Five days later, two Commission members held a closed session with Kilminster, Boisjoly, and Thompson. During the interview Boisjoly gave his memos and activity reports to the Commissioners. After that meeting, Kilminster chastised Thompson and Boisjoly for correcting his interpretation of the technical data. Their response was that they would continue to correct his version if it was technically incorrect.

Boisjoly's February 25 testimony before the Commission, rebutting the general manager's statement that the initial decision against the launch was not unanimous, drove a wedge further between him and Morton Thiokol management. Boisjoly was flown to MSFC before he could hear the NASA testimony about the pre-flight telecon. The next day, he was removed from the failure investigation team and returned to Utah.

Beginning in April, Boisjoly began to believe that for the previous month he had been used solely for public relations purposes. Although given the title of Seal Coordinator for the redesign effort, he was isolated from NASA and the seal redesign effort. His design information had been changed without his knowledge and presented without his feedback. On May 1, 1986, in a briefing preceding closed sessions before the Rogers Commission, Ed Garrison, President of Aerospace Operations for Morton Thiokol, chastised Boisjoly for "airing the company's dirty laundry" with the memos he had given the Commission. The next day, Boisjoly testified about the change in his job assignment. Commission Chairman Rogers criticized Thiokol management: [I]f it appears that you're punishing the two people or at least two of the people who are right about the decision and objected to the launch which ultimately resulted in criticism of Thiokol and then they're demoted or feel that they are being retaliated against, that is a very serious matter. It would seem to me, just speaking for myself, they should be promoted, not demoted or pushed aside" (R.C., V, p. 1586).

Boisjoly now sensed a major rift developing within the corporation. Some co-workers perceived that his testimony was damaging the company image. In an effort to clear the air, he and McDonald requested a private meeting with the company's three top executives, which was held on May 16, 1986. According to Boisjoly, management was unreceptive throughout the meeting. The CEO told McDonald and Boisjoly that the company "was doing just fine until Al and I testified about our job reassignments" (Boisjoly, 1987). McDonald and Boisjoly were nominally restored to their former assignments, but Boisjoly's position became untenable as time passed. On July 21, 1986, Roger Boisjoly requested an extended sick leave from Morton Thiokol.

Ethical Analysis

It is clear from this case study that Roger Boisjoly's experiences before and after the *Challenger* disaster raise numerous ethical questions that are integral to any explanation of the disaster and applicable to other management situations, especially those involving highly complex technologies. The difficulties and uncertainties involved in the management of these technologies exacerbate the kind of bureaucratic syndromes that generate ethical conflicts in the first place. In fact, Boisjoly's experiences could well serve as a paradigmatic case study for such ethical problems, ranging from accountability to corporate loyalty and whistle-blowing. Underlying all these issues, however, is the problematic relationship between individual and organizational responsibility. Boisjoly's experiences graphically portray the tensions inherent in this relationship in a manner that discloses its importance in the causal sequence leading to the *Challenger* disaster. The following analysis explicates this and the implications it has for other organizational settings.

By focusing on the problematic relationship between individual and organizational responsibility, this analysis reveals that the organizational structure governing the space shuttle program became the locus of responsibility in such a way that not only did it undermine the responsibilities of individual decision makers within the process, but it also became a means of avoiding real, effective responsibility throughout the entire management system. The first clue to this was clearly articulated as early as 1973 by the board of inquiry that was formed to investigate the accident which occurred during the launch of *Skylab 1*:

> The management system developed by NASA for manned space flight places large emphasis on rigor, detail, and thoroughness. In hand with this emphasis comes formalism, extensive documentation, and visibility in detail to senior management. While nearly perfect, such a system can submerge the concerned individual and depress the role of the intuitive engineer or analyst. It may not allow full play for the intuitive judgment or past experience of the individual. An emphasis on management systems can, in itself, serve to separate the people engaged in the program from the real world of hardware (Quoted in Christiansen, 1987, p. 23).

To examine the prescient statement in ethical terms is to see at another level the serious consequences inherent in the situation it describes. For example, it points to a dual meaning of responsibility. One meaning emphasizes carrying out an authoritatively prescribed review process, while the second stresses the cognitive independence and input of every individual down the entire chain of authority. The first sense of responsibility shifts the ethical center of gravity precipitously away from individual moral agency onto the review process in such a way that what was originally set up to guarantee flight readiness with the professional and personal integrity of the responsible individuals instead becomes a means of evading personal responsibility for decisions made in the review process.

A crucial, and telling, example of this involves the important question asked by the Rogers Commission as to why the concerns raised by the Morton Thiokol engineers about the effects of cold weather on the O-rings during the teleconference the night before the launch were not passed up from Level III to Levels II or I in the preflight review process. The NASA launch procedure clearly demands that decisions and objections methodically follow a prescribed path up all levels. Yet, Lawrence Mulloy, operating at Level III as the Solid Rocket Booster Project Manager at MSFC, did not transmit the Morton Thiokol concerns upward (through his immediate superior, Stanley Reinartz) to Level II. When asked by Chairman Rogers to explain why, Mr. Mulloy testified:

At that time, and I still consider today, that was a Level III issue,
Level III being a SRB element or an external tank element or Space
Shuttle main engine element or an Orbiter. There was no violation
of Launch Commit Criteria. There was no waiver required in my
judgment at that time and still today (R.C., I, p. 98).

In examining this response in terms of shifting responsibility onto
the review process itself, there are two things that are particularly
striking in Mr. Mulloy's statement. The first is his emphasis that this
was a "Level III issue." In a formal sense, Mr. Mulloy is correct.
However, those on Level III also had the authority—and, one would
think, especially in this instance given the heated discussion on the
effects of cold on the O-rings, the motivation—to pass objections
and concerns on to Levels II and I. But here the second important
point in Mr. Mulloy's testimony comes into play when he states,
"There was no violation of Launch Commit Criteria." In other
words, since there was no Launch Commit Criteria for joint temperature, concerns about joint temperature did not officially fall
under the purview of the review process. Therefore, the ultimate
justification for Mr. Mulloy's position rests on the formal process
itself. He was just following the rules by staying within the already
established scope of the review process.

This underscores the moral imperative executives must exercise
by creating and maintaining organizational systems that do not
separate the authority of decision makers from the responsibility
they bear for decisions, or insulate them from the consequences
of their actions or omissions.

Certainly, there can be no more vivid example than the shuttle
program to verify that, in fact, "an emphasis on management systems can, in itself, serve to separate the people engaged in the program from the real world of hardware." Time and time again the
lack of communication that lay at the heart of the Rogers Commission finding that "there was a serious flaw in the decision making
process leading up to the launch of flight 51-L" (R.C., I, p. 104) was
explained by the NASA officials or managers at Morton Thiokol
with such statements as, "that is not my reporting channel," or "he
is not in the launch decision chain," or "I didn't meet with Mr.
Boisjoly, I met with Don Ketner, who is the task team leader" (R.C.,
IV, p. 821, testimony of Mr. Lund). Even those managers who had

direct responsibility for line engineers and workmen depended on formalized memo writing procedures for communication to the point that some "never talked to them directly" (Feynman, 1988, p. 33).

Within the atmosphere of such an ambiguity of responsibility, when a life threatening conflict arose within the management system and individuals (such as Roger Boisjoly and his engineering associates at Morton Thiokol) tried to reassert the full weight of their individual judgments and attendant responsibilities, the very purpose of the flight readiness review process, i.e., to arrive at the "technical" truth of the situation, which includes the recognition of the uncertainties involved as much as the findings, became subverted into an adversary confrontation in which "adversary" truth, with its suppression of uncertainties, became operative (Wilmotte, 1970).

What is particularly significant in this radical transformation of the review process, in which the Morton Thiokol engineers were forced into "the position of having to prove that it was unsafe instead of the other way around" (R.C., IV, p. 822; see also p. 793), is that what made the suppression of technical uncertainties possible is precisely that mode of thinking which, in being challenged by independent professional judgments, gave rise to the adversarial setting in the first place: groupthink. No more accurate description for what transpired the night before the launch of the *Challenger* can be given than the definition of groupthink as:

> a mode of thinking that people engage in when they are deeply involved in a cohesive in-group, when the members' strivings for unanimity override their motivation to realistically appraise alternative courses of action. . . . Groupthink refers to the deterioration of mental efficiency, reality testing, and moral judgment that results from in-group pressures (Janis, 1972, p. 9).

From this perspective, the full import of Mr. Mason's telling Mr. Lund to "take off his engineering hat and put on his management hat" is revealed. He did not want another technical, reality-based judgment of an independent professional engineer. As he had already implied when he opened the caucus by stating "a management decision was necessary," he wanted a group decision, specifically one that would, in the words of the Rogers Commission, "accommodate a major customer" (R.C., I, p. 104). With a group decision the objections of the engineers could be mitigated, the risks shared, fears allayed, and the attendant responsibility diffused.[1]

This analysis is not meant to imply that groupthink was a pervasive or continuous mode of thinking at either NASA or Morton Thiokol. What is suggested is a causal relationship between this instance of groupthink and the ambiguity of responsibility found within the space shuttle program. Whenever a management system, such as NASA's generates "a mindset of 'collective responsibility'" by leading "individuals to defer to the anonymity of the process and not focus closely enough on their individual responsibilities in the decision chain" (N.R.C. Report, 1988, p. 68), and there is a confluence of the kind of pressures that came to bear on the decision making process the night before the launch, the conditions are in place for groupthink to prevail.

A disturbing feature of so many of the analyses and commentaries on the *Challenger* disaster is the reinforcement, and implicit acceptance, of this shift away from individual moral agency with an almost exclusive focus on the flaws in the management system, organizational structures and/or decision making process. Beginning with the findings of the Rogers Commission investigation, one could practically conclude that no one had any responsibility whatsoever for the disaster. The Commission concluded that "there was a serious flaw in the decision making process leading up to the launch of flight 51-L. A well structured and managed system emphasizing safety would have flagged the rising doubts about the Solid Rocket Booster joint seal." Then the Commission report immediately states, "Had these matters been clearly stated and emphasized in the flight readiness process in terms reflecting the

---

1. A contrasting interpretation of the meeting the night before the launch, given by Howard Schwartz, is that NASA began to view itself as the ideal organization that did not make mistakes. According to Schwartz, "The organization ideal is an image of perfection. It is, so to speak, an idea of God. God does not make mistakes. Having adopted the idea of NASA as the organization ideal, it follows that the individual will believe that, if NASA has made a decision, that decision will be correct" (Schwartz, 1987).

In his testimony before the Rogers Commission, Roger Boisjoly indicated the extent to which NASA procedure had changed: "This was a meeting (the night before the launch) where the determination was to launch, and it was up to us to prove beyond the shadow of a doubt that it was not safe to do so. This is the total reverse to what the position usually is in a pre-flight conversation or a flight readiness review" (Boisjoly, 1986).

As Schwartz indicates: "If it was a human decision, engineering standards of risk should prevail in determining whether it is safe to launch. On the other hand, if the decision was a NASA decision, it is simply safe to launch, since NASA does not make mistakes" (Schwartz, 1987).

views of most of the Thiokol engineers and at least some of the Marshall engineers, it seems likely that the launch of 51-L might not have occurred when it did" (R.C., I, p. 104). But the gathering and passing on of such information was the responsibility of specifically designated individuals, known by name and position in the highly structured review process. Throughout this process there had been required "a series of formal, legally binding certifications, the equivalent of airworthiness inspections in the aviation industry. In effect the myriad contractor and NASA personnel involved were guaranteeing *Challenger*'s flight readiness with their professional and personal integrity" (McConnell, 1987, p. 17).

When the Commission states in its next finding that "waiving of launch constraints appears to have been at the expense of flight safety," the immediate and obvious question would seem to be: Who approved the waivers and assumed this enormous risk? And why? This is a serious matter! A launch constraint is only issued because there is a safety problem serious enough to justify a decision not to launch. However, the Commission again deflects the problem onto the system by stating, "There was no system which made it imperative that launch constraints and waivers of launch constraints be considered by all levels of management" (R.C., 1986, I, p. 104).

There are two puzzling aspects to this Commission finding. First, the formal system already contained the requirement that project offices inform at least Level II of launch constraints. The Commission addressed the explicit violation of this requirement in the case of a July 1985 launch constraint that had been imposed on the Solid Rocket Booster because of O-ring erosion on the nozzle:

> NASA Levels I and II apparently did not realize Marshall had assigned a launch constraint within the Problem Assessment System. This communication failure was contrary to the requirement, contained in the NASA Problem Reporting and Corrective Action Requirements System, that launch constraints were to be taken to Level II (R.C., 1986, I, pp. 138–139; see also p. 159).

Second, the Commission clearly established that the individual at Marshall who both imposed and waived the launch constraint was Lawrence Mulloy, SRB Project Manager. Then why blame the management system, especially in such a crucial area as that of launch constraints, when procedures of that system were not followed? Is that approach going to increase the accountability of individuals within the system for future Flights?

Even such an independent minded and probing Commission member as Richard Feynman, in an interview a year after the disaster, agreed with the avoidance of determining individual accountability for specific actions and decisions. He is quoted as saying, "I don't think it's correct to try to find out which particular guy happened to do what particular thing. It's the question of how the atmosphere could get to such a circumstance that such things were possible without anybody catching on." Yet, at the same time Feynman admitted that he was not confident that any restructuring of the management system will ensure that the kinds of problems that resulted in the *Challenger* disaster—"danger signs not seen and warnings not heeded"—do not recur. He said, "I'm really not sure that any kind of simple mechanism can cure stupidity and dullness. You can make up all the rules about how things should be, and they'll go wrong if the spirit is different, if the attitudes are different over time and as personnel change" (Chandler, 1987, p. 50).

The approach of the Rogers Commission and that of most of the analyses of the *Challenger* disaster is consistent with the growing tendency to deny any specific responsibility to individual persons within corporate or other institutional settings when things go wrong. Although there are obviously many social changes in modern life that justify the shift in focus from individuals to organizational structures as bearers of responsibility, this shift is reinforced and exaggerated by the way people think about and accept those changes. One of the most pernicious problems of modern times is the almost universally held belief that the individual is powerless, especially within the context of large organizations where one may perceive oneself, and be viewed, as a very small, and replaceable, cog. It is in the very nature of this situation that responsibility may seem to become so diffused that no one person, *is* responsible. As the National Research Council committee, in following up on the Rogers Commission, concluded about the space shuttle program:

> Given the pervasive reliance on teams and boards to consider the key questions affecting safety, "group democracy" can easily prevail. . . . [I]n the end all decisions become collective ones (N.R.C. Report, pp. 68 and 70).

The problem with this emphasis on management systems and collective responsibility is that it fosters a vicious circle that further and further erodes and obscures individual responsibility. This leads to a paradoxical—and untenable—situation (such as in the space shuttle program) in which decisions are made and actions are performed by individuals or groups of individuals but not attributed to them. It thus reinforces the tendency to avoid accountability for what anyone does by attributing the consequences to the organization or decision making process. Again, shared, rather than individual, risk-taking and responsibility become operative. The end result can be a cancerous attitude that so permeates an organization or management system that it metastasizes into decisions and acts of life-threatening irresponsibility.

In sharp contrast to this prevalent emphasis on organizational structures, one of the most fascinating aspects of the extensive and exhaustive investigations into the *Challenger* disaster is that they provide a rare opportunity to re-affirm the sense and importance of individual responsibility. With the inside look into the space shuttle program these investigations detail, one can identify many instances where personal responsibility, carefully interpreted, can properly be imputed to NASA officials and to its contractors. By so doing, one can preserve, if only in a fragmentary way, the essentials of the traditional concept of individual responsibility within the diluting context of organizational life. This effort is intended to make explicit the kind of causal links that are operative between the actions of individuals and the structures of organizations.

The criteria commonly employed for holding individuals responsible for an outcome are two: (1) their acts or omissions are in some way a cause of it; and (2) these acts or omissions are not done in ignorance or under coercion (Thompson, 1987, p. 47). Although there are difficult theoretical and practical questions associated with both criteria, especially within organizational settings, nevertheless, even a general application of them to the sequence of events leading up to the *Challenger* disaster reveals those places where the principle of individual responsibility must be factored in if our understanding of it is to be complete, its lessons learned, and its repetition avoided.

The Rogers Commission has been criticized—and rightly so—for looking at the disaster "from the bottom up but not from the top down," with the result that it gives a clearer picture of what transpired at the lower levels of the *Challenger*'s flight review process than at its upper levels (Cook, 1986). Nevertheless, in doing so, the Commission report provides powerful testimony that however elaborately structured and far reaching an undertaking such as the space shuttle program may be, individuals at the bottom of the organizational structure can still play a crucial, if not deciding, role in the outcome. For in the final analysis, whatever the defects in the *Challenger*'s launch decision chain were that kept the upper levels from being duly informed about the objections of the engineers at Morton Thiokol, the fact remains that the strenuous objections of these engineers so forced the decision process at their level that the four middle managers at Morton Thiokol had the full responsibility for the launch in their hands. This is made clear in the startling testimony of Mr. Mason, when Chairman Rogers asked him: "Did you realize, and particularly in view of Mr. Hardy's (Deputy Director of Science and Engineering at MSFC) point that they wouldn't launch unless you agreed, did you fully realize that in effect, you were making a decision to launch, you and your colleagues?" Mr. Mason replied, "Yes, sir" (R.C., 1986, IV, p. 770).

If these four men had just said no, the launch of the *Challenger* would not have taken place the next day. Could there have been any doubt about what was at stake in their decision, or about the degree of risk involved? Not in view of the follow-up testimony of Brian Russell, another Thiokol engineer present at the teleconference. Mr. Russell was asked by Mr. Acheson to give his recollection of the thought process followed in his mind "in the change of position between the view presented in the telecon that Thiokol was opposed to the launch, and the subsequent conclusion of the caucus within the company" (R.C., 1986, IV, p. 821). In the course of his response, Mr. Russell stated:

> But I felt in my mind that once we had done our very best to explain why we were concerned, and we meaning those in the camp who really felt strongly about the recommendation of 53 degrees, the decision was to be made, and a poll was then taken. And I remember distinctly at the time wondering whether I would have the courage, if asked, and I thought I might be, what I would do and whether I would be alone. I didn't think I would be alone, but I was wondering if I would have the courage, I remember that distinctly, to stand up and say no. . . . I was nervous. . . . [T]here was a nervousness

there that we were increasing the risk, and I believe all of us knew that if it were increased to the level of O-ring burnthrough, what the consequences would be. And I don't think there's any question in anyone's mind about that (R.C., 1986, IV, pp. 822–823).

Some pertinent observations that have direct implications for managers in any organization must be made about where the principle of individual responsibility intersects with the structural flaws and organizational deterioration that have been attributed such a prominent role in the *Challenger* disaster. While it is on the basis of these flaws that the Rogers Commission absolved NASA officials of any direct responsibility for the disaster, it must nevertheless be pointed out that such officials "act in the context of a continuing institution, not an isolated incident, and they or other officials therefore may be culpable for creating the structural faults of the organization, or for neglecting to notice them, or for making inadequate efforts to correct them" (Thompson, 1987, p. 46). While it is true that attributing responsibility demands precision in determining the consequences of acts as much as in identifying the agents, this specificity of outcomes "does not preclude responsibility for patterns of decision and decision making" (Thompson, 1987, p. 48). Therefore, among the outcomes for which managers are held responsible, the continuing practices, standards, and structures of their organizations should be included.

Of all the descriptions of the flaws, break downs, and deterioration of NASA's managerial system, none point to any failures that fall outside the well-documented pathologies of bureaucratic behavior (e.g., lack of communication, distortion of information as it passes up the hierarchy, jealousy of existing lines of authority, bias in favor of the status quo, bureaucratic turf protection, power games, inclination to view the public interest through the distorted lens of vested interests, the "think positive" or "can do" syndrome), and, as such, they can be anticipated. That bureaucratic routines "have a life of their own, often roaming beyond their original purpose, is a fact of organizational behavior that officials should be expected to appreciate. The more the consequences of a decision fit such bureaucratic patterns, the less an official can plausibly invoke the excuse from ignorance" (Thompson, 1987, p. 61).

So much has been made of NASA's top officials not being fully informed of the extent of the problems with the O-rings, and specifically of the Thiokol engineers' objections to the *Challenger* launch in cold weather, that an analysis of the disaster in *Fortune* magazine had as its title, "NASA's Challenge: Ending Isolation at the Top" (Brody, 1986). The actual extent of their isolation has been questioned, and even the Rogers Commission is not consistent on this issue. In its findings for Chapter V, the Commission states, "A well structured and managed system emphasizing safety would have flagged the rising doubts about the Solid Rocket Booster joint seal." Nevertheless, it concludes in the next chapter that "the O-ring erosion history presented to Level I at NASA Headquarters in August 1985 was sufficiently detailed to require corrective action prior to the next flight" (R.C., 1986, I, pp. 104 and 148).

Whatever the extent of their ignorance, an important principle comes into play in determining the degree of individual responsibility. It is implied in Richard Feynman's position where he drew the line in not ascribing accountability for the *Challenger* disaster to specific individuals. Referring to Jesse Moore, Associate Administrator for Space Flight, the Level I manager with whom final approval for launch rested, Feynman maintained, "the guy at the top never should have an excuse that nobody told him. It seemed to me he ought to go out and find out what's going on" (Chandler, 1987, p. 50). The moral principle underlying Feynman's position here and which must be considered in tracing the boundaries of individual responsibility vis-à-vis the question of ignorance is the principle of "indirect responsibility."

As applied to the issue of ignorance, this principle confronts anyone in an organization with the inherent expectations of his or her position of power and level of expertise. The contours of indirect responsibility follow in the wake of these expectations because the standards against which to measure a claim of ignorance are precisely the standards of a given position and requisite knowledge. Therefore, to reject an excuse from ignorance it is sufficient to say: You are indirectly responsible for what has transpired because, given your position and professional experience, if you didn't know, you should have (Rosenblatt, 1983).

Although this principle operates in a gray area where the difference between indirect responsibility and pardonable ignorance can be marginal, a tragic, complex event like the *Challenger* disaster demands its application. Like the law, ethical thought must not be willing to accept ignorance as a sufficient excuse when it can be reasonably established that those in the causal sequence or in positions of authority should have known, or found out before acting or rendering decisions. This is especially true for managers who become instruments of their own ignorance whenever they prevent the free and complete flow of information to themselves, either directly by their acts, or indirectly through the subtle messages they convey to their subordinates, in their management style, or by the organizational climate they help create (Thompson, 1987, pp. 60–61).

Although fragmentary and tentative in its formulation, this set of considerations points toward the conclusion that however complex and sophisticated an organization may be, and no matter how large and remote the institutional network needed to manage it may be, an active and creative tension of responsibility must be maintained at every level of the operation. Given the size and complexity of such endeavors, the only way to ensure that tension of attentive and effective responsibility is to give the primacy of responsibility to that ultimate principle of all moral conduct: the human individual—even if this does necessitate, in too many instances under present circumstances, that individuals such as Roger Boisjoly, when they attempt to exercise their responsibility, must step forward as moral heroes. In so doing, these individuals do not just bear witness to the desperate need for a system of full accountability in the face of the immense power and reach of modern technology and institutions. They also give expression to the very essence of what constitutes the moral life. As Roger Boisjoly has stated in reflecting on his own experience, "I have been asked by some if I would testify again if I knew in advance of the potential consequences to me and my career. My answer is always an immediate 'yes.' I couldn't live with any self-respect if I tailored my actions based upon the personal consequences" (Boisjoly, 1987).

References

Boisjoly, Roger M. 1985a. Applied Mechanics Memorandum to Robert K. Lund, Vice President, Engineering, Wasatch Division, Morton Thiokol, Inc., July 31.

Boisjoly, Roger M. 1985b. Activity Report, SRM Seal Erosion Task Team Status, October 4.

Boisjoly, Roger M. 1987. Ethical Decisions: Morton Thiokol and the Shuttle Disaster. Speech given at Massachusetts Institute of Technology, January 7.

Boling, T. Edwin and Dempsey, John. 1981. "Ethical dilemmas in government: Designing an organizational response," *Public Personnel Management Journal* 10, 11–18.

Brody, Michael. 1986. "NASA's challenge: Ending isolation at the top." *Fortune* 113 (May 12), pp. 26–32.

Chandler, David. 1987. "Astronauts gain clout in 'revitalized' NASA," *Boston Globe* 1 (January 26), 50.

Christiansen, Donald. 1987. "A system gone awry," *IEEE Spectrum* 24 (3), 23.

Cook, Richard C. 1986. "The Rogers commission failed," *The Washington Monthly* 18 (9), 13-21.

DeGeorge, Richard T. 1981. "Ethical responsibilities of engineers in large organizations: The Pinto Case," *Business and Professional Ethics Journal* 1, 1–14.

Feynman, Richard P. 1988. "An outsider's view of the *Challenger* inquiry," *Physics Today* 41 (2), 26–37.

Janis, Irving L. 1972. *Victims of Groupthink*, Boston, MA: Houghton Mifflin Company.

Kilminster, J. C. 1985. Memorandum (E000-FY86-003) to Robert Lund, Vice President, Engineering, Wasatch Division, Morton Thiokol, Inc., July 5.

McConnell, Malcolm. 1987. Challenger, *A Major Malfunction: A True Story of Politics, Greed, and the Wrong Stuff*, Garden City, N.J.: Doubleday and Company, Inc.

Mankin, Hart T. 1981. "Commentary on 'Ethical responsibilities of engineers in large organizations: The Pinto Case,'" *Business and Professional Ethics Journal* 1, 15–17.

National Research Council. 1988. *Post*-Challenger, *Evaluation of Space Shuttle Risk Assessment and Management*, Washington, D.C.: National Academy Press.

Report of the Presidential Commission on the Space Shuttle Challenger *Accident*. 1986. Washington, D.C.: U.S. Government Printing Office.

Rosenblatt, Roger. 1983. "The commission report: The law of the mind," *Time* 126 (February 21), 39–40.

Schwartz, Howard S. 1987. "On the psychodynamics of organizational disaster: The case of the Space Shuttle *Challenger*," *The Columbia Journal of World Business*, Spring.

Thompson, Dennis F. 1987. *Political Ethics and Public Office*, Cambridge, MA: Harvard University Press.

Wilmotte, Raymond M. 1970. "Engineering truth in competitive environments," *IEEE Spectrum* 7 (5), 45–49.

11
Rodney King and Use of Excessive Force
Police Work and Organizational Culture
Jerome H. Skolnick and James J. Fyfe

It all started when George Holliday brought home a camcorder, a Sony CCD-F77, on Valentine's Day, 1991. The thirty-three-year-old, recently married former rugby player, general manager of a local office of Rescue Rooter, a national plumbing company, hadn't had time to load it until March 2, the day before one of his employees was scheduled to run in the Los Angeles marathon. After setting his alarm for 6 A.M. so as to arrive in time for the race, Holliday went to bed early and was awakened at 12:50 A.M. by a blast of siren noise and screeching rubber. The racket was coming from Foothill Boulevard, the main thoroughfare of a middle-class, ethnically mixed Los Angeles exurb with a population about 60 percent Latino, 10 percent black, and the rest Asian and white. When Holliday, who is white, pulled the window shade aside, he could scarcely believe what he saw. The powerful spotlight of a police helicopter was shining on a white Hyundai surrounded by a half-dozen police cars. His first thought was, "Hey, let's get the camera!"[1]

The videotape Holliday shot showed a large black man down on hands and knees, struggling on the ground, twice impaled with wires from an electronic TASER gun, rising and falling while being repeatedly beaten, blow after blow after blow—dozens of blows, fifty-six in all, about the head, neck, back, kidneys, ankles, legs, feet—by two police officers wielding their 2-foot black metal truncheons like

1. Mike Sager, "Damn! They Gonna Lynch Us," *Gentlemen's Quarterly,* October 1991. Sager offers a vivid, detailed description of the events preceding, during, and following the beating of Rodney King.

baseball bats. Also visible was a third officer, who was stomping [Rodney] King, and about ten police officers watching the beating along with a number of Holliday's neighbors.

Actually, twenty-three LAPD [Los Angeles Police Department] officers responded to the scene (an interesting number in light of the later claim that the Department is severely understaffed to respond to emergencies). Four officers were directly involved in the use of force; two hovered overhead in a helicopter; ten were on the ground and witnessed some portion of the beating; seven others checked out the scene and left. Four uniformed officers from two other law enforcement agencies—the Highway Patrol and the Los Angeles Unified School District—were also there. . . .

In the ninety-second tape, viewers saw with their own eyes how a group of Los Angeles police officers could act out their anger, frustration, fears, and prejudices on the body of a black man who had led them on a high-speed chase. Like films of the police dogs in Selma or the clubs and tear gas of the 1968 Chicago Democratic Convention, the dramatic videotape gave new credibility to allegations of a sort that many people—including police officers—formerly dismissed as unbelievable. . . .

How can police, who can be exemplary heroes, beat people and then even be prepared to lie about it? We shall explain this paradox with the proposition that two principal features of the police role—danger and authority—combine to produce in them a distinctive worldview that affects the values and understanding of cops on and off the job, sometimes leading to admirable valor, sometimes to brutality and excessive force, and sometimes to a banding together, a cover-up, a conspiracy of silence. . . .

The Work of Police

Like a tribe or an ethnic group, every occupational group develops recognizable and distinctive rules, customs, perceptions, and interpretations of what they see, along with consequent moral judgments. Although some recognitions and prescriptions are shared with everyone else—we all live in the same society—others are mandates peculiar to and appreciated only by members of the craft or

profession. In this sense, a specific world of work is rather like a
game: One has to know the rules in order to play properly. Even
those who play games develop such informal rules. "Baseball has
evolved a set of unwritten and rarely even spoken norms, mores,
habits, and customs," George Will writes. "The code governs such
matters as when it is appropriate to pitch at, or very close to, a batter;
when and how to retaliate for that; which displays of emotion are
acceptable and which constitute 'showing up' an umpire or opposing player; what sort of physical contact, in what sorts of game situations (breaking up a double play at second, trying to score when
the catcher is blocking the plate), is acceptable."[2]

Police also live by a profusion of such unwritten rules. Some
have been adopted by police all over the Western world, such as
customary ways of dealing with people who challenge police authority. Others are the unwritten norms prevailing in a specific department. Every police department has such written and unwritten
guidelines, including the proprieties of accepting gratuities, dis-
counts, bribes, or favors.

Even in those American police departments enjoying a reputation for "legalistic" and therefore incorruptible policing, such as
the Los Angeles Police Department, police may enjoy certain favors
but not others. Basing his observations on years of service as a Los
Angeles police officer and detective, Joseph Wambaugh, in his novel
The Choirboys, observes that one of his characters, an ordinary LA
policeman, "had accepted a thousand packs of cigarettes and as
many free meals in his time. And though he had bought enough
clothing at wholesale prices to dress a dozen movie stars, he had
never even considered taking a five dollar bill nor was one ever
offered except once when he stopped a Chicago grocer in Los
Angeles on vacation."

Like most of us, and unlike economists, police do not make their
choices by a rational calculation of comparative economic values.
Choices are made instead on moral grounds, developed within the
subculture of a police department. Thus, Wambaugh interprets his
character's conduct as being in conformity with a distinction the
police department and its members made "between gratuities and
cash offerings, which were considered money bribes no matter how

2. George Will, *New York Review of Books,* June 10, 1991.

slight and would result in a merciless dismissal as well as citizen prosecution."[3] Robert Daley describes a similar, but more sinister, dichotomy in *Prince of the City,* his account of a New York City narcotics detective's decline into corruption. Among this work group, the elite Special Investigations Unit, it was permissible to steal drug dealers' money and to reward snitches with some of the drugs seized in raids made possible by their information. Money earned from selling drugs, however, was *dirty*.[4] By the same logic, according to the Knapp Commission's report on police corruption, other officers considered bribes from bookmakers and illegal numbers operators to be *clean money* and would have nothing whatever to do with drug dealers.[5] . . .

Policing, particularly because it is a twenty-four-hour-a-day identity, generates powerfully distinctive ways of looking at the world, cognitive and behavioral responses which, when taken together, may be said to constitute "a working personality."[6] How working cops learn to see the world around them and their place in it has come to be acknowledged by scholars of police as an indispensable key to understanding their motives, fears, and aspirations, and the moral codes by which they judge themselves and affect the lives of others. "It is a commonplace of the now voluminous sociological literature on police operations and discretion," Robert Reiner observes, "that the rank-and-file officer is the primary determinant of policing where it really counts—on the street."[7]

Social scientists have studied police in every part of the United States, in Europe and in Asia. The fundamental culture of policing is everywhere similar, which is understandable since everywhere the same features of the police role—danger, authority, and the mandate to use coercive force—are everywhere present. This combination generates and supports norms of internal solidarity, or *brotherhood.* Most police feel comfortable, and socialize mainly, with other cops,

3. Joseph Wambaugh, *The Choirboys* (New York: Dell, 1975), p. 63.

4. Robert Daley, *Prince of the City: The True Story of a Cop Who Knew Too Much* (Boston: Houghton Mifflin, 1978).

5. Whitman Knapp *et al., Report of the New York City Commission to Investigate Allegations of Police Corruption and the City's Anti-Corruption Procedures* (New York: George Braziller, 1973), p. 67.

6. Jerome H. Skolnick, *Justice Without Trial: Law Enforcement in Democratic Society* (New York: Wiley, 1966, 1975).

7. Robert Reiner, *The Politics of the Police* (Sussex, U.K.: Wheatsheaf Books, 1986), p. 99.

a feature of police culture noted by observers of police from the 1960s to the 1990s. Every cop has a story about a social occasion where an inebriated guest would make a joking or half-joking remark that deprecated police or set them apart. Most cops prefer to attend parties with other police, where drinking and carousing can occur without fear of civilian affront or knowledge. Cops don't trust other people—which is practically everybody who is not a cop. "They know the public generally resents their authority," Mark Baker says, "and is fickle in its support of police policy and individual police officers. Older officers teach younger ones that it is best to avoid civilians."[8] Different philosophies and styles can be introduced into policing. . . . Yet cops on patrol in New York, Philadelphia, Los Angeles, London, and Stockholm—with whom we and others have ridden and observed—are remarkably comparable, with kindred occupational perspectives and working personalities. . . .

Robert Reiner, perhaps the leading contemporary British police scholar, has argued that a sense of mission is a central feature of the culture of police. "This is the feeling that policing is not just a job, but a way of life with a worthwhile purpose, at least in principle."[9] Oddly enough, it may be precisely this sense of mission, this sense of being a "thin blue line" pitted against forces of anarchy and disorder, against an unruly and dangerous underclass, that can account for the most shocking abuses of police power.

The Police Role

A by now sizable number of observers of police have made strikingly similar commentaries about the police role and how it shapes its occupants. Forty years ago Colin MacInnes, a British suspense novelist and student of police, portrayed police as neither the courteous, charming English "bobbies" so often portrayed in the British cinema nor as the equally distorted opposite fantasy, the devil-may-care-adventurer. Instead, MacInnes depicted the cop as an

8. Mark Baker, *Cops: Their Lives in Their Own Words* (New York: Fawcett. 1985), p. 211.
9. Reiner, *Politics of Police*, p. 88.

utterly conventional character, averse to risk, who above all prefers a predictable and orderly world. "The true copper's dominant characteristic, if the truth be known," he wrote, "is neither those daring nor vicious qualities that are sometimes attributed to him by friend or enemy, but an ingrained conservatism, an almost desperate love of the conventional. It is untidiness, disorder, the unusual, that a copper disapproves of most of all; more, even, than of crime which is merely a professional matter."[10]

These preferences are understandable, even inevitable. Consider that the world inhabited by cops is unkempt, unpredictable, and sometimes violent. Statistics suggest that the risk of physical injury is greater in many lines of industrial work than in policing,[11] but cops are the ones to whom society accords the right to use, or to threaten to use, force. This assignment and the capacity to carry it out are said to be *the* central feature of the role of police in society. "Whatever the substance of the task at hand," the sociologist Egon Bittner writes, "whether it involves protection against an undesired imposition, caring for those who cannot care for themselves, attempting to solve a crime, helping to save a life, abating a nuisance, or settling an explosive dispute, police intervention means above all making use of the capacity and authority to overpower resistance."[12] Bittner is well aware that police may not use force so very often. But he concludes: "There can be no doubt that this feature of police work is uppermost in the minds of people who solicit police aid or direct the attention of police to problems." It is also in the minds of police, and its potential hazards, however statistically remote, are never far away in the everyday life of the cop.

"You never know what's going to happen," one cop told Connie Fletcher, who interviewed more than a hundred. "The whole world can come to an end in your last few minutes of duty, right before you leave your watch. Or—right before you retire from the force. We've had cases of police officers working their last tour before

10. Colin MacInnes, *Mr. Love and Justice* (London: New English Library, 1962), p. 74.

11. See, for example, H. J. Caudill, "Manslaughter in a Coal Mine," *The Nation*, 224 (April 23, 1977): 492–97, and C. Gersuny, *Work Hazards and Industrial Conflict* (Hanover, NH: University Press of New England, 1981).

12. Egon Bittner, *The Functions of the Police in Modern Society* (Cambridge, MA: Oelgeschlager, Gunn & Hain, 1970), p. 40.

going on pension. And they've run into a situation where they're killed."[13]

Every arrest, every handcuffing, involves an imposition of force on an essentially unwilling person, no matter how compliant. The volatility of even routine police field investigations—as well as the degree to which they dehumanize their subjects—is made plain by Jonathan Rubinstein:

> [The patrol officer] may not only circumscribe a person's liberty by stopping him on the street, he may also completely violate the suspect's privacy and autonomy by running his hands over the man's entire body. The policeman knows that a frisk is a humiliation people usually accept from him because he can sustain his authority by almost any action he feels necessary. While he does not frisk people often just to humble them, he can do so; when he feels obliged to check someone for a concealed weapon, he is not usually in a position to request their permission, even if this were desirable.[14]

Understandably, police prefer to encounter citizens who appear stable, well-dressed, normal, and unthreatening enough not to warrant a field patdown. But precisely because they are society's designated force-appliers, police often encounter those who are unstable, ill-dressed, pugnacious, and threatening.

Students of police have frequently remarked upon the *machismo* qualities of the police culture. The typical police recruit is chronologically and temperamentally young, male, and athletic. Recruits often lift weights—like football players—so as to offer a more formidable appearance on the street. They are trained in self-defense. They are trained to handle a variety of offensive weapons, including deadly ones. They are taught how to disable and kill people with their bare hands. No matter how many warnings may be issued by superiors about limitations on the use of force, no matter how much talk about policing as a profession, police training continually reminds recruits that coercive power is a central feature of police life.

---

13. Connie Fletcher, *What Cops Know: Cops Talk About What They Do, How They Do It, and What It Does to Them* (New York: Villard, 1991), p. 47.

14. Jonathan Rubinstein, *City Police* (New York: Farrar, Straus & Giroux, 1973), p. 271.

The Paradoxes of Coercive Power

The informal norms that cops develop on the street are, at least in part, a paradox noted by William Ker Muir: "The nastier one's reputation, the less nasty one has to be"; in other words, *the stronger one's reputation for being mean, tough, and aggressive, the less iron-handed one actually has to be.*[15] Cops and everyone else understand the reality of this paradox. And whether or not they actually articulate it, cops develop styles of policing in response to it. One style . . . was used by Southern police to keep the African-American population in a subordinate position. The cops made clear how nasty and brutal they could be. As a result, the Southern black population was, by and large, compliant to the rules of caste subordination.

Nevertheless, when police rely on coercive power to control a population, they may not be successful. The Southern police of the 1930s were agents of the power elite, and those who might have opposed them were virtually powerless. That is no longer true even in the South, and it is certainly not true in Northern cities. However much racist opinions may be expressed in private, the caste society of the Southern United States of the 1930s, a society of legal segregation of the races, is no longer acceptable to the wider society. Our laws will not tolerate explicit racism. Nor can police publicly resort to coercive power without eliciting criticism from portions of the citizenry and the public, and from higher police and public officials. They may also subject themselves to criminal and civil liability.

Furthermore, even when iron-handed law enforcement proves effective in general, it also invites retaliation by those who are *not* intimidated by it. Abusive police must then raise the force ante, employing ever more severe violence to continue to seem formidable. This, for Muir, generates a competing paradox: *Police who rely on coercive force to make the world a less threatening place make it more dangerous place for themselves and for other cops.* Those who are being policed do not distinguish among blue uniforms. All cops

15. William Ker Muir, Jr., *Police: Streetcorner Politicians* (Chicago: University of Chicago Press, 1977), pp. 101–26.

come to be defined as brutal, and thus appropriate targets for retaliation. Hated cops are not safer cops.

William Ker Muir was the first police scholar to call attention to the paradoxes of coercive power. He saw how police who are gifted with maturity, empathy, and interpersonal skills could escape from the trap of relying on the threat of force. As he had seen in his observations of police, some accomplished cops could intuit how to handle even the most difficult and potentially explosive situations. He believed that appropriate "training and enhanced language skills" could diminish police violence.[16] . . .

In connection with the need to use force, police and their culture are a complex and often contradictory combination of cautious values and risky undertakings. Mark Baker, who unscientifically, but convincingly, interviewed more than a hundred cops for his book on police and their lives, concludes that police lean to the right politically and morally. "They advocate the straight and narrow path to right living," he writes. "They believe in the inviolability of the marriage vows, the importance of the family, the necessity of capital punishment." In this, cops are in tune with the constituency that elected Ronald Reagan and George Bush to be President of the United States, that most politically conservative portion of the majority of Americans whom Anthony Bouza calls "the overclass."

The occupational vision of police and its culture is grounded in these beliefs. But cops do not necessarily abide by the apple-pie-and-motherhood values that they assert. As with most human beings, spoken values are often an aspiration, not necessarily something to embody. At least half the married male police officers whom Baker interviewed told him about their girlfriends and mistresses. After a few years on the job the cops interviewed developed a distinctive, but scarcely exemplary, hierarchy of wrongfulness: "dead wrong, wrong but not bad, wrong but everybody does it."[17] Skepticism, cynicism, mistrust—all are words observers of police apply to them and that they apply to themselves, especially after years on the job.

---

16. William Ker Muir, Jr., "Power Attracts Violence," *Annals of the American Academy of Political and Social Science*, 452 (November 1980): 48.

17. Baker, *Cops*, pp. 6–7.

Suspicion and skepticism are especially congruent with the capacity to use force and enforce the laws. We all make distinctions between the normal and the abnormal, the safe and the unsafe, the appropriate and the inappropriate. Police are, however, specially trained and required to make these interpretations. The distinction between what is "normal" and what is threatening or "abnormal" usually depends upon the context in which it appears. Is a man with a gun in a bank "abnormal"? That depends. The possession of a deadly weapon is appropriate for a bank security guard, but not for an armed robber. Similarly, we expect to see an electric light switched on to illuminate a room at night. But if the room is in a warehouse, and it is two in the morning, the policeman must understand whether the lighted room signifies that someone is, as usual, working late, or whether the warehouse is being burglarized. We want police to draw such distinctions and to act upon them.

Complaints about police conduct do not usually arise because police are apprehending burglars in the middle of the night, or robbers who are holding up a bank. Trouble arises out of social interactions, especially when cops encounter people who may not be engaging in criminal activity, but whose conduct suggests that they might be, or might be the sort of people who would if they could. A police manual cautions police to attend to the unusual, listing among the persons and conditions for which to be especially watchful and cautious: "suspicious persons known to the officer from previous arrests, field interrogations, and observations"; "persons who loiter about places where children play"; "known troublemakers near large gatherings"; and "cars with mismatched hub caps, or dirty cars with clean license plates (or vice versa)." Years ago, in our studies of police, one of us observed that because police work requires cops continuously to be alert, they become much attuned to deviations from the normal, especially those suggestive of potential violence. As a necessity and a consequence of maintaining this high state of readiness, police develop a perceptual shorthand to identify certain kinds of people as "symbolic assailants," that is, as persons whose gestures, language, or attire the police have come to identify as being potentially threatening or dangerous. This sort of apprehension and sensitivity sets police apart and tends to isolate them from those whom they are policing. Such isolation may be especially pronounced when police are patrolling in vehicles, rather than on foot, since the vehicle segregates the police from the people who are being policed. Well before community and problem-oriented policing became as acceptable as it has become in some police circles, the 1967 Civil Disorder Commission advised patrolmen to get out of their cars, into the neighborhoods, and on the same beat or assignment long enough to know the people and the neighborhood's prevailing conditions.

But even when police know the people with whom they are dealing, they still must distinguish the known from the unknown or unfamiliar. How much latitude police enjoy in making such distinctions and acting upon them has been a continuing issue in the constitutional law of search and seizure. When police do not have grounds for an arrest, do they have the right to stop and question suspects without their consent? . . .

Imagine standing up to armed police. . . . Most of us learn early to respect the authority of a police officer, and that it is impolitic for a citizen to challenge that authority. When he or she does, especially when he does, he may find himself occupying Van Maanen's . . . most evocative category, that of "the asshole," that is, a person who denies, resists, or questions the authority of the police. The following story, offered by Van Maanen, exemplifies the category: A cop stops a motorist for speeding and politely asks for license and registration. "Why the hell are you picking on me," says the motorist, "and not somewhere else looking for real criminals?"

"Cause you're an asshole," replies the policeman. "But I didn't know that until you opened your mouth."

Paul Chevigny similarly explains the origins of much police brutality in *Police Power,* his classic study of police abuses in New York City in the 1960s.[18] Following an extensive two-year study of complaints against police, Chevigny identified as "the one truly iron and inflexible rule" he could deduce from the cases he reviewed was this: "any person who defies the police risks the imposition of legal sanctions, commencing with a summons, on up to the use of firearms."[19]

Chevigny goes on to describe a three-step process leading to excessive force. Step One involves a perception by police of a chal-

---

18. Paul Chevigny, *Police Power: Police Abuses in New York City* (New York: Vintage, 1969).
19. Ibid., p. 136.

lenge to authority. Those who take the police on high-speed chases are, of course, among the most extremely confrontational. But Chevigny reports instances of much lesser defiance, such as merely questioning an officer. Such a person, in the New York of the 1960s, was called a "wise guy," a term that seems in retrospect antiquated and mild but conveys the appropriate connotation. The speaker is thought by the police officer to be presenting himself as superior to the cop. In the parlance of the police studied by Van Maanen, he is said to be an "asshole, creep or bigmouth," or any number of other dismissive names used by cops to describe a person who resists police authority."[20]

In Step Two, when police have so defined the malefactor, as in, "So you're a wise guy," an arrest, according to Chevigny's respondents, would almost invariably follow.

Whether it did or not depended on the offender's response (Step Three). If the citizen admitted that he was, in fact, a wise guy, or turned polite and complied with the officer's request, he was usually released. If he persisted in defying police authority, an arrest would typically follow. If he further persisted, he would be taught a lesson of compliance by being beaten, and then charged with resisting arrest, in addition to the original charge.

Albert Reiss, Jr., who with Donald Black conducted a systematic observational study of police coercion for the President's Commission on Law Enforcement and Administration of Justice, reported that, of the incidents of excessive force recorded by observers, nearly half occurred when the victims verbally defied police authority. The authority that was defied was not "official" but the personal authority of the individual officer. Reiss was surprised to find that in 40 percent of the cases of what the police considered open defiance, the police never executed an arrest, nor did they file charges of resisting arrest to "cover" their improper use of force. Reiss inquired further into what police interpreted as defiance. "Often he seems threatened," Reiss observed, "by a simple refusal to acquiesce to his own authority. A policeman beat a handcuffed offender because, when told to sit, the offender did not sit down. One Negro woman was soundly

20. John Van Maanen, "The Asshole," in Peter K. Manning and John Van Maanen, eds., *Policing: A View from the Street*, pp. 221–37 (Santa Monica, CA: Goodyear Publishing, 1978).

slapped for her refusal to approach the police car and identify herself."[21]

Recently, one of us was riding alongside a patrol officer in a Midwestern city. The officer saw a young white woman seated behind the driver's seat of a car parked in the area of a predominantly black housing project noted for drug dealing. Since the cop suspected that the woman was picking up drugs, the officer waited until she left, determined to stop her for something, anything, such as running a red light, so he could search her car. He noted that one of the taillights on her car was slightly damaged and stopped her for that. He checked out the car on his computer and discovered that the owner, her boyfriend, had failed to pay three parking tickets.

The officer asked to search the car, and she reluctantly consented, clearly unaware of what rights she had, if any. He found no drugs, and she denied ever using or selling them. She did act annoyed, talked back to the officer, and complained that she was being harassed. In return for her seeming insolence, the officer committed no act of brutality but had the car towed, arrested her for a traffic violation, and booked her at the police precinct. In reality, she had committed two police cultural crimes: She was a white driver in a black neighborhood where drugs were sold, and she had challenged the authority of the officer, a serious transgression in the police cultural statute book, where it is an offense to talk back to a cop.

Chevigny was sensitive in his three-step paradigm to two other important considerations. First, an ordinary citizen begins to assume the status of a pariah only when actively defying the police, while an outcast group member may be presumed to be a potential offender. Consequently, when such a person is arrested, the arrest can be considered the ethical, if not the legal, equivalent of arresting a criminal. The arrest can be justified on grounds that even if the outcast has not committed a crime this time, he has been guilty many times in the past.

Second, Chevigny notes that it also may be more difficult for members of minority groups to show the submissive qualities middle-class people learn to use when dealing with authorities.

21. Albert J. Reiss, Jr., "Police Brutality: Answers to Key Questions," *Trans-Action*, July–August, 1968, p. 12.

He further observes that the words "Sorry, Officer" often feel like galling words of submission to the downtrodden and are especially hard for African-Americans to say. "The combination of being an outcast (step one)," he writes, "and refusing to comply in step three is explosive; thereby hangs the tale of many police brutality cases."[22]

The Underclass

Chevigny's is a book of the 1960s and reflects the deep social divisions of those troubled and turbulent years. The economic and social conditions of America's inner-city ghettos have cruelly worsened in the intervening years. "The urban black poor of today," Wacquant and Wilson wrote in 1989, "differ both from their counterparts of earlier years and from the white poor in that they are becoming increasingly concentrated in dilapidated territorial enclaves that epitomize acute social and economic marginalization." This "hyperghettoization" has brought in its wake a tangle of unfathomed social miseries, including crime, drug use and sale, high rates of unemployment, high teenage pregnancy rates, the highest homicide rates in American history, and unprecedented homicides and interpersonal violence among young black males. For several years, black-on-black homicides have been the leading cause of death for young black males.[23] . . .

Cops usually resonate to what they see happening in front of them, not to underlying causes or sociological explanations, although many cops are surprisingly sensitive to these. Yet, no matter how discerning, when doing their policing job cops do not interpret *why* someone is mugging, raping, or selling drugs on the street, just that they are doing it or are threatening to do it. If cultural beliefs shape the working personalities of police, as we have argued they do, the cop, like the majority of Americans, is unlikely to define the street drug dealer as a victim of inequality, structural

22. Chevigny, *Police Power*, p. 138.

23. Centers for Disease Control, "Homicide Among Young Black Males: United States, 1978–1987," *Morbidity and Mortality Weekly Report*, vol. 39 (December 7, 1990); Jewell Taylor Gibbs, *Young, Black and Male in America: An Endangered Species* (Dover, MA: Auburn House, 1988), pp. 260–65.

unemployment, and exploitation. What the cop perceives is a bad and dangerous person who preys on the *deserving* poor and exacerbates the social conditions found in the inner cities. Such preconceptions profoundly influence police behavior, especially their use of force.

Still, problems of excessive force rarely arise when police address actual crime and criminals. A clean, straightforward apprehension of a robber or of a drug dealer who has been busted following an undercover police officer's "buy" is rarely an occasion for exercising excessive force. Abuses occur when police develop two visions of their work that are often a prelude to excessive force. One is described by the Christopher Commission as a "siege mentality."[24] The other is "the Dirty Harry" vision, which rationalizes vigilante justice.

The Siege Mentality

In the course of its investigation, the Christopher Commission, the 1991 blue-ribbon commission headed by Warren Christopher to investigate the LAPD following the Rodney King beating, found general agreement among all sources, from senior and rank-and-file police to the general public, that the LAPD reflected an organizational culture, based on its time-honored notion of "professionalism," that "emphasized crime control over crime prevention and isolated the police from the communities and the people they serve."[25] This organizational culture insisted on both the aggressive detection of such major crimes as murder, burglary, and auto theft and a rapid response to calls for service. Officers were rewarded for the number of calls they handled and arrests they made, as well as for being "hardnosed." As a result, the LAPD consistently outperformed other big-city police departments in the number of violent crime arrests per officer, but at the risk of creating what the Commission calls a "siege" (us–them) mentality that alienates the

24. Warren Christopher et al., *Report of the Independent Commission on the Los Angeles Police Department*, July 9, 1991, p. 95.
25. Ibid., p. 98.

officer from the community. Obviously, not every police depart-ment encourages a siege mentality. But the Los Angeles Police Department's policing style for many years served nationally as an important model of police professionalism. Consequently, its vision of hardnosed and impersonal policing influenced the train-ing of thousands of American cops—so much so that its vision and values became entrenched as an element of traditional police culture.

The Dirty Harry Problem

The Dirty Harry dilemma was so named by the sociologist Carl B. Klockars, who drew its name from a 1971 Warner Brothers film. "Dirty Harry" Callahan, played by Clint Eastwood, is on the trail of a psychopathic killer who has kidnapped a fourteen-year-old girl and buried her with just enough oxygen to keep her alive for several hours. Harry meets the kidnapper with the ransom. The kidnapper reneges on his bargain, wounds Harry's partner, and escapes. Harry manages to track him down, illegally searches his apartment, finds guns and other evidence of his guilt, and captures the kidnapper on a football field. He shoots the kidnapper in the leg and tortures him, twisting the injured leg, into revealing where the girl has been hidden. Unfortunately, she is already dead, and the killer must be set free because none of the evidence—the gun, the confession—was legally obtained.

Released in 1971, *Dirty Harry* could properly be interpreted as a right-wing attack on "legal technicalities." But, as Klockars astutely saw, it also raises a fundamental problem constantly confronting police, namely, "When and to what extent does the morally good end warrant or justify an ethically, politically, or legally dangerous means for its achievement?"

The Dirty Harry dilemma faces every cop in the course of his or her career, and its ultimate resolution is always problematic and subject to hindsight criticism. Extralegal resolution of the Dirty Harry dilemma is difficult enough when the "bad guy" is an identi-fiable and factually guilty individual. It is most problematic when the criminal is not an individual but a loosely defined gang or criminal organization, where the consequences of a mistake can be tragic for innocent individuals or bystanders, and where a gut-level racism can be imputed to the officers involved. . . .

The Code of Silence

We have both heard comments that, in near mystical terms, describe or speculate about a highly conspiratorial police code of silence. Those who propound this theory assert that, like gangsters who understand that death is the penalty for violations of *omerta*–the Mafia rule of absolute secrecy–police officers risk their lives when they violate their brotherhood's unwritten regulations. . . .

. . . Although it probably has occurred at some point in American police history, we know of no . . . cases in which police have punished those who betrayed the code of silence with anything as extreme as a shooting. Instead, the code–and there is a code–typically is enforced by the threat of shunning, by fear that *informing* will lead to exposure of one's own derelictions, and by fear that colleagues' assistance may be withheld in emergencies.

In our experience, this last incentive to silence–denial of help in street emergencies–is more often imagined than real. Officers who by their own admission "do not see eye-to-eye" with their work groups frequently complain that colleagues intentionally fail to respond promptly to their calls for urgent assistance. On close examination, however, these complaints usually reflect a variety of paranoia that itself accounts for these officers' unpopularity among their peers. In other words, some officers perceive situations as more threatening than they are (or, through bungling, make them worse than they began), call urgently for help, and draw the rapid response of colleagues who arrive and can't figure out what all the fuss was. After a few such incidents, such officers' credibility is damaged, and their colleagues come to regard their calls for help like that of the boy who cried wolf too often.

The first two disincentives to violating the code of silence–shunning and exposure of one's own derelictions–are real. . . . For now, having claimed that the police code of silence is not a mafia-style life-or-death pact with the devil, we shall confine ourselves to some observations about what the police code of silence is.

Most important, a code of silence is not unique to the police. In every identifiable group, there exists an unspoken understanding that one reports on members' misconduct only at some risk. The sociologist and police scholar Albert J. Reiss, Jr., has suggested that even his Yale University students share such a set of understandings.[26] In the pressure cooker of elite academic institutions, Reiss points out, students sometimes are tempted to cheat to maintain the grades necessary for a big job or a slot at a prestigious professional or graduate school. On occasion, other students become aware of such cheating but, despite academic codes of honor, rarely will call their peers' misconduct to official attention.

In our own university discussions of the code of silence, we regularly ask for students who have become aware of classmates' cheating at some point in their educational careers to raise their hands. Invariably, almost every hand in the class is raised. When we ask for only those who have called such cheating to teachers' attention and have been willing to be publicly identified as accusers, virtually every raised hand is lowered.

The point, of course, is that it is not easy in any group to be identified as the *rat,* the *squealer,* the *busybody,* the one person who cannot be trusted absolutely. Doctors rarely expose the incompetence of their colleagues, even though, as the great frequency and size of medical malpractice verdicts suggests, it certainly must come to their attention. College athletes don't usually talk about alumni boosters' under-the-table payments to superstars, and office workers do not inform on co-workers who take supplies home. Similarly, real estate agents and banks remain mum about de facto discrimination and redlining in apartment rentals and mortgage lending. Regardless of where, any member of any group who considers becoming a *whistle-blower* must know that, however laudable one's motives, doing so will forever change one's own life and status in the group.

In the closed society of police departments, especially in departments or units that see themselves and the public in terms of "us

26. Albert J. Reiss, Jr., interview with James J. Fyfe, June 6, 1992.

and them" and adopt the siege view of the world, the pressure to remain loyal is enormous. In such societies, there is no need for violent means of enforcing the code, because, having subsumed their individual identities into the whole, cops know that betraying the group betrays themselves and destroys their identities. . . .

The code of silence, then, is not one that is enforced by assassins lurking in dark alleys or arranging for drug dealers to terminate cops who inform. The police code of silence is an extreme version of a phenomenon that exists in all human groups. It is exaggerated in some police departments and some police units because cops so closely identify with their departments, their units, and their colleagues that they cannot even conceive of doing anything else. . . . They live in a world of desperately conflicting imperatives, where norms of loyalty wash up against standards of law and order. So mostly, like the cops who witnessed the beating of Rodney King, they see, hear, and speak no evil.

IV
Reactions

Preview of the Readings

Before any audience will define a given governmental or corporate act as deviant, many individuals and groups must become participants. At the outset, some people may become whistle-blowers and call attention to the act, while others who took part may publicly defend what they did. The media may highlight, ignore, or explain the act in various ways, and accused organizations may try a cover-up or wage a war of attrition in the courts. The readings in this section examine such reactions to corporate and governmental deviance.

Selection 12, "Ten Whistleblowers" by Professor Myron Glazer, examines the experiences of people who went public with evidence of their organizations' wrongdoing. He tells us why these people blew the whistle and shows how personal and occupational consequences unfold for these whistle-blowers. Although publicly exposing deviant organizational acts is difficult and allows no going back, Professor Glazer notes that it is not the end of the road for the careers of many of the people who tell the rest of us about deviance by large organizations.

Selection 13, "Rely Tampons and Toxic Shock Syndrome," traces how Procter & Gamble responded to news about a tampon for which the company had great plans. Although P&G was widely praised for voluntarily withdrawing Rely from the market, Alecia Swasy demonstrates that the company actually dragged its feet and that the delays caused injuries and deaths.

Selection 14, "Chained Factory Fire Exits," examines newspaper coverage of a chicken-processing plant fire that killed 25 workers and injured 56 others. The authors evaluate the changing ways a cross section of the nation's major newspapers explained the tragedy, with a special focus on the failure to clearly communicate that what happened was manslaughter.

Selection 15, Craig Calhoun and Henryk Hiller's paper "Asbestos Exposure by Johns-Manville," explores varied reactions to a major corporation knowingly exposing millions of people to deadly asbestos dust. The authors recount discovery of the problem in the early 1900s, Johns-Manville's efforts to cover problems up in the 1960s, an explosion of litigation starting in the 1970s, and the company's bankruptcy and name change (to Manville Corporation) in 1982. They conclude by arguing that we must leave the "deep pockets" of large corporations intact, so that victims can receive adequate compensation.

Annotated Bibliography

Baker, Wayne E., and Robert F. Faulkner. "The Social Organization of Conspiracy: Illegal Networks in the Heavy Electrical Equipment Industry." *American Sociological Review* 58 (1993): 837–60. Quantitative analysis of the networks in the illegal price-fixing case described in Selection 5.

Braithwaite, John. *To Punish or Persuade: Enforcement of Coal Mine Safety.* Albany: State University of New York Press, 1985. Offers data and arguments that efforts to persuade and educate usually reduce violations and increase safety more effectively than efforts to punish.

Ermann, M. David, and William H. Clements II. "The Interfaith Center on Corporate Responsibility." *Social Problems* 32 (1984): 185–96. The deviance-defining process as illustrated by a church group's effective campaign against the marketing of infant formula in the developing world.

Fisse, Brent, and John Braithwaite. *The Impact of Publicity on Corporate Offenders.* Albany: State University of New York Press, 1983. What happens when corporations are caught in the unwelcome glare of negative publicity.

Grabosky, P. N., J. B. Braithwaite, and P. R. Wilson. "The Myth of Community Tolerance Toward White-Collar Crime." *Australian and New Zealand Journal of Criminology* 20 (1987): 33–41. Clear evidence from both Australia and the United States that members of the general public view white-collar crime as more serious and more deserving of serious punishment than most ordinary crimes.

Landy, Marc K., Marc J. Roberts, and Stephen R. Thomas. *The Environmental Protection Agency: Asking the Wrong Questions.* New York: Oxford University Press, 1990. A history of the EPA, with special attention to major issues and cases.

Macey, Jonathan R. "Agency Theory and the Criminal Liability of Organizations." *Boston University Law Review* 58 (1993): 315–40. Legal review of Sentencing Commission guidelines for corporations in light of some theories of organizational behavior.

Magnuson, Jay C., and Gareth C. Leviton. "Policy Considerations in Corporate Criminal Prosecutions After People v. Film Recovery Systems, Inc." *Notre Dame Law Review* 62 (1987): 913–39. Review of the impact of an important and well-publicized case.

Mann, Kenneth. *Defending White-Collar Crime: A Portrait of Attorneys at Work.* New Haven, Conn.: Yale University Press, 1985. How white-collar crime specialists defend clients by helping them control information flows to prosecutors.

Mokhiber, Russell. *Corporate Crime and Violence: Big Business Power and the Abuse of the Public Trust.* San Francisco: Sierra Club Books, 1988. Thirty-six clearly written case summaries and more than 50 suggestions for reform and control.

Scott, Wilbur J. "Competing Paradigms in the Assessment of Latent Disorders: The Case of Agent Orange." *Social Problems* 35 (1988): 145–61. A description and analysis of the deviance-defining process as it applies to the effects of the herbicide Agent Orange.

Seymour, Sally. "The Case of the Willful Whistle-Blower." *Harvard Business Review* (1988): 103–6. A case-study teaching tool about a long-buried design flaw, an employee who went public with evidence of the defect, and the personal and organizational consequences of that employee's action.

Sherman, Lawrence W. *Scandal and Reform: Controlling Police Corruption.* Berkeley: University of California Press, 1978. The healing power of scandal in the context of police corruption.

Szasz, Andrew. "The Process and Significance of Political Scandals: A Comparison of Watergate and the 'Sewergate' Episode at the Environmental Protection Agency." *Social Problems* 33 (1986): 202–17. Asserts that most political scandals are like professional wrestling because "political bodies fly through the air, mete out incredible punishments, and crash noisily to the canvas" with no lasting consequences.

Vaughan, Diane. *Controlling Unlawful Organizational Behavior: Social Structure and Corporate Misconduct.* Chicago: University of Chicago Press, 1983. Control of an episode of corporate deviance.

Wheeler, Stanton, Kenneth Mann, and Austin Sarat. *Sitting in Judgment: The Sentencing of White-Collar Criminals.* New Haven, Conn.: Yale University Press, 1988. Factors shaping the sentencing of white-collar criminals.

Winters, Paul A. (ed.). *Policing the Police.* San Diego: Greenhaven Press, 1995. Overview of efforts and ideas to control and reform deviant police organizations.

Yeager, Peter. *The Limits of Law.* Cambridge: Cambridge University Press, 1991. Thorough study of water pollution, legislation, and legal liability.

12
Ten Whistleblowers
What They Did and How They Fared
Myron Peretz Glazer

In 1959, Frank Serpico joined the New York City police force. For Serpico, the police had always represented the meshing of authority and service. His early days on the force propelled him into the conflict between the norms governing police behavior set by department regulations and the actual "code" generated by the police. Formal regulations precluded the taking of any items from neighborhood stores and sanctioned the acceptance of bribes. In the station house and out on patrol a different set of rules applied. "Shopping" for items of food at local stores was clearly acceptable and taking money to pardon a lawbreaker became standard fare. Serpico was caught in a dilemma that faces many rookie police. Which set of norms should he uphold?[1]

Like many other whistleblowers in industry, government, and the academic world, initially Serpico was caught between his desire to follow his moral beliefs and the organizational pressures to conform. How do workers handle such a conflict? And what happens to their personal lives and their careers once they have blown the whistle? In an effort to understand the dynamics of the process, I have interviewed or exchanged letters with nine prominent whistleblowers and have corresponded with the wife of a tenth, who

From "Ten Whistleblowers and How They Fared," *The Hastings Center Report,* December 1983, pp. 33–41. Copyright © 1983 by The Hastings Center. Reprinted by permission.

1. Peter Maas, *Serpico* (New York: The Viking Press, 1973). For a participant observation account of police training, see Richard Harris, *The Police Academy: An Inside View* (New York: John Wiley, 1973). Other studies of the police support Serpico's experiences and observations. See Lawrence W. Sherman, *Police Corruption* (New York: Anchor, 1974).

is deceased.[2] Their cases portray three distinct paths through which individuals move toward public disclosure:

Unbending resisters protest within the organization about unethical or illegal behavior that they have observed. They maintain a strict commitment to their principles, despite efforts to cajole or coerce them. Ultimately, as a consequence of neglect and retaliation within the organization, they take a public stand.

Implicated protesters speak out within their organizations, but acquiesce when they are ordered to conform. They find themselves drawn into illegal or unethical behavior, which they expose when they fear legal liability.

Reluctant collaborators become deeply involved in acts they privately condemn. They seek public remedy and personal expiation only when they leave the organization.

Once an employee has blown the whistle, the responses of his or her superiors can take two broad forms. There are "degradation ceremonies" to punish and alienate resisters and protesters, and "ceremonies of status elevation," which reinforce the whistleblower's feeling that what he or she is doing is right. Whether and when someone will blow the whistle will depend on the peculiar mixture of sustenance and punishment, as well as the person's courage and the circumstances of his or her life. My observations also reveal that the whistleblower's fate need not be grim.

Blowing the Whistle

Like Serpico, Bob Leuci, the protagonist of *The Prince of the City*, was also caught in a net of conflicting loyalties. He has aptly de-

---

2. In those instances where the whistleblowers lived beyond driving distance, I exchanged letters with them and did a lengthy, taped, telephone interview during the summer of 1982. Unless otherwise noted all quoted material is from the interviews or letters. Since I was interested in the whistleblowers' perceptions of their experience, I did not interview other people involved in the cases. The material on Frank Serpico derives from published sources.

Three of the whistleblowers discussed in this article—Joseph Rose, Grace Pierce, and Frank Camps—also described their experiences in Alan Westin, ed. *Whistle Blowing? Loyalty and Dissent in the Corporation* (New York: McGraw-Hill, 1981).

For a study that reports on 51 cases of whistleblowers, see Lea P. Stuart, "'Whistle Blowing' Implications for Organizational Communication," *Journal of Communication* 30:4 (Autumn 1980), 90–101. For an intensive case study, read Robert M. Anderson, Robert Perrucci, Dan D. Schendel, and Leon E. Tractman, *Divided Loyalties: Whistle-Blowing at BART* (West Lafayette, Ind.: Purdue University, 1980).

scribed to me the "erosion process" by which young police officers
became "bent":

> I remember the first time I was in a situation that scared me. We
> were in a police car and there was a fight in the street. I was work-
> ing with this big, strong guy. I was nervous when I got out of the
> car and approached the fight. "Am I good enough to handle this
> kind of thing?" Two guys were going at each other with knives. I
> backed off a bit, but one guy came at me. My partner pushed me
> aside. "You move toward my partner again, and I'll kill you." And
> all of a sudden I got this feeling. He didn't say "You move toward
> me," but he said, "You move toward my partner." Whether he would
> have killed this guy or not, had the guy come at him, I don't know.
> But he would have killed him if the guy came at me. When hearing
> that, in that sort of context, you have this feeling of something very,
> very special about working with someone when your life may be in
> danger. So I was with a guy who was fifteen years my senior and a
> wonderful policeman. The first time he went in to get dinner, and
> came out with a sandwich I asked, "Did you pay for it?" He answered,
> "No, it's okay." It was in fact okay coming from him. It *was* okay.
> This man would not do anything wrong; he would not do anything
> criminal certainly, and what was so terrible about this? But what
> happens is that emotionally things are going on that you don't
> realize. There is an erosion process that is taking place, and it is
> changing you. That is something that I certainly didn't notice for
> many years. But it was happening to me—happening to a lot of
> people around me.[3]

Serpico felt similar pulls of loyalty born of comparable experiences. Yet he began to drift from the others on the force as he
tired of the endless shoptalk. In a search for outside interests he
took courses for a degree in sociology and moved to Greenwich
Village where he spent time with aspiring women artists and danc-
ers. Serpico's disenchantment peaked when, as a plainclothes officer,
he accidentally received a $300 payoff, which he immediately took
to one of the top men in the New York City Department of Investigation. The captain told Serpico that he could go before the grand
jury, but that word would get out that he had been the chief witness and he might end "face down in the East River." Or, the captain continued, Serpico could forget the whole thing.

3. Bob Leuci's experiences are recounted by Robert Daly, *Prince of the City* (Boston: Houghton
Mifflin, 1978). This statement is taken from a class visit to Smith College, March 12, 1981.
Since then, I have had numerous other discussions with Leuci.

This is a crucial decision for the whistleblower. The organization counts on the threat of punishment to exercise control. But this can often backfire. Serpico's alienation toward the police force intensified. He felt powerless to require others to live up to their responsibilities. Doubting his own belief in the honesty of his comrades and leaders and knowing that serious rule-breaking was endemic at all levels of the department, he felt increasingly isolated from those whose trust was essential for his survival. He refused, however, to complete the cycle of self-alienation by turning his back on his own beliefs of proper police conduct. Serpico resisted the temptation to go along with the group, even though the pressure increased markedly when he transferred to the South Bronx with assurances by high-level police officials that it was free of corruption.

The combination of blatant police wrongdoing and the extreme poverty of the neighborhood aggravated his dilemma. In desperation, he bluffed to a superior that he had gone to "outside sources" about police payoffs. This threat generated an investigation and eight of his peers were eventually tried. But no higher-ups were indicted, despite promises from the district attorney. Ostracized by most police after testifying and feeling increasingly vulnerable, Serpico convinced his immediate superior to accompany him to the *New York Times*. This led to a series of front-page articles on police corruption and ultimately to the establishment of the Knapp Commission. Its lengthy, independent investigation verified all of Serpico's charges and led to important changes in the New York City Police Department. Serpico would leave his mark.[4]

Several months later, Serpico was shot and seriously wounded during a drug raid. Had he been set up by his comrades? He retired, received a pension, and left the country for a time. Serpico still maintains that a principled officer must resist. Serpico reappeared in 1981 and reported on a television news program that he was writing a book. Since Serpico's experiences, another police officer, detective Robert Ellis, has assisted investigators in the apprehension of corrupt fellow police. He reports the difficulty of his activities and the subsequent threats made upon his wife and daughter. "I don't want my friends in other commands to think that for eight years

4. David Burnham, "Graft Paid to Police Said to Run into Millions, *New York Times*, April 25, 1970. New York City, *The Knapp Commission Report on Police Corruption* (New York: George Braziller, 1973).

they were dealing with a spy," he said. "I want it simply to be said that I am an honest cop" (*New York Times,* July 3, 1977, p. 1).

The experience of other unbending resisters shows similar links between initial protest, retaliation against the whistleblower from one's superiors, and a continuing search for affirmation of professional ideals. In 1973 Joseph Rose, an experienced lawyer, joined the Associated Milk Producers Incorporated (AMPI) as an in-house attorney. Rose quickly became aware of illegal political payments to the Nixon reelection campaign, which were part of the Watergate investigation. In a phone interview in 1982, he told me:

> My assignment in the corporation included fiduciary responsibilities. When I found out that so much money had gone under the table, I might have been able to take a moral posture of "All right—that's a past offense that I can indeed defend." But the criminal conspiracy was ongoing, and the law concerning criminal conspirators states that you don't have to participate in the original crime to be indicted as a coconspirator later. All you need is to know about it and take steps to cover it up or otherwise further the conspiracy. Second, money was misused. The Watergate televised proceedings had started. An airline retrieved money that it had paid for similar purposes. When that broke, I went to the law books and became convinced of the duty to recover these assets. A whole chain of events led me more and more to believe that the current executives were in very deep themselves. I talked to a lawyer and former judge here in San Antonio named Joe Frazier Brown. He urged me to start keeping notes on everything I did. He also urged me to gather all of the documents that supported my position, to bypass the general manager, and to take the evidence to the board of directors. I was never allowed to do that. My attempt [to talk to the board] happened on a weekend during their convention in Minneapolis. Labor Day followed, and then Tuesday I went into work. I found a guard posted at my door; locks had been changed. The general manager demanded to see me. My services had become very, very unsatisfactory. When I was fired, I felt virtually a sense of relief. I was glad to be out of it, and I planned to keep my mouth shut. Then I had a call from one of the lawyers involved in an antitrust case against AMPI. He said, "They are really slandering you—making some very vicious attacks on you." I had indicated to AMPI executives that if the board would not listen to me, I would go right to the dairy farmers and they obviously felt my career and credibility had to be completely destroyed to protect their own tails. After I was terminated, I had a call both from the Watergate Special Prosecutor's office and from the Congressional Committee's Subcommittee, wanting to know if they could fly down and talk to me. My

answer was absolutely, unequivocally not. They both said they had subpoena power, and I said, "You have it. I suggest you use it if you want to talk to me." Of course, I was subpoenaed, first to Congress and then to Mr. Cox's grand jury.

Unlike Serpico who came forth on his own, Joseph Rose correctly feared he would be charged with breaking attorney-client privilege if he testified voluntarily. For Rose the path to public disclosure had been triggered by a series of events–his refusal to engage in illegal and unethical actions, corporate retaliation, and the government requirement that he testify against his former associates. Afterwards Rose was forced to confront the shame of being disreputable in the eyes of others, for as a result of his testimony he remained underemployed for eight years. Potential employers, who accepted AMPI's explanation that Rose had been disloyal, were unwilling to hire him. His father died believing that his son had irrevocably lost his ability to earn a living. A once-successful attorney and his family were forced to live on food stamps.

Rose's career opportunities began to improve appreciably only after the *Wall Street Journal* publicized his case. In the meantime, the AMPI was found guilty and heavily fined, and two of its officers were convicted and sentenced to prison terms. Its finance officers sought and received immunity from prosecution to testify against others.

Rose now looks at American society with cold cynicism.

> I believe I can make a contribution to the young people in this country by continuing to respond with a strong warning that all of the public utterances of corporations and indeed our own government concerning "courage, integrity, loyalty, honesty, and duty" are nothing but the sheerest hogwash that disappear very rapidly when it comes to the practical application of these concepts by strict definition. The reason that there are very few Serpicos or Roses is that the message is too clearly out in this society that white-collar crime, or nonviolent crime, should be tolerated by the public at large, so long as the conduct brings a profit or a profitable result to the institution committing it. . . .

Public disclosure can also come about in an effort to clear one's personal reputation and establish the legitimacy of professionals to resist what they see as their superiors' unethical directives. Dr. Grace Pierce joined the Ortho Pharmaceutical Corporation, a division of Johnson & Johnson, in 1971 after eleven years in private medical practice, service in the Food and Drug Administration, and experience with another drug firm. In 1975 she was assigned to direct a research team attempting to develop Loperamide, a drug for the relief of acute and chronic diarrhea. The liquid Loperamide formulation originated with Janssen, a Johnson & Johnson company in Belgium, and had a very high saccharin content to hide the bitter taste. Dr. Pierce and all the Ortho team members agreed that there was a need to reformulate the drug to diminish the saccharin concentration, particularly with the ongoing controversy over its carcinogenic potential. While her colleagues ultimately acceded to management pressures to accept the high saccharin formulation, Dr. Pierce refused. As the only medical person on the team, she would not agree to begin clinical trials with what she considered a questionable formulation.

After her refusal, Dr. Pierce charged that her immediate superior questioned her judgment, loyalty, and competence. Later, he accused her of misusing company funds on a research trip and of taking an unauthorized vacation. Although she rejected and refuted the accusations, the critique was a clear signal of her diminished prospects.

> When the situation came up and I couldn't get other people to go along with me, I asked my superior whether we could get three objective consultants outside the company. If they say it's okay, I'll do it. Or if you'll permit me to go to the FDA and put the situation to them openly and they say okay, I'll do it. I think I offered alternatives for a reasonable compromise. He refused. Use of saccharin remains a question yet. Nobody knows where this problem of carcinogens is heading. It probably won't be resolved soon, if ever. I was on the spot. I had to get with it or get out. I hated that. I was cornered. There was no compromise. Nobody from higher up came and said, "Why don't we do that or do this." They were just riding roughshod all over me. I always like to feel I'm a person, not a cog in a machine. . . . One of my colleagues said, "Grace, you're nuts. Why not write a lengthy memo for the files, make sure you're on record. They're responsible." If I do the research, I'm responsible. I feel responsibility as a physician first. My responsibility to the corporation is second. I think my colleagues' attitude is commonplace. People salve their conscience. They keep the benefits of the job. This memo gives them an escape hatch.

Pierce resigned. Unlike Joseph Rose, she was quickly approached by a colleague to affiliate in a group medical practice, which she joined on a part-time basis. Later the vice president of Personal Products, another subsidiary of Johnson & Johnson, invited her to join his research staff although she alerted him that she might sue Ortho. Within six months she had become director of research. While Dr. Pierce felt vindicated of charges against her integrity and competence, her work situation changed dramatically when she actually filed her suit for "damage to her professional reputation, dissipation of her career, loss of salary, as well as seniority and retirement benefits."[5]

Despite their excellent relationship, the vice president's attitude cooled. Not unexpectedly, he summoned her at the end of one work day.

> I was fired. He said it was unconscionable that any one working for Personal Products would sue a sister company. I said I didn't think so. He had been aware of the legal thing with Ortho. He was dejected and hurt by the whole thing. The next morning he seemed very sad about seeing me go. . . . I haven't seen him since.

Dr. Pierce carried her suit to the New Jersey Supreme Court, which broke constitutional ground by affirming a professional's right to challenge superiors where professional ethics are at stake. In Grace Pierce's case, however, five of the six judges for the New Jersey Supreme Court ruled that her judgment and Ortho's were simply at variance. Professional ethics were not the issue, according to the court, which sustained Ortho's actions.

Postponing the Whistle

Some professionals delay taking a path of direct confrontation and, as a result, they become involved in unethical or illegal behavior. Implicated protesters include those who have spoken up within their organizations, have capitulated and gone along with the policies of their superiors, and have subsequently publicized inappropriate actions when they have become fearful of the consequences of their own involvement.

5. Alfred G. Feliu, "Discharge of Professional Employees: Protecting Against Dismissal for Acts Within a Professional Code of Ethics," *Columbia Human Rights Law Review*, 11 (1979–1980). See especially pp. 186–187.

In the late 1960s, Kermit Vandivier, a technician, assisted in the production of an airplane brake whose faulty design could have endangered Air Force test pilots. He asserted that, despite his repeated pleas and those of several engineers including his supervisor, other engineers and managers in the Goodrich Corporation pushed a false report. When Air Force pilots tested the brakes with near fatal results, Vandivier approached a lawyer who advised him to go to the FBI.

Though Vandivier's account has been reprinted many times in the last decade,* he recently provided additional insight. Note how—as a relatively uneducated technician—he felt alienated and powerless. Note also his sense of anomie as people he trusted simply backed off, and his anxiety over his isolation.

> At the time of the Goodrich fiasco I had six children of school age at home. My salary, if I remember correctly, was around $125–$135 per week. My only outside source of income was the pay I received from the *Troy Daily News* [TDN]—$15 for the three columns per week I wrote. High principles notwithstanding, I couldn't—at that time—subject myself and my family to "retaliation." Please note I said "at that time," because I think there is one factor which I perhaps have not made entirely clear in the Goodrich story. I don't think anyone within the Goodrich organization really believed—until the moment it actually happened—that the report was going to be issued to the Air Force. Until such time as it was published and delivered to the Air Force, none of us who actually had a part in preparing the phony report was guilty of any criminal act. True, my attorney offered his opinion that we might be guilty of conspiracy to defraud, but qualified that opinion by adding there would have to be proof we knew at the outset a fraud would ultimately be committed. I can't describe the sense of incredulity I (and I'm sure others) experienced when I learned the report had really been issued, that Goodrich was actually going to try and pull this thing off. . . . Naturally, my editors at TDN knew what was going on right from the start. When the situation had developed sufficiently we considered whistleblowing in the TDN, but TDN attorneys were concerned that there was simply not enough proof of any wrongdoing at that time and felt that a libel suit could be certain. Meanwhile, I was gathering incriminating data, photographs, charts, movie film, notes of meetings and telephone conversations. I smuggled them out of the plant each day, copied them at night, and returned the originals the following day. Altogether, I amassed more than 1,000 documents and other items

*ED. NOTE: See Selection 6 in this volume.

(I still have them), which were invaluable evidence at the Senate hearing. When I finally was ready to blow the whistle I had all the evidence necessary to make a strong case. No one was indicted or charged in connection with the hearing, but the day following the hearing the Department of Defense quietly initiated sweeping changes in its inspection and procurement procedures. A DOD official later confirmed the changes were made as a direct result of the hearing. . . .

Vandivier's testimony underscores that the ties of loyalty can be broken and public criticism undertaken when the dangers of continued inaction appear more serious than the fears of retaliation. Under such circumstances, those who contemplate blowing the whistle have a potentially powerful and omnipresent ally in the weight of the law, which holds companies and individuals responsible for the production of faulty products.[6] Many implicated protesters might resist the orders of their superiors were there greater likelihood of apprehension, conviction, and severe punishment for white-collar crimes.[7]

In the early 1970s another serious breach of professional and managerial ethics unfolded. Frank Camps, a senior principal design engineer, was directly involved in the development of the Ford Pinto, which proved to have an unsafe windshield and a gas tank that might explode on impact. He questioned the design and testing procedure and later charged publicly that his superiors who knew of this danger were so anxious to produce a lightweight and cheap car to compete with the imports that they were determined to overlook serious design problems. Camps's level of anxiety grew as he contemplated the consequences of his own involvement.

We were still in the development stage. I had a certain degree of resentment; these people were not listening although we were having problems with the car. I can remember I went into my manager's office. He said, "Look, we're in the business of selling cars and every time we barrier crash a car and it causes problems, then we have one failure. If we get another car to crash, to see how the first failure happened, we may have two failures. This would compound

6. For a discussion of the recent legislation to protect and encourage whistleblowing, see Westin, *Whistle Blowing?* pp. 131–167.

7. For a pertinent instance, see Eberhard Faber, "How I Lost Our Great Debate about Corporate Ethics," *Fortune*, November 1976, pp. 180–188.

itself until my bonus would be reduced." Now this was the kind of
thinking—the corporate attitude—that my immediate superior had.
He didn't say anything about crashing for occupant safety. He just
didn't want his bonus to be cut down. I said to my wife, "This guy
is a bad actor. This guy is going to get me in trouble if I don't start
documenting and protecting myself." This was colossal arrogance,
callous indifference toward the safety of people. It bothered me even
if only one person should die or be disfigured because of something
that I was responsible for.

Camps was a respected and longtime member of Ford's engineering staff and thus not totally without influence. Yet he felt
powerless to affect company policy. To avoid complete absorption
into a system of relationships and definitions that calibrated human
life on a scale of company costs and to protect himself against legal
liability, he sued the company.

Camps described the response of fellow engineers, a response
that mitigated his sense of isolation.

Most of the working engineers were very supportive of me at that
time. They are still supportive of me. I can recall, right after I filed
the suit, other engineers said—"Go get 'em, we wish we could do it,
there goes a man with brass balls." While I had tacit support, I was
looking for an honest man to stand with me. I found that these guys
were suddenly given promotions, nice increases in salary. Next thing
I knew, I did not have the support any more.

Camps wasn't alone in his agony over the Pinto. From 1971 to
1978 fifty lawsuits were filed against Ford because of gas-tank
explosions in rear-end accidents. In 1980 Ford was brought to trial
on a criminal charge in the death of three Indiana girls. The case
created national headlines and featured the testimony of a former
high-ranking Ford engineer whose statements were similar to
those made by Frank Camps within the company.[8] While Ford was
found innocent in this trial, the Pinto has come to symbolize
management's drive for profits over customer safety. Had Camps
been treated as a voice to be heeded rather than a protester to be
ignored and punished, Ford might have avoided fatalities and
serious injuries, years of litigation, and the stigma of corporate
irresponsibility.

---

8. Richard T. DeGeorge, "Ethical Responsibilities of Engineers in Large Organizations: The
Pinto Case," *Business Professional Ethics Journal* 1 (Fall 1981), 1–17.

Whistling Late in the Game

Many professionals who participate in illegal or unethical acts only blow the whistle once they have left the organization and have reestablished their careers in other companies or fields of work. They seek to make up for their past timidity and to ease their consciences.

The late Arthur Dale Console studied at Cornell Medical College and later practiced neurosurgery. In search of less strenuous work after a serious illness, he joined the E. R. Squibb and Sons pharmaceutical company in 1949 as associate director of research. He found Squibb an ethical company, still run by its founder and maintaining an orientation in which the physician in charge of research was defined as a "physician's physician." During the ensuing years, according to Dr. Console, much changed in the pharmaceutical industry. Larger companies bought out the smaller ones and the search for profit became more intense. The transformation affected all members of the company staff including the director of research, a position that Dr. Console had by then assumed. As he worked, he experienced an increasing tension between his sense of what was appropriate medical decision making and what was required by his more business-oriented superiors. He was particularly disturbed by those instances in which he had pressured physicians to certify drugs that they had not sufficiently tested. He resigned from his position in 1956 after six and a half years in the drug industry, and soon after began to train for a new career as a psychiatrist.

During the 1960s, Console's continuing sense of self-estrangement led him to take the initiative and testify several times before congressional committees. At one hearing he was asked why he had left Squibb. His answer captures the process of capitulating to the pressures of multi-national corporations and the disillusionment that follows.

> I believe that the best answer can be found in my unfinished essay of *The Good Life of a Drug Company Doctor*. Toward the end I said: "These are only some of the things a drug company doctor must learn if he is to be happy in the industry. After all, *it is a business*, and there are many more things he must learn to rationalize. He must learn the many ways to deceive the FDA and, failing in this, how to seduce, manipulate or threaten the physician assigned to the New Drug Application into approving it even if it is incomplete. He must learn that anything that helps to sell a drug is valid even if it

is supported by the crudest testimonial, while anything that decreases sales must be suppressed, distorted and rejected because it is not absolutely conclusive proof. He will find himself squeezed between businessmen who will sell anything and justify it on the basis that doctors ask for it and doctors who demand products they have been taught to want through the advertising and promotion schemes contrived by businessmen. If he can absorb all this, and more, and still maintain any sensibilities he will learn the true meaning of loneliness and alienation." During my tenure as medical director I learned the meaning of loneliness and alienation. I reached a point where I could no longer live with myself. I had compromised to the point where my back was against a wall and I had to choose between resigning myself to total capitulation, or resigning as medical director. I chose the latter course.[9]

After he left the pharmaceutical industry, Dr. Console received a grant from Squibb to train for a career in psychiatry, which placed him outside the authority of all corporate structures. Console's widow, a respected psychiatrist in her own right, has provided additional insight into Dr. Console's background, his commitment to Squibb, and his ultimate decision to blow the whistle several years after entering private practice.

He was one of two surviving brothers who both carried out their father's ambitions to complete medical school. Arthur did so with great distinction. . . . In spite of two bouts of tuberculosis during this period he went on and completed a neurosurgical residency— the first resident chosen in this separate specialty considered the most prestigious in surgery. Trouble really began when, in attempting to establish a practice, he fell ill a third time, necessitating complete bed rest at home. We had an infant son with club feet requiring frequent surgical intervention and casts, absolutely no income except mine from an also newly established practice, and the resulting pressure on me from multiple conflicting responsibilities was overwhelming. It was apparent that he had to find a less physically demanding and an economically sound alternative. It was at this time he accepted the offer to join Squibb as an associate medical director. The decision to give up neurosurgery as a career was a bitter and lasting defeat. The coincidence of Dr. Console's tenure as medical director of Squibb with its changeover from an ethical drug house to a competitive business-oriented company

9. "A. Dale Console," in Ralph Nader, Peter J. Petkas, and Kate Blackwell, eds., *Whistle Blowing* (New York: Bantam, 1972), pp. 122–123. Also see Hearings before the Subcommittee on Monopoly of the Select Committee on Small Business, United States Senate, Ninety-first Congress, First Session on Present Status of Competition in the Pharmaceutical Industry, Part II, March 13, 1959, pp. 44–84.

could not have been foreseen, but his sense of having been con-
demned to second-class medicine then became more and more
intolerable. Because of Dr. Console's increasing and outspoken
alienation from the drug industry it was clear that an open break
was pending. It was imperative for him to look elsewhere for the
future. The choice of psychiatry was made after considerable discussion together. . . . When the opportunity arose to testify in the
Kefauver hearings, Dr. Console had already distanced himself from
almost all his former colleagues. . . . The real problem was one of
conflict from some sense of loyalty to Squibb, which had been very
generous to him, and the pressure of his need to speak out. I did
not share this intensity and had some misgivings but felt that he
had to follow his own conviction. His moments of "speaking out"
appeared then to be an opportunity to vindicate himself in his own
eyes before the world.

Dr. Console *chose* to reveal his own complicity in a large-scale effort
to profit from unethical marketing procedures. Whistleblowing of this
kind can result when people believe deeply that they should have acted
earlier to resist illegitimate authority.[10] Although Dr. Console testified over a decade ago, recent scholarship reveals that many of the
problems he highlighted continue to characterize the drug industry,
particularly in its relationship with Third World countries.[11]

Taboos and Degradation Ceremonies

Those willing to breach the taboo against informing face potent
challenges.[12] Their superiors have the power to harass them by
questioning their competence and judgment, to terminate their
employment, and to blacklist them from other positions. Attorney
Joseph Rose learned that the extensive influence of the Associated
Milk Producers could bring his career to a standstill.

10. Other reluctant collaborators now have become international figures. See Philip Agee,
Inside the Company (New York: Bantam Books, 1976). His decision to identify publicly CIA
agents makes him the country's most controversial whistleblower. For a debate on his actions,
see "On Naming C.I.A. Agents," *The Nation* (March 14, 1981), pp. 295–301.

11. See Ray H. Elling, "The Political Economy of International Health with a Focus on the
Capitalist World-System," in Michael Lewis, ed. *Social Problems and Public Policy*, Vol. II (Stam-
ford, Conn.: JAI Press, 1982).

12. For a recent and illuminating study of the role of the informer, see Victor Navasky, *Naming Names* (New York: Viking, 1980).

After I left AMPI, they weren't content with the firing, they wanted to call my ex-employers and completely ruin me. There was an attorney up in New York and I answered one of his ads. It turned out that he was a friend of an executive of AMPI, and indeed his secretary was one of the executive's nieces. I accepted the job and he and I went out on one case. He said right in front of a client, "He doesn't know it yet, but at Christmas time, I am going to fire him." I thought he was kidding, and I didn't pay any attention to it, and then lo and behold, right at Christmas time, right on target before Christmas, he fired me. After he dismissed me, I had been under fire so long that I was about to have a damned nervous breakdown. I did a very peculiar thing. President Ford was in office, and I wrote Ford and said, "This is happening to me, because I wouldn't be a crook." The next thing I knew, John Sales of the Watergate prosecutor's office called me and he said, "How are you?" and the clear implication was "Are you keeping your sanity?" And I said, "John, I'm holding on, but it sure as hell isn't easy." And he said, "Well, we've got an interview for you with the Department of Labor in Dallas." I thought, all of a sudden, there is justice in the world, maybe somebody does care. So I drove to Dallas, and I interviewed with the guy who was the head of the Department of Labor there, and I'll be damned if he didn't know some of the AMPI people. He made the comment, "I didn't request to interview you, as far as I am concerned, I can throw your resume up to the ceiling and hope it sticks there."

AMPI's influence seemed also to extend into religious organizations. Rose, a devout man, was particularly hurt by this.

My wife and I were attending Castle Hills First Baptist Church in town. I was in very bad emotional shape. I mean *very* bad and one of the high guys at AMPI attended the same church. I went to talk to the leader of the church. I guess I just wanted somebody to talk to, to get this thing out of my system. The man literally turned his back on me and started talking to other people. I felt that I certainly was not abandoning Jesus Christ by abandoning the specific church building.

As Joseph Rose learned through bitter experience, those who break the taboo will experience degradation, which recasts the social identity of whistleblowers, labeling them as unreliable, of poor judgment, and of dangerous character.

Joseph Rose worked in private industry. What of the government employees? A prime example is Ernest A. Fitzgerald, a staff analyst in the Pentagon. In 1969, he appeared before Proxmire's Senate subcommittee investigating the production of the C5A air transport. Fitzgerald "committed truth" by answering affirmatively that there had been a two-billion-dollar overrun in the plane's development.[13] He could have sidestepped the question or lied to the Senator. Had he done so, Fitzgerald would have avoided being labeled as someone who no longer had a future at the Pentagon. Such a designation came from the highest levels of government, including the Secretary of the Air Force and the President of the United States, Richard M. Nixon.

A statement by Alexander Butterfield, White House aide (and the man who later revealed the existence of the secret Nixon tapes), best summed up the official view toward Fitzgerald.

> Fitzgerald is no doubt a top-notch cost expert, but he must be given very low marks in loyalty, and after all loyalty is the name of the game. Only a basic "nogoodnik" would take his official grievances so far from normal channels. We should let him bleed for a while at least.[14]

While such retaliation did not break Fitzgerald, it extracted a heavy price from him and his family. In a recent conversation he has spoken of the impact on his children as comparable to radiation—difficult to measure but potentially very damaging.

Butterfield's statement implicitly highlights some of the central characteristics of "successful degradation ceremonies" that Harold Garfinkel has identified: the whistleblower's actions are "out of the ordinary" and in contrast to those of a loyal employee or peer; the actions are not accidental and reflect on the entire person of the whistleblower; the denunciation reinforces the values of the group, which stress silence and loyalty.[15] The message is clear. Whether in industry or government or academia, the whistleblower who is determined to reject self-estrangement despite the attacks of superiors must be able to withstand the charge of being labeled incompetent and disloyal.

13. A. Ernest Fitzgerald, *The High Priests of Waste* (New York: W. W. Norton, 1972). For a pertinent study, see Mark Ryter, *A Whistle-blower's Guide to the Federal Bureaucracy* (Washington: Institute for Policy Studies, 1977).

14. Media Transcripts Incorporated Program 20/20. December 18, 1980, p. 14.

15. Harold Garfinkel, "Conditions of Successful Degradation Ceremonies," *The American Journal of Sociology* 61 (January 1956), 420–424; Victor W. Turner, *The Ritual Process* (Chicago: Aldine, 1969), pp. 168–203.

Ceremonies of Status Elevation

New York City detective Bob Leuci received crucial encouragement from government prosecutors Scoppetta and Shaw in his decision to do undercover work against racketeers and corrupt police. Note how Leuci's sense of self is directly tied to his identification with these two men.

> I undertook this investigation because of the support that I received from Scoppetta and Shaw, incredible support. It was the same kind of support that I received from my partners when I was working out on the street. You have a sense that there is somebody who truly cares about you.

The experiences of James Boyd and Marjorie Carpenter offer a sharp example of the way in which efforts toward status elevation can alleviate the pressures toward self-estrangement. Boyd and Carpenter are credited with exposing and bringing down the powerful Senator Thomas Dodd of Connecticut in the late 1960s. Boyd, Dodd's assistant for twelve years, and Carpenter, Dodd's secretary, suspected that the Senator was pocketing large amounts of campaign funds.[16] According to Boyd, Dodd sensed their suspicions, fired them both, and spread the word that they were disreputable employees who were dismissed when he discovered that they were engaged in a sordid love affair. Boyd suspected that the Senator also intended to blacklist him from employment in Washington.

> I didn't come to the decision to really go at it, tooth and nail, until I saw him trying to keep me from getting a job. I didn't want to go back with him. I was trying to get away from him for some time, but he tried to use the power to keep me from getting a job, and then, in a roundabout way, boasting to me what he was doing, toying with me as if I were some kind of a creature, instead of a partner as we had started out.

Boyd had decided to expose Senator Dodd but could not act until he was approached by Drew Pearson and Jack Anderson.[17] The two

16. James Boyd, *Above the Law* (New York: New American Library, 1968).

17. Drew Pearson and Jack Anderson, "Portraits of a Senator," in *The Case Against Congress* (New York: Simon and Schuster, 1968). The Dodd case was one among other factors leading to the Senate's ultimate reconsideration of its principles of behavior and the revision of its own code of ethics. See the special section entitled "Revising the U.S. Senate Code of Ethics," *Hastings Center Report* (February 1981), pp. 1–28.

journalists assessed his suspicion, and encouraged him to act against Dodd with their explicit promise that they would define the case as their highest priority, would never back off no matter how great the heat, and would continue to demand an investigation by the Senate and other legal authorities.

After this careful agreement, Boyd and Carpenter obtained keys to Dodd's office, and removed and copied thousands of documents that contained evidence of Dodd's financial dealings with major corporations and others who sought his intervention on their behalf. Boyd and Carpenter had taken bold and controversial action, which resulted in Dodd's eventual censure by the Senate.

Healing the Wounds

The available literature on whistleblowers often emphasizes the dead end that awaits those who break with peers and superiors. My evidence provides a more intricate mosaic. Virtually all the individuals discussed here have been able to rebuild their careers and belief in their competence and integrity. They found an escape hatch in private practice, consulting, and the media. Ironically perhaps the diversity of American economic and social institutions provides opportunities to those who have dared defy the authority of the established ones.

Although Frank Serpico never sought to develop a new career, he is a national figure who continues to be respected for his courageous stand. His name is synonymous with police integrity. Bob Leuci completed his twenty years in the New York City Police Department, is a popular speaker on college campuses, and is currently writing a novel about police work.

Joseph Rose is a successful attorney in San Antonio. Former colleagues who avoided him and believed the accusation that he had betrayed AMPI now treat him with respect. Some clients seek him out expressly because they know of his past difficulties and admire his toughness. When we spoke in the winter of 1983 his practice was flourishing.

Grace Pierce works exclusively in clinical medicine. She has expanded her work in the group clinic by opening an office in her home, believes she provides an important service to local patients, and has time to enjoy her garden.

"I really lucked out," she says. Her skills, the support of the medical community, and the receptiveness of her patients have provided an up-beat continuity to her work and personal life. She does, however, harbor many troubling questions about whistleblowing and its effectiveness in changing organizational policies. . . .

> And now that the "whistleblowers" have been re-established or resettled into other pursuits of living what has happened to the persons, institutions or corporations that created these dilemmas? Have there been corrective steps taken to avoid similar episodes of employee disenchantment? Have those offenders to the whistleblowers changed in any way—have there been any recriminations? Is there less deception or corruption or is it better concealed? Have the pathways of whistleblowers been kept open, or even broadened for other employees who may be confronted with similar ethical issues? Are the courts any more or less supportive? Were these struggles really worth it? Have our little pieces of the world actually improved because of these actions? Are there other ways and means available to resolve the whistleblower's conflicts—perhaps more effectively and perhaps less painfully with less personal sacrifice? Is there still a place for "idealists" in a world quite full of "realists"?

Unique opportunities arose for both Kermit Vandivier and Frank Camps after their break with former superiors. Vandivier has built a new career at the *Troy Daily News*.

> Looking back, I would say probably the best thing that ever happened to me was the Goodrich thing. That gave me the push I probably wouldn't have had otherwise. When you have six kids and you've got a job that looks fairly secure, and you like it—which I did—I liked the Goodrich job—and you feel like you're accomplishing something —you don't feel like quitting or starting a new career. I went into a different field. I would never have gotten a job at Goodyear or Bendix, the other two brake manufacturers. I don't think anyone in private industry would touch me. I am a troublemaker, you know. I went to work for the *Troy Daily News* the day following my abrupt departure from BFG. I have served as a general assignment reporter and have covered a variety of beats, including the police, city hall and political beats. . . . Two years ago the TDN became involved in cable television. I was named cable news director and given the responsibility of organizing and implementing the project.

Like Vandivier, Frank Camps found that others were interested in his skills and eager to hire him. Camps now serves as a consult-

ant to attorneys involved in product liability litigations. He underscores how important those relationships have become in recreat-
ing his career and his sense of himself.

> When I filed my suit, six months before I left Ford, it gained wide
> publicity, not only in the Detroit papers but in many papers and in
> many television outlets in the cities where the Ford plants were
> located. It also got into the *Wall Street Journal.* I began getting calls
> from attorneys all over the country, and I couldn't quite compre-
> hend what they were driving at until one of the attorneys said he
> would like me to help him on a case. He came up with an hourly
> figure and a retainer that was absolutely staggering, based on what
> I was making at Ford. He became my mentor. . . . All of those feel-
> ings I had—the anxiety, resentment, anger, helplessness, that's all
> gone, because of what I now accomplish. I am doing what I want to
> do, when I want to do it. I can speak my mind truthfully and openly
> in a court of law. There is nothing more gratifying than to know
> that you are now involved in due process. Incidentally, in all of the
> cases I have been involved in, I have not been on the losing side
> even one time.

Ernest Fitzgerald has spent more than a decade in litigation to
secure his former position. He has defeated a bureaucracy committed to his expulsion and banishment. An out-of-court settlement
with former President Richard Nixon, the return to previous duties,
and the court-directed government payment of his legal fees have
all provided clear evidence for his complete and public vindication.
Fitzgerald has survived as the nation's best-known whistleblower.

Finally, James Boyd has taken a more circuitous route. He has
published a book about his experiences in the Dodd case, has directed
the Fund for Investigation Journalism, has written for the *New York
Times Magazine,* and has completed several projects with Jack Anderson. He and Marjorie Carpenter Boyd live with their two children
in a rural area far from Washington. She continues to believe that
they acted appropriately and were guided by their need for a sense
of inner satisfaction, which she finds characteristic of many whistleblowers. As Boyd reflects on the last fifteen years, he can count some
of the costs and gains of his decision to take on a United States
Senator.

> I have friends from that period of my life who are now retired. If I
> had done that, I would have been retired now for three years, and
> I would have been getting $35.000 a year. I realize that there is a

tremendous material loss involved. Also you lose something—there's something in an institution, various supports—professional, friendship, life-support type things—that you lose when you are separated from that institution. What I have gained is a whole new outlook on life—a feeling of independence—of "being my own man"—working at my own hours—and all that sort of thing, which I find enormously attractive. . . .

In a recent note Rose aptly summarized his views.

Gandhi said that noncooperation with evil is as much a duty as cooperation with good; Burke said the only thing necessary for the triumph of evil is for good men to do nothing. Both concepts are still viable . . . although expensive.

For each of these whistleblowers there was no going back. Yet there was a future.[18] That message is as vital as the severe price they paid.

---

18. These findings are confirmed by a recent government report. The U.S. Merit Systems Protection Board, *Whistle Blowing and the Federal Employee* (Washington, D.C.: U.S. Government Printing Office, October 1981), particularly p. 41.

13

Rely Tampons and Toxic Shock Syndrome
Procter & Gamble's Responses

Alecia Swasy

Pat and Michael Kehm had a good life. The Cedar Rapids, Iowa, couple worked on sketches of their dream house where they could raise their two daughters.[1] The white house would sit on a hill, over-looking a pasture where Pat could ride her horse.[2]

They talked about their plans and dreams at a family outing on Labor Day 1980, when they took the children, Andrea and Katie, to a local park. The Old McDonald's Farm exhibit was a favorite of three-year-old Andrea. "It was a nice quiet day the four of us spent together," Mike Kehm recalled.[3]

But their storybook life began to collapse the next day. Pat had taken her sister Colleen's advice and tried Rely tampons,[4] a popu-lar brand with many women.

Four days after she began using Rely, Pat Kehm was dead at age twenty-five, a victim of toxic shock syndrome.[5] About two weeks after she was buried in Cedar Memorial Cemetery, P&G pulled the tampons from the market. They had been linked to the disease that killed the young mother.[6]

From *Soap Opera: The Inside Story of Procter & Gamble*. Copyright © 1993 by Alecia Swasy. Reprinted by permission of Times Books, a division of Random House, Inc.

1. Testimony of Rebecca Spore, childhood friend of Patricia Kehm, in *Michael L. Kehm, Administrator of the Estate of Patricia Ann Kehm, Deceased* v. *Procter & Gamble Manufacturing Co., Procter & Gamble Distributing Co., Procter & Gamble Paper Products Co., and Procter & Gamble Co.*, U.S. District Court for the Nothern District of Iowa. Cedar Rapids Division. Trial held in April 1982. References to the Kehms' life are found on page 1,127 of trial transcript.

2. Ibid., testimony of Colleen Jones, p. 1,079.

3. Testimony of Michael Kehm in 1982 trial, p. 1,408 of transcript.

4. Kehm trial transcript, testimony of Jones, p. 1,077.

5. Kehm trial transcript, p. 1,439.

6. Testimony by Dr. Bruce Dan, CDC researcher on toxic shock, pp. 199–200.

P&G was lauded for taking such a drastic and costly step.[7] It was one of the largest product recalls in U.S. business history, requiring P&G to take a $75-million charge to cover the cost of discontinuing the product.[8] "I am personally proud of the way our people in all concerned departments have behaved under the pressure of real concern for human life," said Edward Harness, then chairman of P&G, in a letter to employees.[9]

But P&G has little reason to be proud. A closer look at the episode and the court cases that followed paint a different picture of P&G: a corporate bully that showed carelessness, indeed recklessness, toward consumer safety. P&G wants to win at any price, and the Rely case shows how far it will go to achieve victory.

The full story of the Rely debacle has never been told because P&G effectively silenced most of its victims and their families through out-of-court and confidential settlements, which imposed on P&G and its insurers as much as $85 million in payments to claimants and defense costs.[10] And it locked up scientific research on toxic shock with millions of dollars in P&G grants. Those who spoke out were offered stipends to keep their research quiet.[11] By the late 1980s more than 1,100 lawsuits and claims had been filed against P&G because of Rely.[12] "P&G lucked out. Had the truth come out back then, they would've been nailed for everything they have," said Dr. Philip Tierno, a New York University microbiologist who has studied toxic shock. "And justifiably so. They didn't do their homework." He calls Rely a "toxin factory."[13]

The Kehm case was one of the few that ever went to trial, providing a glimpse into how far P&G will go to protect its image. "They looked pretty bad in the toxic shock litigation," said Tom Riley, attorney for the Kehm family and about 140 other plaintiffs in toxic

7. Speech by Jere E. Goyan, commissioner of Food and Drug Administration, before the Health Industry Manufacturers Association, Washington, D.C., Oct. 2, 1980.

8. Jane Brazes, *Cincinnati Post*, Sept. 23, 1980.

9. Ed Harness letter to P&G employees, Sept. 24, 1980.

10. William Gruber, *Chicago Tribune*, March 27, 1989, and Paul Souhrada, *Cincinnati Business Courier*, March 27–April 2, 1989.

11. Interviews with Dr. Philip M. Tierno and others.

12. Paul Souhrada, *Cincinnati Business Courier*, March 27–April 2, 1989, p. 1.

13. Tierno interview.

shock cases. "They could've saved a lot of lives, including Pat Kehm's. But they're too damn greedy."[14]

The story of Rely began in the early 1960s, when researchers started studying how to make a superabsorbent tampon that would outsell other brands. Once P&G developed the product, it considered names such as Sure, Merit, Certain, Always, and Soft Shape, but chose Rely,[15] which instilled confidence. "Hopes run high in Cincinnati that the tampon named Rely will take a major share of the market from Tampax and Kotex," wrote *Fortune* magazine in July 1974. "Demonstrating the new product, P&G executives plunk Rely and Tampax into separate beakers of water to demonstrate their own product's superiority. They are confident enough about the outcome to make an explicit claim on the package: 'Rely absorbs twice as much as the tampon you're probably using now.'"[16]

Tampons date back to an invention by Dr. Earl Haas, a Denver barber turned physician who got the idea to roll up cotton and sew it together with string. He sold the invention, called Tampax, for about $30,000 in the 1930s.[17] Rely was different. Instead of cotton, it contained superabsorbent synthetic chips of polyester and carboxymethylcellulose, a derivative of wood pulp. It was shaped like a tea bag, with a net to contain the synthetic chips that absorbed menstrual blood.[18] "Rely could absorb an entire menstrual flow in one tampon," Dr. Tierno said.[19]

It was just the breakthrough P&G wanted in order to continue building its paper division. In the late 1970s "it was one success after another," recalls Marjorie Bradford, a former manager in the public relations department. "Some of it was almost embarrassing." The company had the dominant share in the diaper market with Pampers. Indeed, P&G lawyers worried about the Federal Trade Commission crying foul about its near monopoly. Rely was such an immediate hit, P&G figured it would soon lock up another category

14. Interview with Tom Riley, attorney who handled the Kehm case and about 140 other toxic shock cases.

15. Reference to other tampon trademarks found in "Marketing: What's Next for P&G?" *Wall Street Journal*, Oct. 2, 1980.

16. Peter Vanderwicken, *Fortune*, "P&G's Secret Ingredient," July 1974.

17. Tom Riley's opening statement, Kehm trial transcript, p. 69.

18. Kehm trial transcript, pp. 71 and 66.

19. Tierno interview.

and boast the country's number-one tampon. "There was a feeling of invincibility," Bradford said.[20]

But women like Judy Braiman, a mother of five and a Rochester, New York, consumer advocate, began to question Rely's safety in 1975. The product was being test marketed in her city when Braiman began to receive complaints from women. The housewife had become an outspoken consumer advocate after her own health crisis in 1966. A severe cough prompted doctors to diagnose her ailment as lung cancer. Tests revealed sixty lesions in each lung but no cancer. Her lungs were covered with boils, which doctors linked to inhaling aerosol hairspray. It changed her life.

Braiman founded a small group called the Empire State Consumer Association. Most days, she and a couple of friends are its only volunteers. The group's checking account balance hovers around $100. When she has a complaint, she prefers press conferences to noisy demonstrations. She appears more like a Junior League member than one of Ralph Nader's Raiders, serving coffee in yellow china cups, with biscotti and linen napkins on the side.

Braiman is anything but demure in her campaigns, however. In 1971 she began what became an annual hunt for unsafe toys at Christmas. That first year she found thirty-nine toys in Rochester stores that were dangerous for children. She began testifying at government hearings about product safety. In 1975 she was asked to serve on the product safety council for the Consumer Product Safety Commission, a watchdog agency. She isn't popular with some. "The day before one hearing, the local sheriff came to the door to say he had a report of a bomb exploding at my house," she said. It proved to be a false alarm.

Rochester women began to call Braiman's home with reports of vomiting and diarrhea after using the free sample of Rely tampons.[21] Then she read a July 1975 local newspaper report that said Rely contained polyurethane, an ingredient that had been linked to cancer.[22]

P&G was aware of the concerns before the newspaper reports. In an internal memo of February 28, 1975, from R. B. Drotman to

20. Interview with Marjorie Bradford.

21. Interview with Judy Braiman.

22. Armand Lione and Jon Kapecki, *Rochester Patriot*, July 23–Aug. 5, 1973, p. 1.

F. W. Baker, the company outlined "possible areas of attack on Rely." The list said components were cancer-causing agents. It also noted that Rely affected the natural microorganisms and bacteria found in the vagina.[23]

P&G invited Braiman in 1975 to a meeting to discuss her concerns. She had been speaking out about Rely and contacted the company for more information about the product. Braiman had small children at home, so she told P&G officials that she wouldn't be able to leave home for a meeting. Company officials volunteered an employee's spouse to baby-sit her kids while she attended the meeting.

She questioned the use of polyurethane, but P&G assured her the product would be reformulated. She asked to see safety testing results and for an explanation of why women were vomiting when they used the product. But P&G wouldn't provide the data. "They were very condescending," she recalled. Braiman also questioned whether P&G would introduce a deodorant version of Rely. She pointed out that it was unnecessary to put a deodorant in a tampon, because the fluid has no odor as long as it remains in the body. P&G did have plans to introduce a deodorant Rely but did not disclose this in the meeting. "She was right," Bradford admitted. "Even the scientists knew that deodorant tampons were a crazy idea." But P&G also knew they would sell.

Braiman surveyed about fifty women on tampon usage. P&G wanted the names of those who'd suffered adverse reactions. She wouldn't give out the information. P&G "blamed their problems on allergies," she said. The company didn't mention that it had been receiving one hundred complaints per month since June.[24]

Despite these problems, the national rollout proceeded as scheduled. About 60 million sample packages of Rely were sent to 80 percent of U.S. households, at a cost of $10 million.[25] The campaign worked. By mid-1980 Rely had gained about 24 percent of the tam-

23. P&G memo by R. B. Drotman to F. W. Baker, "Possible Areas of Attack on Rely," Feb. 28, 1975.

24. Information on the number of consumer complaints about Rely found in Kehm trial transcript, Martin Cannon testimony, p. 2,361.

25. *Wall Street Journal*, Sept. 19, 1980.

pon market and threatened to overtake the leading brand, Tampax, in a very short time.[26]

But Rely's star was already beginning to fade. In the spring of 1980 the Centers for Disease Control, the government agency that tracks disease, issued its *Morbidity and Mortality Weekly Report,* or *MMWR.* It listed fifty-five cases of toxic shock syndrome since October 1979 and noted that the disease was predominant among young, menstruating women.[27] Despite the warning signs, that same spring P&G president John Smale sent chairman Edward Harness a memo requesting approval to move forward with its plans to introduce a deodorant version of Rely.[28]

In early June the CDC contacted P&G's paper division for information on tampon usage for a study of toxic shock. At the time, a doctor from the agency mentioned speculation by a *Los Angeles Times* reporter that tampons might be associated with toxic shock. While P&G continued to assuage consumers' worries, it had been receiving as many as 177 complaints per month since 1975.[29]

The company instructed its sales force not to discuss toxic shock with customers, including doctors. But if asked, the salespeople were given canned answers that denied any link between tampons and toxic shock.[30]

Complaints about the product were deemed routine by P&G. The company always got a lot of calls after introducing new products. Some managers likened the Rely calls to the reports of rashes and other skin irritations that had followed P&G's introduction of Bounce fabric softener in the mid-1970s. They figured it was nothing serious.[31]

But toxic shock *is* serious. Symptoms of the disease, first identified by Dr. James Todd in Denver, include high fever, a sunburnlike rash, vomiting, and low blood pressure. After a while, a victim's

---

26. Market share information found in Dean Rotbart and John Prestbo, "Killing a Product, Taking Rely off Market Cost Procter & Gamble a Week of Agonizing," *Wall Street Journal,* Nov. 3, 1980.

27. P&G memo on chronology of key events on toxic shock and Rely.

28. Smale memo to Harness about introduction of Rely deodorant, May 14, 1980.

29. P&G memo from G. T. Davis to M. G. Leman, Feb. 22, 1980, about consumer comments.

30. P&G memo to sales personnel, June 27, 1980.

31. Interviews with P&G managers familiar with the calls.

skin peels off the hands and feet. Breathing becomes difficult, and the lungs fill with fluid until she suffocates or her heart stops. The name is derived from the severe prolonged shock that accompanies the illness.

Scientists found that the disease begins with *Staphylococcus aureus,* bacteria commonly found in the vaginas of up to 15 percent of all women. Men and nonmenstruating women can get the disease from an abscessed infection where the staph produces the toxin. In menstrual toxic shock, the tampon creates a haven for the bacteria that are present, allowing them to grow and produce deadly toxins.[32]

Superabsorbent synthetics—carboxymethylcellulose, or CMC, and polyester—made Rely especially dangerous. In addition, CMC is partially degradable, which contributed to the bacteria growth. Though CMC is safe enough to be used as an additive in ice cream, P&G didn't test to see how it would react with bacteria. "Rely turned on the production of certain poisons; produced toxins that were absorbed into the blood," Dr. Tierno explained.[33]

When tampon makers were first invited to a meeting with the CDC in late June 1980, they heard a presentation on a toxic shock study, but no particular brand was linked to the disease. P&G sued CDC to get the names and addresses of patients, but the agency refused on the grounds of confidentiality. Instead P&G got some information from doctors and state health departments, while continuing to badger the CDC with requests under the Freedom of Information Act. Company officials were getting increasingly annoyed, especially with a young physician named Dr. Kathryn Shands. She had joined the CDC in July 1979 in the special pathogens department, where researchers tackle unknown pathogens, or disease-producing agents. It was the same group that had dealt with the Legionnaires' disease.[34]

Six months into her new job, Shands found herself facing off against P&G's senior management from Cincinnati, whom she described as "fairly intimidating." P&G's attitude was "you guys are freshmen, and you don't know what you're talking about," she

32. Description of toxic shock syndrome comes from Kehm trial transcript, opening statement by Tom Riley, pp. 62–67.

33. Interview with Tierno and pp. 71–72 of opening statements of Kehm trial.

34. Information on P&G's meetings with the Centers for Disease Control gathered from memos and interviews with Dr. Kathryn Shands and Tom Riley.

recalled. But Shands aggressively fought P&G's request for the names of patients in the studies, citing the obvious invasion of their privacy. In a P&G memo, officials complained that Dr. Shands said she would go public with a statement that this request by P&G "will greatly hinder their work on TSS."[35]

In July P&G distributed 2 million free samples of Rely and planned a high school promotion for late August.[36] That month the company got the news that a woman had died from toxic shock after using Rely. Tom Laco, then executive vice president, called Marjorie Bradford into his office. "Read this," he said tersely, handing her a wire service report tying P&G's product to the victim's death.

"How do you feel about it now?" Laco asked Bradford.

"This changes things," she replied.

"Looking back, Bradford said, For the first time, a company product had been linked to a death. There was no way we [could] get around the public perception of Rely linked to a fatal disease."[37]

That same month P&G considered placing a warning label on the product, as well as sponsoring public service advertisements warning about the symptoms of toxic shock. But according to a P&G memo, company lawyers warned that the ads should be worded so that "we do not leave ourselves open for other tampon manufacturers to make claims against us." The solution: Don't mention tampons in the ads. Another memo that month cautioned against slowing Rely's momentum, declaring "We should continue our planned activity to support this brand and build its share to leadership status."[38] P&G never issued the warning label or ads, despite the growing evidence of problems. "That was corporate murder," Attorney Tom Riley said.[39]

Women continued to complain. Some reported that they were deathly ill each time they used Rely. A July 1980 memo by Owen Carter, a P&G chemistry safety expert, describes how P&G officials met with doctors and county health department workers in Lima,

35. Interview with Shands.

36. Kehm trial transcript, pp. 61–62.

37. Bradford interview.

38. P&G August file memo by P. F. Wieting on warning statement and Wieting memo about expansion of Rely Moderate.

39. Riley interview.

Ohio, to quiet rumors that "mistakenly" linked the tampon to health problems. They heard about a twenty-seven-year-old woman, mother of a six-week-old baby, who fell into a deep shock when she used Rely. Yet P&G officials insisted that Rely was blamed merely because of "unfortunate circumstances of timing involving the sample drop and introductory promotional advertising of the new tampon" and newspaper reports of the disease.[40]

In mid-September the CDC called again to report on a second study, in which 70 percent of the women with TSS reported using Rely. P&G asked the CDC not to mention Rely when it published the results. "It would be realistic to say that P&G would have very much preferred to keep their name out of the study," said Dr. Bruce Dan, then an infectious disease specialist at the CDC.[41]

P&G resisted pulling the product from shelves, believing that such a measure "would've sent the wrong signals," Bradford said. P&G contended that Rely was wrongly linked because so many women had been using free samples, so that when they were asked questions about tampon use, they naturally mentioned Rely. "Rely was one of the biggest ad campaigns that P&G ever had," Bradford said.[42]

In Rochester, consumer advocate Judy Braiman was telling women to stop using Rely. "My phone was flooded with hundreds of calls," she said. Another concern surfaced: The superabsorbent tampon swelled so much that one woman likened it to "trying to remove an open umbrella from her body," Braiman said. When she learned of the deaths, "I was physically ill. I kept thinking, What could I have done to make someone pay attention to me? If someone had listened, some women would still be alive," she said, wiping away tears.[43]

Because the company was making little progress in swaying national regulatory agencies,[44] P&G's Washington office began to lobby for congressional support to save Rely. Bryce Harlow, a former Nixon aide and P&G lobbyist, was still active in Washington

40. Owen Carter file memo, July 25, 1980.

41. Information on study and Dr. Bruce Dan quote from "P&G's Rely Tampon Found Implicated in Rare Disease by U.S. Disease Center," *Wall Street Journal.* Sept. 18, 1980.

42. Bradford interview.

43. Braiman interview.

44. Interviews with various P&Gers and Shands.

circles. But his Democratic counterpart, Walt Hasty, took the lead to find allies in the Carter administration and Congress who could help override the Food and Drug Administration and CDC.

Ed Harness called top scientists for a scientific advisory group meeting at the Hilton Hotel at Chicago's O'Hare airport on September 21, 1980. From 8:30 A.M. to 7:30 P.M., five doctors from Harvard, the University of Southern California, and other universities debated in room 2027 about whether Rely was the cause. No one could guarantee the chief executive that P&G's product wasn't to blame.[45]

The next day P&G announced it was pulling Rely from the market. Harness wrote the press release himself. "He was just devastated," Bradford said. "I've never seen a man age so quickly."[46]

P&G knew it had to act. The FDA was getting antsy. "The FDA said it would give P&G the opportunity to do something," Bradford said. The message: "If you don't we will," she said. "We knew that meant a recall."

The day after the announcement, P&G met with the FDA, which said the company had yet more work to do. But P&G spent much of the meeting debating whether the action would be called a withdrawal or a recall. P&G disliked "recall" because it seemed to imply safety violations. Exasperated FDA officials finally said, "If you don't want to call it a recall, we'll call it a *banana*." During the meeting, that's exactly how they referred to it. "We just wanted it off the market," said a former FDA official who attended the meetings.[47]

P&G signed a consent agreement in which it didn't admit that Rely was defective or that the company violated any laws. The FDA forced it to undertake a massive ad campaign to notify women to stop using the tampons. In addition, P&G had to buy back the product.[48]

About 3,000 P&G employees were involved in the effort to get Rely off the shelves. Back at company headquarters, managers told of orders to shred documents on Rely. "We were told that all the

45. Information on the Chicago airport hotel meeting gathered in interviews and from the following *Wall Street Journal* story: Dean Rotbart and John A. Prestbo, Nov. 3, 1980, p. 1.

46. Bradford interview.

47. *Wall Street Journal*, Nov. 3, 1980, p. 1.

48. Ibid.

records shouldn't be kept," said a former top officer of the company. It became known as the "Ides of September." When asked about document shredding, a P&G spokesman expressly denied any order to shred and said the company had an obligation not to dispose of Rely documents during pending litigation. P&G said it retained over one million pages of documents related to Rely.

"My faith was shaken," said one woman manager. "I wanted to know what the company knew and when did it know it." But many got swept up in the accolades of how P&G had done the right thing, pulling out of a very successful market.[49]

It had been a popular product. Pat Kehm's sister, Colleen, had pestered her during their Monday shopping trips to buy Rely. The two women weren't just sisters; they were best friends. Often their mother and Pat's husband, Mike, would join them for lunch on his noon break from the service department at Bruce McGrath Pontiac.[50]

The day after Labor Day, Pat began to use Rely tampons. By Wednesday, she was sluggish and went to bed early. By Friday, Mike was staying home from work to care for her. She had been vomiting and running a high fever the night before. "I ran up to the store and got her 7-Up, but she couldn't keep that down," he said.[51]

When Pat's mother came to pick up the kids for the weekend, she took little Andrea to Pat's bedside to say good-bye. Pat could hardly raise her hand to wave good-bye one last time.[52]

Mike took Pat to the emergency room, but the doctors gave her penicillin and sent her home. Saturday she made an appointment to see her doctor. Her legs were so discolored that she asked Mike to help her put on a pair of his loose-fitting jeans. He had to carry her to the car.[53]

In the doctor's office, the nurse couldn't find her blood pressure. She called an ambulance, even though the hospital was just two blocks away. "That's when I became frightened," Mike said. "I

49. Interviews with numerous P&G officials, including retired officers who were on the administrative committee at time of crisis.

50. Kehm trial transcript, p. 1,079.

51. Ibid., Mike Kehm testimony, p. 1,412.

52. Ibid., p. 1,433.

53. Ibid., p. 1,428.

couldn't imagine why—how all of a sudden she became so sick that she had to be taken in an ambulance."[54]

In the hospital, doctors had a hard time finding a vein to start an IV. Her condition grew worse. The nurses asked if Mike wanted to call their priest. "I had never seen Pat like this; she was starting to turn black and blue," he said.[55]

Pat Kehm died around 3:45 Saturday afternoon. The doctor said he suspected it might be toxic shock related to tampons. Mike gave his permission for the physician to perform an autopsy to solve the mystery of his wife's death. He also consented to have her organs donated. But most of her organs had been severely damaged by the disease. Only Pat's eyes could be donated.

Mike went back to the their Bowling Street home. In the bathroom he saw the box of Rely and threw it in the wastebasket.[56] "After she died, Andrea kept asking, 'When is Mommy coming home?'" Kehm recalled.[57]

54. Ibid., pp. 1,430–31.
55. Ibid., p. 1,437.
56. Ibid., pp. 1,440–41.
57. Interview with Mike Kehm.

14

Chained Factory Fire Exits

*Media Coverage of a Corporate Crime
That Killed 25 Workers*

John P. Wright, Francis T. Cullen, and Michael B. Blankenship

The news media are frequently chastised for presenting a mislead-ing portrayal of crime (Graber 1980; Lotz 1991; Marsh 1989). In this view, the media function as a "carnival mirror" (Reiman 1990) who distort reality by focusing disproportionately on street crime, particularly violent offenses. The media thus neglect other types of crime, especially corporate lawlessness (Garofalo 1981; Marsh 1989; Reiman 1990). This omission, the argument goes, helps to reproduce inequality by directing public attention away from the enormous costs—including violent costs—associated with the "crimes of the powerful" (Hills 1987; Reiman 1990).

Although criminologists have argued that corporate illegality has largely been ignored by the media, it is possible that this situation is changing. Over the past 15 years, observe various commentators, there has been a social movement against white-collar and corpo-rate crime (Cullen, Maakestad, and Cavender 1987; Katz 1980; Kramer 1989). This movement arguably has altered public senti-ment against—and aroused interest in—acts of corporate crime. In this context, the media not only may have provided an outlet for the dissemination of information about corporate lawlessness but also may have facilitated the continuation of the social movement.

These considerations raise the issue of the extent to which the media have changed their coverage of corporate violence. Do they continue to present distorted images of crime or are they in fact contributing to the continued social movement against corporate

From "The Social Construction of Corporate Violence: Media Coverage of the Imperial Food Products Fire," *Crime and Delinquency*, Vol. 41, pp. 20–36. Copy-right © 1995 by Sage Publications. Reprinted by permission.

misconduct? In particular, are they defining corporate harms—including violence—as criminal? . . .

Building on previous research, our study attempts to address these issues by exploring newspaper coverage of an incident of corporate violence: the deaths and injuries resulting from the fire at the North Carolina plant of Imperial Food Products, Inc. As a case study, the generalizability of our research is inherently limited. Even so, the features of this case may make it especially useful in discerning the extent to which the news media are willing to construct corporate violence as criminal. . . .

Death in the Workplace

Chicken processing plants dot the southern region of the United States. The Imperial Food Products, Inc., plant was no exception to this pattern. Located in Hamlet, North Carolina, close to the state's southern border, the plant was the primary employer in the community.

On September 3, 1991, the plant caught fire. After workers had repaired a hydraulic line located above a large vat of grease, the line burst, spraying a flammable liquid into the 400° oil in the vat. The fire spread rapidly, and thick soot-filled smoke engulfed the plant. Of the plant's 230 workers, 90 were in the plant at the time the fire started. Of these, 25 died and 56 were injured. The plant suffered extensive damage, and the community lost its largest employer (see Aulette and Michalowski 1993).

Immediately, survivors reported that exit doors had been either locked or blocked and that their escape from the plant had been severely hampered. Apparently, the firm's owner, Emmett Roe, had authorized the doors to be padlocked due to suspected employee's pilferage of chicken parts.

The locked doors, however, were only part of the problem. The building, which was over 100 years old, did not have a plantwide sprinkler system. The plant had no windows to provide an alternate escape route and too few exit doors in critical areas. In its 11 years of operation, the plant had never been inspected by the state's Occupational Safety and Health Administration (OSHA).

An inquiry into the plant fire was initiated almost immediately—on September 4—under the direction of the State Bureau of Investigation. A week later, the AFL-CIO petitioned the federal OSHA to withdraw North Carolina's approval to operate independently from federal OSHA. After a series of meetings, the labor department did just that, taking over part of the state's workplace safety program on October 24, 1991. In response, the state agreed to hire 27 new safety inspectors, and, in August of 1992, the state legislature, amid controversy, enacted 12 workplace safety bills. Federal OSHA withdrew its threats to take over the state's OSHA program.

In the interim period, however, the State Department of Insurance found that the plant was in violation of nine sections of building codes and six state laws. In response, the state labor department fined Imperial Food Products, Inc., $808,150 for its willful and serious violations. Concurrently, on March 10, 1992, Emmett Roe, his son Brad, and the plant manager, James N. Hair were indicted on 25 counts each of involuntary manslaughter. If convicted, each man could have been sentenced to 250 years in prison.

After a series of negotiations with the state, Emmett Roe pleaded guilty to 25 counts of involuntary manslaughter. Under the plea agreement, Brad Roe and James N. Hair were not prosecuted. Emmett Roe received a 19-year, 6-month sentence but could be paroled in 2½ years.

Method

Sample

To assess coverage of the Imperial Food Products case, we conducted a content analysis of 10 newspapers: the *Boston Globe,* the *Chicago Tribune,* the *Los Angeles Times,* the *New York Times,* the *Wall Street Journal,* the *Washington Post,* the *Cincinnati Post,* the *Cincinnati Enquirer,* the *Cleveland Plain Dealer,* and the *Louisville Courier Journal.* These newspapers represent a cross-section of the United States and include several newspapers with national readership. . . .

Content Categories

After reviewing the literature on corporate crime, we developed content categories that measured important dimensions of the case: cause, harm, intent, responsibility, and sanctions. These were used to code the stories on the case. Each line of each story was coded by the first author and a trained assistant. In case of disagreement, which occurred infrequently, an impartial third party was used to solve the disagreement.

Cause. Early reports questioned whether the fire could have been prevented if the workers had followed more rigorous safety standards. Thus, the content category *cause* is divided into three dimensions: worker negligence of safety an issue, worker negligence not an issue, and none or no discussion of cause. The two categories gauge how the cause of the fire was portrayed. References to improper maintenance were coded as worker negligence an issue. Characterizations of the cause of the fire as an accident were coded as worker negligence not an issue.

Harm. Swigert and Farrell (1980) found that the personalization of harm played an important role in media depictions of the Ford Pinto trial. As a result, we analyzed stories for reference to three types of harm. First, direct harm refers to reports on those killed in the fire. Second, residual harm relates to references to the negative effects experienced by the victims' families and friends. Third, community harm covers depictions of the harm suffered by the community, such as the loss of jobs and the subsequent fiscal impact. Finally, a subcategory labeled "none" measured the absence of any reference to harm.

Intent. Traditionally, intent has played a pivotal role in the criminal prosecution of corporate crimes (Cullen et al. 1987). By using the term *intent,* we do not mean to infer that those responsible maliciously calculated the deaths of their employees. Instead, intent refers to the circumstances surrounding the incident that were responsible for the case being defined as manslaughter and not as an accident. We therefore constructed the intent category using two dimensions: references to overt intent, such as padlocked doors, and references to indirect intent, such as no sprinkler system and general plant conditions. A subcategory labeled "none" measured the absence of any reference to intent.

Responsibility.   Morash and Hale (1987) and Evans and Lundman (1983) both found that the media concentrates on the acts of individuals and largely neglects the context within which the acts take place. To construct this category, we used three dimensions that reflect different realms of responsibility. First, management refers to instances in which responsibility for the workers' deaths was placed on individual plant owners and managers. Second, company refers to references that the company (Imperial Food Products, Inc.) was responsible for the deaths. Third, given the importance of regulatory agencies in this story, we included a dimension labeled regulatory. This dimension includes instances in which regulatory agencies were held responsible for the workers' deaths. A subcategory labeled "none" measured the absence of any reference to responsibility.

Sanctions.   This category was composed of three elements. First, the criminal element relates to references to possible or actual criminal charges. Second, civil relates to instances in which stories made reference to the possibility of civil sanctions. Third, regulatory refers to possible or actual sanctions leveled by regulatory agencies. A subcategory labeled "none" measured the absence of any reference to sanctions.

Time intervals.   As illustrated by Swigert and Farrell (1980), news coverage is a dynamic process that changes over time. We therefore categorized three distinct time intervals that corresponded to important happenings (see Table 14.1). The first time interval began on the first day of coverage, September 4, 1991, and ended 1 week later. This period was chosen to allow newspapers time to cover the incident. The second interval began at the end of Interval 1 and continued through to the day before the criminal conviction was announced, September 13, 1992. During this time, the prosecutor announced indictments of the plant owner and managers on manslaughter charges. The third interval began on the day the conviction was announced and ended 1 week later. This method allowed us to gauge the evolution of the story and to provide the basis for comparisons in the degree of coverage.

Results

Coverage

Of the 10 newspapers in the sample, 9 covered the plant fire. Of these, 5 ran the initial news of the fire on the front page. Over the course of the week, however, the priority of the story faded as follow-up reports were placed further back in the paper. This finding holds across time intervals. As seen in Table 14.1, the mean page number for Interval 1 is page 6, the mean page number for Interval 2 is page 14, and the mean page number for Interval 3 is page 15. It is clear that as the story continued to unfold, newspapers accorded it less priority. This is especially noteworthy given that the sentence was handed down in Interval 3, the interval with the least amount of coverage.

The mean number of lines and paragraphs per story reflects a qualitative shift in reporting styles. Interval 1 encompassed most of the coverage, with 68% ($n = 34$) of the 50 total stories falling within the first week after the fire. The mean number of lines per story (111.4) and paragraphs (17.2), however, do not reflect the wide

TABLE 14.1
Newspaper Coverage of the Imperial Food Products Fire

	Time interval		
Characteristic of coverage	First week	After first week and before conviction	Criminal conviction
Mean page number	6.0	14.0	15.0
Mean number of lines	111.4	125.0	61.8
Mean number of paragraphs	17.2	20.0	10.5
Number of newspapers covering story	9.0	3.0	4.0
Total number of stories	34.0	10.0	6.0

variation in reporting length. For instance, the number of lines per story ranged from 17 to 312; the number of paragraphs ranged from 1 to 44.

Table 14.1 indicates that in Interval 2, there was a substantial reduction in the number of stories ($n = 10$), but an increase in mean line and paragraph length. In short, stories were fewer, but those that were written were lengthier than in Interval 1. Again, however, variation in coverage is apparent, with the number of lines ranging from 38 to 435 and number of paragraphs from 5 to 68.

In Interval 3, we see a further reduction in the number of stones ($n = 6$). Not only were there fewer stories, but also the mean length of the stories was substantially reduced. As we will discuss later, the ramifications of the lack of coverage may have important implications for social policy.

Harm

Table 14.2 indicates that the media focused quite heavily on the harm produced by the fire. References of direct harm to victims outpaced all other subcategories in each time interval. Significant differences exist, however, in the media's portrayal of both residual and community harm between Interval 1 and Interval 2. During Interval 1, the newspapers focused primarily on the victims of the blaze. In Interval 2, however, references to residual and community harm significantly increased. Interval 2 can be characterized by a qualitative shift in reporting. Stories in this period concentrated on the damage done by the fire, on the lives of the survivors, and on the memories of the deaths of family and friends.

Culpability

Cause. As seen in Table 14.2, the origin of the fire was largely ignored in news reports (i.e., whether or not worker negligence caused the hydraulic line to burst and set the plant on fire). Of the stories in Interval 1, 47% ($n = 16$) did not mention the cause of the fire. This pattern holds across intervals. For example, 50% ($n = 5$) of the stories in Interval 2 and 33% of the stories in Interval 3 did not mention the cause of the fire.

TABLE 14.2
Incident Characteristics by Time Interval

Incident characteristic	First week	After first week and before conviction	Criminal conviction
Harm			
Direct	10.9	11.2	4.0
Residual	3.0	8.3	3.0
Community	1.5	7.5	1.2
Number of stories not mentioning harm	0.0	0.0	0.0
Immediate cause of fire			
Worker negligence—not an issue	3.9	3.2	1.5
Worker negligence—an issue	0.0	2.1	1.0
Number of stories not mentioning cause	16.0	5.0	2.0
Intent			
Overt	7.3	5.4	3.2
Indirect	7.4	8.3	1.7
Number of stories not mentioning intent	1.0	0.0	0.0
Responsibility			
Management	1.5	3.0	2.2
Company	0.3	0.4	0.3
Regulatory	6.9	6.8	1.2
Number of stories not mentioning responsibility	8.0	0.0	0.0
Sanction			
Criminal	0.9	3.0	5.2
Civil	0.1	1.6	0.8
Regulatory	0.0	2.4	1.3
Number of stories not mentioning sanction	23.0	1.0	0.0

Note: Mean number of lines per story reported unless otherwise indicated.

Intent. A distinctive feature of this industrial tragedy was that a number of the plant's exit doors had been padlocked. Table 14.2 indicates that such "overt intent" was widely depicted in the media. However, the media did not limit its coverage to the doors being locked; they also focused on the unsafe conditions of the plant. As seen in Table 14.2, in the first two intervals, indirect intent, such as plant conditions, was focused on as much if not more than the doors being locked. It was not until Interval 3, the time of the criminal conviction, that the media focused more attention on the importance of the locked doors.

These findings suggest that the media attempted to bring to light the excessive risks associated with working in this particular plant. The padlocking of the doors was typically portrayed as part of a larger problem of management indifference and/or of lax regulatory oversight. In other words, the reports did not exclude the context in which the event transpired, a finding that differs from past research. We should note, however, that the final shift in the proportion of attention given to the locked doors occurred in Interval 3, exactly when coverage was at its lowest.

Responsibility. Again, past research suggests that the media will focus on the acts of individuals and remove them from the context in which the acts took place (Evans and Lundman 1983; Morash and Hale 1987). Our data, however, do not support such a contention. Early on, blame for the fire was assigned to the state's regulatory agency. The state of North Carolina OSHA had never inspected the plant in its 11 years of operation, even though the building was over 100 years old and lacked modern safety equipment, such as a sprinkler system.

Table 14.2 indicates that coverage critical of the actions of regulatory agencies emerged immediately and continued through Interval 2. In Interval 1, coverage attributing the plant fire to lax regulation was over four times more likely than coverage blaming a lack of management accountability. Even in Interval 2, coverage of regulatory responsibility was twice as likely as coverage of management culpability. It was not until Interval 3, when the conviction of the defendant was announced, that a shift occurred in assessing blame. In short, throughout much of its initial coverage, the media primarily laid blame for the fire on a lack of state regulatory oversight and inspection that allowed unsafe and hazardous conditions to exist.

Sanctions

Overall, Table 14.2 indicates that coverage of possible or actual sanctions was minimal across all time periods. In Interval 1, for example, 72% of the stories failed to mention any sort of possible sanctions. When they did, the coverage amounted to an average of 1 line. Even though this incident was potentially criminal, and even in the wake of numerous deaths and injuries, the media did not initially define the act as criminal. It was not until the second interval, when manslaughter indictments were announced, that discussions of criminal sanctions emerged in the stories. And only in the third interval did discussions of criminal penalties receive a strong priority. It is instructive, however, that as depictions and definitions of criminal penalties emerged in the latter time periods, coverage became even more limited.

It appears that the media are hesitant to label acts of corporate violence as criminal—or are not conscious of this possibility—even with the clear presence of aggravating circumstances. Instead, the reports did not define the deaths as criminal until the government deemed the act as a potential and then an actual criminal violation. Of course, this stands in contrast to forms of traditional violence where the press immediately ask if criminal charges will be filed.

We should also note that when the plea agreement was reached, and the sentence was handed down, only 40% of the newspapers covered the story. Further, the coverage can be characterized as minimal, with only 5 stories highlighting the sentence. Not only was the mean page number pushed back to page 15, but also the mean number of lines and paragraphs was significantly reduced from previous time intervals. The newspapers in our sample did not see the event as a priority for coverage, even though the criminal penalty was one of the most severe sentences ever given to a corporate executive.

Discussion

. . . The newspaper coverage of the Imperial Food Products case clearly detailed the enormous harm from the fire: the deaths and injuries, the suffering of family members and relatives, and the damage to the social fabric and economy of the community. It is noteworthy, moreover, that the newspaper reports did not define the case simply as an industrial accident or as being due to worker negligence. In short, the reports readily depicted corporate violence and did not seek to localize responsibility in terms of bad luck (accident) or blaming the victim (the workers).

Even so, the newspapers showed little consciousness that corporate violence might be seen as a crime. The reports did not initially define the deaths as homicides, nor did they raise the possibility that the corporation or individual executives might be eligible for prosecution. In essence, the media was not proactive, but reactive: It was not until the government announced the manslaughter indictments and, in particular, the plea bargain that the criminality of the violence was reported. This attention, however, occurred after the first time interval, during which the coverage was the least extensive and least prominently placed in the newspapers.

Instead of a potential criminal offense, the news reports socially constructed the worker deaths as a breakdown in government safety regulation. The reports thus focused not only on the padlocked doors, which might have served as a safety exit, but also on the plant's general hazardous conditions and the failure of OSHA to conduct an inspection of working conditions.

This construction of corporate violence likely was not inconsequential. Although we do not know how media coverage influenced subsequent policy decisions, it is instructive that, under pressure from OSHA in Washington, DC, substantive regulatory reform was undertaken in North Carolina. As noted, the legislature enacted 12 new workplace safety laws and 27 additional safety inspectors were hired. If nothing else, the media coverage served to reinforce, not question, these policy initiatives.

Yet, again, the newspaper reports did not serve to transform the consciousness of the public and business community so that corporate violence would be seen as criminal—a transformation that scholars since Ross (1907) have argued is necessary (Hills 1987; Mokhiber 1988). Even though the violence was enormous and the grounds for a prosecution were apparent (e.g., locked safety exits), and even though precedents existed for prosecuting workplace deaths (Cullen et al. 1987; Farber and Green 1988; Frank 1985), the national media did not focus on the potential criminality of the corporate managers.

The lack of coverage devoted to the outcome of the case—the manslaughter convictions—also is noteworthy. Again, although it was a major case of corporate violence, the criminal conviction of the company's owner either was not covered or was conveyed in a relatively short report placed deep within the pages of the newspaper. This coverage thus limited the power this conviction might have had to exert educative or deterrent effects; that is, to have educated the public about the moral boundaries of corporate risk-taking and to have shown corporate managers that creating or tolerating safety hazards can make them criminally liable (Cullen et al. 1987; Swigert and Farrell 1980).

In short, although the role of the media might vary under other circumstances, the Imperial Food Products case suggests that reporters—including those at the nation's most influential newspapers—are unlikely to be instrumental in defining corporate violence as criminal and, more broadly, of leading efforts to implement policies that would make the use of the criminal law against corporate personnel more prevalent. Instead, as in this case of workplace violence, which saw the district attorney file manslaughter charges, it seems that local prosecutors, not the media, may be the key actors in socially constructing corporate violence as lawlessness.

. . .

Although we have endeavored to analyze the data objectively, the discerning reader will detect that a prescriptive message informs our discussion: the news media *should* have been more proactive in criminalizing the harms of the Imperial Food Products fire and, more generally, should play a role in the movement against corporate violence. This critical appraisal of the media is value-laden but is not idiosyncratic: It reflects three themes common to the criminological literature.

First, as noted above, the news media have not traditionally treated corporate violence as criminal despite the enormous costs this form of violence imposes on society. Arguably, a duty exists for them to do so (see Linsky 1988). Second, because the media often distort the reality of crime—street as well as corporate lawlessness—they have a shaky claim to objectivity, "to merely reporting the facts." The issue is not if the media will construct a reality about crime, but rather which reality they will set forth (Elias 1994; Fishman 1978, 1980; Marsh 1989). Third, the reality constructed by the media frequently does not serve noble ends but is shaped by occupational/organizational self-interest (e.g., advancing careers, boosting ratings) and by larger power structures in society (Barak 1988; Leiber, Jamieson, and Krohn 1993). With these themes as a background, the failure of the press to criminalize the plant workers' deaths in North Carolina is seen not as judicious reporting but as part of an institutional pattern detrimental to the commonweal.

In fairness, a more sympathetic assessment of newspaper coverage of the Imperial Food Products fire is possible. Reporters legitimately could be praised for exercising restraint in not criminalizing this incident and in providing local prosecutors with the space to weigh the existing evidence and to let justice run its course (restraint that seems in short supply in cases involving rock stars and football heroes). Prematurely portraying corporate managers as crass criminals may have caused these individuals unfair public shame and spurred their unwarranted prosecution. Before casting accusations against corporations, moreover, reporters also must weigh whether they will expose their employers to legal liability and public embarrassment (Weiser 1993).

This perspective is weakened, however, by two considerations emphasized previously. First, the reporters covering the plant fire did not remain neutral compilers of facts but rather quickly developed as their angle—their paradigm for explaining the fire—the theme of regulatory breakdown. In short, they socially constructed the case, not as a crime in and of itself. Second, and perhaps most important, the newspapers can be criticized for the lack of coverage given when the case officially became a crime (i.e., when the plea agreement and prison sentence were announced). This disinterest undoubtedly is not peculiar to corporate violence—"journalists take to heart the old saying that yesterday's newspaper wraps today's fish" (Linsky 1988, p. 215)—but nonetheless, it is consequential. Although many citizens across the nation may have heard about the tragic loss of life in the chicken-processing plant, how many ever were informed that the workers' deaths were manslaughters? . . .

Whether the media had a duty to raise the prospect that the deaths at the Imperial Food Products plant were "criminal" is a value question of consequence. Admittedly, in cases involving corporate violence, criminologists—and we are no exceptions—may be overly ideological and perhaps too quick to criticize when news reporters do not immediately define such harms as criminal. At the same time, criminologists may well serve the commonweal when they unmask the implicit biases of reporters and challenge the media to join the public discourse concerning the seriousness and potential criminality of corporate violence.

References

Aulette, Judy R. and Raymond Michalowski. 1993. "Fire in Hamlet: A Case Study of a State-Corporate Crime." Pp. 171–206 in *Political Crime in Contemporary America,* edited by K. D. Tunnell. New York: Garland.

Barak, Gregg. 1988. "Newsmaking Criminology: Reflections on the Media, Intellectuals, and Crime." *Justice Quarterly* 5:565–87.

Cullen, Francis T., William J. Maakestad, and Gray Cavender. 1987. *Corporate Crime Under Attack: The Ford Pinto Case and Beyond.* Cincinnati, OH: Anderson.

Elias, Robert. 1994. "Official Stories: Media Coverage of American Crime Policy." *The Humanist* 54:3–8.

Evans, Sandra S. and Richard J. Lundman. 1983. "Newspaper Coverage of Corporate Price-Fixing." *Criminology* 21:529–41.

Farber, Stephan and Marc Green. 1988. *Outrageous Conduct: Art, Ego, and the Twilight Zone Case.* New York: Morrow.

Fishman, Mark. 1978. "Crime Waves as Ideology." *Social Problems* 25:531–43.

——. 1980. *Manufacturing News.* Austin: University of Texas Press.

Frank, Nancy. 1985. *Crimes Against Health and Safety.* New York: Harrow & Heston.

Garofalo, James. 1981. "Crime and the Mass Media: A Selective Review of Research." *Journal of Research in Crime and Delinquency* 18:319–50.

Graber, Doris A. 1980. *Crime News and the Public.* New York: Praeger.

Hills, Stuart L. 1987. *Corporate Violence: Injury and Profit for Death.* Totowa, NJ: Rowman and Littlefield.

Katz, Jack. 1980. "The Social Movement Against White-Collar Crime." Pp. 161–84 in *Criminology Review Yearbook,* edited by E. Bittner and S. Messinger. Beverly Hills, CA: Sage.

Kramer, Ronald C. 1989. "Criminologists and the Social Movement Against Corporate Crime." *Social Justice* 16:146–64.

Leiber, Michael J., Katherine M. Jamieson, and Marvin D Krohn. 1993. "Newspaper Reporting and the Production of Deviance: Drug Use Among Professional Athletes." *Deviant Behavior* 14:317–39.

Linsky, Martin. 1988. "The Media and Public Deliberation." Pp. 205–27 in *The Power of Public Ideas,* edited by R. Reich. Cambridge: Harvard University Press.

Lotz, Roy. 1991. *Crime and the American Press.* New York: Praeger.

Lynch, Michael J., Mahesh K. Nalla, and Keith W. Miller. 1989. "Cross-Cultural Perceptions of Deviance: The Case of Bhopal." *Journal of Research in Crime and Delinquency* 26:7–35.

Marsh, Harry L. 1989. "Newspaper Crime Coverage in the U.S.: 1893–1988." *Journal of Criminal Justice* 19:67–78.

Mokhiber, Russell. 1988. *Corporate Crime and Violence: Big Business Power and the Abuse of the Public Trust.* San Francisco: Sierra Club Books.

Morash, Merry and Donna Hale. 1987. "Unusual Crime or Crime as Unusual? Images of Corruption at the Interstate Commerce Commission." Pp. 129–49 in *Organized Crime in America: Concepts and Controversies,* edited by T. S. Bynum. Monsey, NY: Criminal Justice Press.

Reiman, Jeffery. 1990. *The Rich Get Richer and the Poor Get Prison.* 3rd ed. New York: Wiley.

Swigert, Victoria L. and Ronald A. Farrell. 1980. "Corporate Homicide: Definitional Processes in the Creation of Deviance." *Law and Society Review* 15:161–82.

Weiser, Benjamin. 1993. "TV's Credibility Crunch: NBC's Staging of a GM Truck Crash Puts the Focus on Television News Ethics." *Washington Post National Weekly Edition,* March 8–14, pp. 6–8.

15

Asbestos Exposure by Johns-Manville
Cover-ups, Litigation, Bankruptcy, and Compensation

Craig Calhoun and Henryk Hiller

The new technologies and large-scale markets that have prolifer-
ated since the industrial revolution have been mechanisms of new
kinds of injuries on a growing and often extraordinarily large scale.
The progression of coal mine accidents, collapsing bridges, railway
and airplane crashes, and factory explosions forms a frightening
counterpart to industrial progress. . . .

Insidious Injuries and Legal Responsibility

Injuries are "insidious" when the links between their causes and
manifest symptoms are obscure. This is particularly common where
the symptoms are those of a general disease rather than a specific
trauma, for example, lung cancer rather than a broken bone. Identifying such diseases as injuries is often difficult. Insidious injuries
(a) appear only after a period of latency, like asbestosis and silicosis;
(b) strike only a segment of the exposed population, either randomly
or patterned by varying individual vulnerabilities, like diseases caused
by pollution; (c) manifest themselves by raising rates of risk for diseases that also have other causes, as occupational exposure to various toxins may multiply cancer risks, and/or (d) affect victims widely
dispersed through the population, like the results of faulty pharmaceutical products. Some injuries, like those stemming from exposure
to asbestos dust, are insidious in all four senses.

From "Coping with Insidious Injuries: The Case of Johns-Manville Corporation
and Asbestos Exposure," *Social Problems*, Vol. 35, pp. 162–81. Copyright © 1988
by the Society for the Study of Social Problems. Reprinted by permission.

Insidious injuries are associated with increased scale of social organization and with introduction of complex and dangerous new technologies, but they are not simply reducible to such impersonal forces. They are injuries caused by people and often by corporate "persons." For this reason, attempts to seek redress for insidious injuries fall into the province of tort law. In the United States, the absence of any national health care or universal health insurance system means that victims are often led to file tort suits simply as a way of coping with extraordinary medical costs. Litigation is, however, generally a slow and difficult means of securing compensation, which is further complicated by the pursuit of deterrence and/or punishment. . . .

Asbestos-related diseases offer an advantageous starting point for analysis of the changing nature of insidious injuries and their implications for tort law and public policy. First, asbestos-related litigation combines several dimensions of insidiousness in a very large-scale mass tort. Second, it raises interesting questions about what it means to treat corporations as responsible actors, both because asymmetry distorts suits between corporations and natural persons and because of the anthropomorphism of arguments that corporations ought to be punished and made to feel pain for their misdeeds. Third, largely because of the tort and bankruptcy litigation involving Johns-Manville,[1] it offers a wealth of documentary evidence. A particularly interesting feature of the Manville case is the unusual strategy the firm adopted to protect its assets from the millions of dollars of claims produced by tort litigation. It sought protection in the bankruptcy courts while still clearly solvent and profitable. Manville was not the first firm to employ this defense against tort liability, but it was the first Fortune 500 firm to do so. . . .

The Manville Corporation and Asbestos-related Disease

Asbestos is a fibrous material useful primarily as a fire retardant. The resilient fibers are removed from mined rock and are flexible

---

1. Hereafter referred to as Manville, in accord with its 1982 change of name.

enough to be woven, sprayed, or packed. End-products include fire-proof textiles, construction materials, brake linings, and other surfaces for coping with high friction.

Henry W. Johns pioneered commercial applications for asbestos in the late 1860s. In 1901, Johns's successors merged his firm with the Manville Covering Company, an insulation firm. The newly-formed Johns-Manville Corporation rapidly increased its annual sales to some forty million dollars by 1925. The business concentrated on asbestos roofing and pipe insulation and operated a huge asbestos mine in Quebec. By 1934, the company was manufacturing 1,400 products (most with asbestos); as of 1981, asbestos had thousands of commercial applications (U.S. Congress: House Committee on Education and Labor [HCEL], 1981:9).

Throughout the twentieth century, Manville dominated many of its markets and expanded rapidly abroad, gaining a two-thirds share of total U.S. sales for insulation material composed partly of asbestos. Manville claimed as recently as 1982 to be the largest asbestos processor and the largest asbestos-cement manufacturer in the free world (Moody's, 1982:3995). Raw asbestos fiber, insulation, pipe, and roofing constituted the largest portion of its sales. Asbestos remained a major ingredient in most of these products even after litigation concerning its health effects was well under way; a rapid decline began in the middle 1980s (Goodwyn, 1972:12-13; Johns-Manville Annual Report, 1978 et seq.). The company has been on *Fortune* magazine's list of the 500 largest corporations in the United States from its inception and was for many years among the 200 largest. Its sales peaked at $2.2 billion in 1979, and in 1981 its assets totaled $2.3 billion.

In the early years of the asbestos industry, the mineral seemed an unalloyed good. Gradually, however, the picture darkened. Shortly after 1900, evidence began to show dangers associated with asbestos use. Mining, milling, weaving, transportation, and other uses all create asbestos dust. This dust is composed of tiny asbestos fibers that are easily inhaled by exposed individuals. The very properties that render asbestos strong and fire-retardant make it very difficult for the body's defense mechanisms to dispose of it; up to one-half of the inhaled fibers become lodged in the lungs (U.S. Congress: HCEL, 1979:49). These fibers and the body's reaction to them can result in various asbestos-related diseases. The three most common are asbestosis, lung cancer, and mesothelioma. Precise specification of each disease and its relation to asbestos exposure is still a matter of some dispute.

Asbestosis is a breathing difficulty resulting from the formation of fibrous, scarlike tissue around asbestos fibers lodged in the alveolar tissue of the lung. It generally progresses over a period of 10 to 30 years. Symptoms are slow to develop, and the fibrous tissue growth can be detected by X-ray only in advanced stages. Asbestosis itself is seldom fatal, but the decreased lung efficiency it causes often contributes to fatal respiratory disease such as pneumonia or to heart failure. It has been estimated that 10 percent of those working with asbestos die from these and other complications associated with asbestosis (U.S. Congress: HCEL, 1978:134). Asbestosis is dose-related; that is, lower levels of exposure produce lesser problems. Contrary to earlier belief, however, no "safe" exposure levels exist (see U.S. Congress: HCEL, 1979:51).

Lung cancer and, less often, gastro-intestinal cancer are also related to asbestos exposure. Though the statistical connection has appeared since the 1930s, the precise mechanism by which asbestos exposure contributes to malignant formations is unclear. The coupling of cigarette smoking and asbestos exposure greatly increases cancer risks, though exposed non-smokers are also apparently at risk. In most cases, the cancer will be latent for 20 to 30 years after first exposure and upon manifestation will quickly result in the victim's death. Of those heavily exposed to asbestos dust (including factory workers and those installing asbestos products), 20 to 25 percent are estimated to die of lung cancer (U.S. Congress: HCEL, 1978:134).

Mesotheioma is a cancer of the mesothelial cells in the pleura (which lines the chest cavity) or the peritoneum (which lines the abdominal cavity). The tumor remains latent for 20 to 40 years and then quickly spreads throughout the chest or abdomen. Breathlessness and severe pain occur, vital organ function is affected, and death results very quickly. Mesothelioma occurs almost exclusively among those exposed to asbestos and was not recognized in the medical literature until the 1940s. The incidence of this cancer appears to be increasing, and it is estimated that 7 to 10 percent of heavily exposed workers die from it (U.S. Congress: HCEL, 1978:134).

Approximately eleven million people in the United States have been exposed to asbestos dust at work. Most of the intensive exposures occurred in shipyards during the Second World War. Dust exposure levels varied over time and work area in the shipyards and other places where asbestos was used. It is estimated that asbestos-related diseases will claim the lives of 40 percent of the four million workers heavily exposed to asbestos dust and 15 percent of the four to seven million with less intense exposure (U.S. Congress: HCEL, 1978:135; see also Vermeulen and Berman, 1982:21). Because of the long latency periods, however, the connection between diseases and asbestos exposure was slow to be discovered, remaining both disputable in court and unclear to the general public for many years.

Corporate Responses to Asbestos-related Disease

Since awareness of asbestos related health hazards developed slowly, Manville and other firms in the asbestos industry had the opportunity to develop a four-stage strategic response.

Controlling the Spread of Information. The first phase began in the early 1930s with the initial medical evidence linking asbestos exposure to disease and lasted until conclusive independent research from Mt. Sinai School of Medicine in New York began appearing in the mid-1960s. During this period the dangers of asbestos exposure became increasingly clear to Manville executives. Their response was two-fold: to limit the dissemination of information on potential health dangers and to challenge unfavorable research findings through industry-sponsored research.

The first case of asbestosis was reported in England in 1906; subsequently, a report of this was published in a 1918 Bulletin of the U.S. Department of Labor Statistics with a call for further research (U.S. Congress: House Committee on the Judiciary [HCJ], 1980:42). By 1930, studies in the United Kingdom had strongly suggested a link between asbestos exposure and pulmonary disease (U.S. Congress: HCEL, 1978:26, 1979:97; U.S. Congress: HCJ, 1980:42). Indeed, early studies in the United States, including those sponsored by Manville and the asbestos industry, supported the existence of such a link (U.S. Congress: HCJ, 1980:492, 493).

Executives at Manville and other industry firms interpreted adverse research findings so as to minimize their importance, arguing that the English findings did not bear on the U.S. situation and that the problem was one of "individual susceptibilities" (U.S. Congress: HCEL, 1978:152; U.S. Congress: Senate Committee of Labor and Human Resources [SCLHR], 1980:206). In addition, they repeatedly and successfully prevented publication of those findings in the trade journal *Asbestos,* read by those in the industry as well as by users of asbestos products (e.g., U.S. Congress: HCJ, 1980:103). The company's general counsel (and later, secretary) Vandiver Brown stated in a 1935 letter to Sumner Simpson, president of the second largest asbestos producer, Raybestos Manhattan: "Our interests are best served by having asbestosis receive the minimum of publicity" (printed in U.S. Congress: HCEL, 1978:152). Consequently, most compensation claims were settled out of court; only one suit reached the appellate level before 1970 (*Vogel v. Johns-Manville Products Corp.,* 1936).

Manville also limited the information reaching its workers as to their own physical condition. There is evidence indicating that as late as the 1960s employees were not being warned of dust dangers (U.S. Congress: HCEL, 1979:151; see also U.S. Congress: HCJ, 1980:533). Medical indications of disease were not revealed to affected workers, and even the outside physician for one Manville plant was reportedly not aware asbestos was used there until 1972 (*Johns-Manville Products Corp. v. Superior Court,* 1980; U.S. Congress: HCEL, 1979:151; U.S. Congress: HCJ, 1980:508–10, 533, 538; Berman, 1978:3).

Company executives realized as early as the 1930s that minimizing public awareness of the hazards of asbestos exposure was an inadequate strategy by itself, given the steadily increasing flow of non-industry research (notably Hueper, 1956, printed in U.S. Congress: HCEL, 1979:153). Manville began to sponsor its own research in 1928 with a small study using only non-human subjects and examining only possible links to cancer (i.e., not to asbestosis). The explicit aim of the industry-sponsored research was to provide scientific evidence to combat the negative non-industry findings as well as to defend against workers' compensation claims and tort suits (Brown, 1934; Hobart, 1934). In 1936, Brown and Simpson proposed a joint research program to an industry group which they dominated. As Simpson (1936) wrote,

We could determine from time to time after the findings are made whether we wish any publication or not. My own idea is that it would be a good thing to distribute the information among the medical fraternity, providing it is of the right type and would not injure our companies.

The resulting research agreement with the Saranac Laboratories in New York State stipulated that the funders:

will determine whether, to what extent and in what manner they [results] should be made public. In the event it is deemed desirable that the results be made public, the manuscript of your study will be submitted to us for approval prior to publication (quoted in Brown, 1939).

The medical professionals involved were clearly willing to cooperate with the asbestos industry. Funding requests by these professionals to asbestos trade associations in the 1950s suggested that research be undertaken to defend against claims or to counter negative non-industry studies. In 1955, for example, the Saranac director requested funds from an industry trade association, suggesting the relationship between asbestos and cancer be studied in animals in order to provide facts "to combat unjust compensation claims" (*Dishner v. Johns-Manvile Corp.,* 1978:850). The next year, Manville's medical director recommended that the association fund a study on the cancer link "in order that we could procure information which would combat current derogatory literature now being circulated throughout the United States and Canada" (quoted from U.S. Congress: HCEL, 1979:153). Results of industry-sponsored research were submitted to Manville and other firms for review and withheld from publication if they did not satisfactorily advance these goals (e.g., U.S. Congress: HCJ, 1980:52–53). Moreover, the results that were published were sometimes carefully misleading. For example, studies published in the 1950s emphasized that *asbestosis* did not cause cancer. This obscured the very real relationship found between the substance asbestos and cancer (U.S. Congress: HCJ, 1980:52, 53; Smith, 1955:202–3).

By the mid-1960s, managing information was no longer a viable strategy. Many of those exposed to asbestos in the past were manifesting disease. Most importantly, research first published in 1964, principally by Dr. Irving Selikoff of the Mt. Sinai School of Medicine, clearly established the widespread and long-term danger of asbestos exposure (e.g., Selikoff et al., 1964). Manville was forced to deal with this public knowledge, reversing in 1964 its long-standing policy against attaching health warnings to its asbestos products. Moreover, union concern for health and safety issues increased, combining with the new scientific evidence to dramatically increase the number and size of compensation claims. Selikoff joined the unions in lobbying for federal dust regulations, and the 1972 standards were among the first to be established under the Occupational Safety and Health Act (Brodeur, 1973:29–31; Ashford, 1976:5–6).

Confronting the Litigation Explosion. The second phase in Manville's response was to confront the explosion of asbestos-related litigation. In 1973, an appellate court first held that asbestos manufacturers could be liable to those using asbestos products for failing to warn of or test for dangers that were reasonably foreseeable (*Borel v. Fibreboard Paper Products,* 1973). This touched off an avalanche of product liability suits. Manville, as the major manufacturer, was named as a defendant in perhaps 13,000 of 20,000 suits industry-wide between 1968 and 1982 (Lublin, 1982; Johns-Manville Debtor's Petition, 1982), although fewer than one hundred reached the trial stage.

By the late 1970s, these suits had become a significant financial threat. In 1976, 159 new lawsuits were filed against the corporation; in 1978, the number reached 792. Crucially, in 1977, a plaintiff attorney discovered the existence of the "Sumner Simpson Papers" (several of which are cited above), which included correspondence among industry executives from as far back as the 1930s coordinating action to limit the spread of information concerning the health hazards of asbestos products and production processes. These letters undermined Manville's argument that there was insufficient medical evidence of health dangers until 1964 to warrant warnings and testing beyond what was done. The tide turned against the company; jury awards ran as high as $750,000 (Soloman, 1979:198), and legal costs mounted. Nonetheless, Manville continued to fight every case vigorously, exhausting every legal option open to it—an approach that plaintiff attorneys regarded as stalling and attempting to fight not on the merit of cases but on relative financial capacity to continue litigation.

Perhaps the most critical threat to the firm came in 1976 when Manville's insurers refused to renew their policies, claiming they were unable to estimate future liability expenses adequately to arrive at an appropriate fee (see U.S. Congress: HCJ, 1980:59, 1982:208). Manville was forced into self-insurance. This not only removed its buffer against liability payments, it made the company immediately responsible for all defense costs. Insurance and asbestos companies entered into litigation to determine whether an asbestos "injury" arose at initial exposure to asbestos (rendering those insuring Manville in the 1930s and 1940s liable) or at manifestation of disease (rendering those insuring at time of manifestation liable). No court decision was forthcoming until 1980; in the late 1970s, the company faced the possibility that a manifestation theory would be accepted, which would leave it liable as self-insurer for all diseases manifested after 1976, and thus for the majority of claims.

Impending Disaster and Protective Legislation.   In the third phase of its response to the developing awareness of the health hazards of asbestos, the company sought relief from its severe immediate and long-term problems by helping to draft federal legislation that would create a fund for the settlement of claims from victims of asbestos-related disease. Representative Millicent Fenwick of New Jersey sponsored the 1977 Asbestos Health Hazards Compensation Act (H.R. 2740), and Senator Gary Hart of Colorado sponsored its 1980 successor (S. 2847). Manville was a principal drafter of both these bills, as Fenwick and Hart readily acknowledged (U.S. Congress: HCEL, 1979:2; U.S. Congress: SCLHR, 1980:172). Neither bill reached the legislative floor. Manville viewed them as legitimate efforts to share the burden created by changing social standards as to what constitutes reasonable business practices as well as changing medical knowledge about the dangers of asbestos. To many critics, however, including legislators, the bills were mere attempts to avoid responsibility for the costs of past corporate practices.

Manville and other supporters of the compensation bills argued that workers' compensation programs and product liability litigation were inadequate to compensate victims. They attempted to show that victims sued manufacturers of products they had used rather than their employers because workers' compensation benefited only a fraction of those with legitimate claims and provided severely limited benefits even in those few cases (U.S. Congress: SCLHR, 1980:169, 207, 227). They similarly faulted tort litigation for failing to provide adequate compensation for victims (U.S. Congress: SCLHR, 1980:205). Since legal expenses (including attorneys fees and court costs) exceeded the compensation received by victims by 66 percent, litigation seemed to them an ineffective and inefficient means of providing compensation (U.S. Congress: HCEL, 1982:202; Kakalik et al., 1983, 1984; see also *Harvard Law Review,* 1980).

The Fenwick and Hart bills similarly called for standardized payments to confirmed victims of asbestos-related disease. Each contained a clause prohibiting all persons eligible for compensation under the proposed statute from bringing suits against employers, manufacturers, insurers, unions, or the government; in other words, the bills proposed to create an exclusive remedy. Each bill provided for some means by which payments would be rendered predictable as well as adequate. This predictability was crucial; it would allow the company to plan its business activities with some clear notion of future liabilities and probably allow it to reinsure itself.

The Fenwick bill proposed to provide compensation by means of a federally administered fund; companies would pay in a fixed percentage of their sales from fifteen years before. Under the Hart bill, payments would be made by companies into state-administered workers compensation programs in amounts corresponding to nationally standardized "percentage rates of liability" for current and expected future claims. The Fenwick bill would have been preferable for Manville because past sales are a more certain indicator of liability than future claims, but each would have provided the needed level of predictability.

Under the Fenwick bill, Manville had no incentive to reduce asbestos dust levels because the corporation's financial contribution to victims would be based directly on its level of sales, not its workers' health. Similarly, under the Hart bill, firms would pay a percentage of total liability which, though not necessarily based on market share, would at least provide for insurance at something close to an industry-wide rate.

Each bill included an attempt to make tobacco companies share some of the cost of asbestos-related disease, primarily on the basis of research showing that cigarette smoking greatly increases the risk of lung cancer for those exposed to asbestos. However, the proposals evaded two key issues. First, were tobacco companies responsible for workers' smoking (an individual choice) in the same sense in which asbestos companies were responsible for spreading asbestos dust? Second, should the asbestos industry share in this liability because it had systematically minimized the chances that workers had to find out about the combined risks of asbestos exposure and smoking?

Finally, the bills sought to have the federal government contribute to the compensation fund. About one-half of all workers occupationally exposed in any intense way to asbestos dust worked in shipyards owned or controlled by the government, especially during the Second World War (Hart, 1983). The government, moreover, had done some early research and failed to do much to implement recommendations that greater precautions be taken (U.S. Congress: HCEL, 1978:38-39). The government would acknowledge liability only for victims directly employed at federal facilities, that is, not for employees of contractors. In the absence of any relevant court decisions, the extent of government liability remained unclear.

Bankruptcy.   Manville's failure to secure financial protection by legislation forced the corporation to try a final and more drastic action. In August 1982, the company filed for protection from its creditors while it reorganized under Chapter 11 of the Federal Bankruptcy Code. At about the same time, the company changed its name from Johns-Manville to the Manville Corporation in an attempt to symbolically distance the corporate identity from the asbestos litigation. This was newsworthy because it was a highly unusual move for a company far from bankrupt in current account terms. In December 1981, as noted, Manville's assets totaled $2.3 billion.

Filing for protection under bankruptcy statutes was an extreme measure but, at least in the short term, an effective one. It immediately froze action on all creditors' claims, including pending and future tort claims. The corporation's longer-term goal was to keep its main operating assets from possible seizure to pay claim settlements. The bankruptcy proceeding, in short, saved the corporation from more or less rapid dissolution as litigation costs and settlements cut increasingly into capital. It was not a painless solution, however, and Manville chose it pretty much as a last resort.

By 1981 the company faced prosecution in some 9,300 cases brought by 12,800 separate plaintiffs. The average award was $16,000 per claim. Total costs were more than twice that, however, as defense costs reached the level of $23,400 per claim (Johns-Manville Debtor's Petition, 1982:5, 6: see also Kakalik et al., 1983, 1984). Moreover, the award ceiling kept rising. In 1981, a Los Angeles County jury awarded a plaintiff $1.2 million in compensatory damages alone (U.S. Congress: HCEL, 1982:204). Much more importantly, in 1981 Manville was first found liable for punitive damages at the trial court level. If the awards were upheld on appeal, Manville would be responsible for full payment no matter when the injury took place because punitive damages generally are not insurable (Stone, 1975:56; though this question is often litigated). . . .

For over 30 years, Manville executives resisted many paths of action that might have prevented or alleviated the suffering of the victims of asbestos related diseases. Because the diseases have long latency periods, the impact of these corporate decisions continued well beyond that 30-year period. It is important to note that since the mid-1960s, no decisions with regard to ordinary company operations could have undone the bulk of the damage for which the corporation now faces liability. Any change in operating procedures, such as the phasing out of asbestos use or the adoption of higher safety standards, could only have reduced the incidence of disease years in the future.

The most important point is not that Manville or its executives were distinctively bad, but that the scale of the company's operations and the danger of its products made the bad actions of its executives distinctively efficacious. . . .

The Corporation as Defendant

Insurance made the compensatory focus of modern tort law possible; the large corporation made it especially important. First, large corporations helped to transform the scale of social organization. Single production facilities grew to employ thousands of people, single companies hundreds of thousands. Organizational and technological complexities helped to make accidents likely; structural rigidity in bureaucratic hierarchies often inhibited efforts to prevent them (Sherman, 1978; Clinard, 1983; Ermann and Lundman, 1987). The very scale of operations in any case was such that even seemingly low probabilities of accidents might produce large absolute numbers of injuries; it was necessary to think in terms of statistical risk rather than only particular cases (Perrow, 1984; Huber, 1985). As the NASA space shuttle disaster recently showed, public bureaucracies can have problems similar to those of private industry.

Beyond this, the corporate form of organization created a basic asymmetry between the two sorts of "persons" who faced each other in litigation. On the one hand were the "natural persons" and on the other were legally created corporations. Each sort of person had the same basic status in tort litigation, but strict liability doctrine came to be invoked to secure compensation precisely when "the typical tort claim arose out of an interaction between persons with unequal power, no previous contractual relations or customary dealings, and imperfect information about risks" (White, 1980:219). Coleman (1982) treats such extreme disparities in wealth, power, and longevity between corporations and human individuals as a defining characteristic of modern society. They also create obvious problems for natural persons who must challenge large corporations in the courts.

One of the crucial ways in which corporations and individuals are asymmetrical is in their ability to control and/or gain access to information. In the asbestos-related cases, individuals faced difficulties in finding out about the nature and causation of injuries done to them and in pursuing legal remedies (Schroeder and Shapiro, 1984). Even without the sort of manipulation and bad faith practiced by Manville executives, individuals are unlikely to be able to gather sufficient knowledge to inform their own decision-making adequately without creating still other large-scale collective actors. Unions and "disinterested" medical research organizations were thus instrumental in bringing an effective challenge to Manville's practices. Potential victims of asbestos-related diseases are widely dispersed and knit together only loosely. In the ordinary course of events, information—to the extent it is available at all—will spread only slowly and unevenly among potential victims (see Stone, 1975: ch. 18). The exposed population has little social organization through which to undertake collective action.

Even when individuals learn of the possible consequences of exposure, they face substantial costs in any effort to challenge the corporation. They may succeed in obtaining counsel from attorneys willing to take their cases on a contingency basis (something that is easy to do only after a fairly considerable momentum has built up), but they are unlikely to be able to match the financial resources a large corporation can use in litigation. Plaintiff lawyers do have a certain interest in taking on some early cases they will likely lose, because this enables them to prepare better for (and advertise their availability for) eventual winning cases. Nonetheless, plaintiffs are at a disadvantage, especially in the early years of litigation. In the Manville cases it took decades of preparation and trial work before the tide turned in favor of plaintiffs. Moreover, the legal system allows defendants almost unlimited opportunities to increase the costs of the proceedings for their opponents, while it simultaneously restricts the interest of plaintiffs' attorneys in their own work (Rosenberg, 1984:904–5; see Galanter, 1975, on the advantages of corporations in such litigation).

Individuals also face difficulties in gathering and analyzing information. Major personal injury cases can involve millions of documents and computerized records: statistics on production, distribution and use of hazardous substances, statistics on the health of thousands of workers, testimony or written evidence from hundreds of sources. Gathering such information requires substantial resources and/or enormous time and dedication. A RAND Corporation study indicates that between the early 1970s and the Manville bankruptcy filing in August 1982, the industry and its insurers had spent $606 million to defend asbestos-related cases; plaintiff's litigation expenses amounted to $164 million (Kakalik et al., 1983:39; net compensation was $236 million with some cases still pending).

Longevity is another relevant asymmetry between corporations and individuals. Individual life spans are limited while corporations may "live" indefinitely. A corporation may choose to drag litigation on for years, regarding the additional legal costs it pays as negligible compared to its potential liability. Its liability, after all, must be understood not in terms of the single case but as magnified by the thousands of others to which it might lead (Galanter, 1975). Corporate executives, moreover, have little incentive to see a potentially expensive case settled during their tenure of office. Since corporate executives often move from one position to another within a company, or among firms, this can be a major issue. No official wants the extraordinary costs of a disadvantageous settlement to threaten his reputation. Each would rather leave the case pending, as he found it (see Stone, 1980; Roe, 1984:9–10). This is an issue of particular force in the case of long-latent diseases. In the Manville case, no senior actors in the original plan of concealment and manipulation of information are alive to face the consequences of their actions.

This bears on one major argument about how to make corporations more responsible. Simply fining corporations and/or making them pay damages to victims does not produce the intended deterrent effect, this argument goes, because such expenses do not translate into direct financial liability for the individuals who made the blameworthy decisions. Critics of corporations have generally viewed corporate status as a shield illegitimately deflecting punishment from culpable individuals and simultaneously depriving deserving victims of compensation (Nader and Green, 1973; Nader, Green, and Seligman, 1976). Many have called for a legal apparatus (e.g., for Nader, a charter) that affirms the right of government to reach inside the corporations to enforce its own standards of good behavior.

Some defenders of corporations have claimed that they should be exempt from this level of government interference because they are essentially creatures of private contract rather than public concession (Hessen, 1979). In this view, the corporation is neither an entity in itself nor a legal fiction in the sense of Justice Marshall's classic description (in *Dartmouth v. Woodward*) of "an artificial being, invisible, intangible, and existing only in contemplation of law." Ironically, this "defense" of corporations harbors serious dangers for them. If the corporation is merely a private association of its members (by which is usually meant its shareholders), then doctrines of limited liability must be called into serious doubt. Either individual employees would be liable (perhaps following some version of the old common law of master and servant) or individual owners would be fully liable, that is, liable to the extent of their assets rather than merely the amount of their initial investment. Yet the modern large company presumably depends on limited liability for its shareholders, if not perhaps for its executives (see Orhnial, 1982).

Corporate charters might be used to build a variety of requirements into the very constitution of corporations. Nader's proposal to use them to reach inside to bring legal action against individuals has little bearing on cases of injuries involving long latency periods, however, though pressing tort and/or criminal charges against corporate officers may be efficacious in some other cases. Charters might, however, be used to promote corporate social responsibility through internal structural reforms and to produce a more ethical corporate culture (Stone, 1975; Ackerman, 1975). The insidious injury cases lend some support to this idea. Charter provisions could be designed to promote structures that encourage corporations to monitor product and process safety and issue early warnings of potential dangers. But any such provisions would in many ways run counter to the tendency of the tort law to encourage corporations to treat all such information as a potential legal risk and thus minimize both its collection and its dissemination. Of course, it may be desirable that high moral standards rather than minimum criteria of legal acceptability be the goal for managerial (as for all other) behavior.

Punishment vs. Compensation

Whatever the desirability of such reform efforts, they are not likely to be the direct product of tort litigation against corporations. In insidious injuries cases, tort law is best suited to providing compensation to victims. What place, we now need to ask, is left for punishment?

Deciding that compensation should be provided to victims still leaves the question of who should pay? Conventional notions of justice would have blameworthy parties pay. In other words, payment would punish those who have caused injuries; publicizing this punishment would deter others. The Manville case, however, suggests that considerable complexities challenge attempts to apply this simple principle in concrete cases. Focusing solely on the company's blameworthiness leads some to propose dissolving it, thus limiting funds available to compensate future claimants.

Clearly, since the pursuit of profit produces the risk, it seems reasonable to argue that even the least blameworthy corporation is the appropriate source of compensation. It is one-sided for the *New York Times* (1982) to describe asbestos-related diseases as a tragedy for "the companies, which are being made to pay the price for decisions made long ago." But those who speak of making the company "suffer" should be pressed to make clear what this means. A company is not a sensory agent capable of "feeling" punishment; any presumed punishment of a corporation must translate into the bad feelings of some set of individuals, whether owners, managers, or other employees. Even though investors might reasonably be held voluntarily to assume the risks associated with financial problems such as those now confronting Manville, punishing them would seem to be plausible primarily as an expiatory ritual, not as a deterrent or source of compensation. At best, the prospect of such "punishment" might encourage future investors to impose demands for clear information as to the "good practices" of firms, that is, to ask for a social audit or certification of due care to minimize actionable injuries. It is not clear that very many investors could conceivably enforce such demands unless they were aided by public monitoring and sanctions for failure to comply. The public information which Manville provided right up to the time of bankruptcy filing was certainly misleading, though apparently not to the point of illegal misrepresentation.

Indeed, insisting on using tort law to effect "punishments" of corporations might lead officers to further restrict or distort information and to resist prompt and just settlement of tort claims. This may include keeping certain top executives ignorant of such information so that they can honestly claim not to know of their own firm's practices or their consequences. "Digging in" of managerial heels is a major problem to be considered in any attempt to deal with insidious injuries. Businesses themselves will be in the best position to detect early signs of insidious diseases. Some form of government regulation may be required to get them to act positively on their knowledge.

There is good reason to think that corporations, unlike individual criminals, will discriminate effectively among severe penalties (see Clinard and Yeager, 1980; Ermann and Lundman, 1982); for instance, between dissolution and large financial costs. As Rosenberg (1984:855) has pointed out, "mass exposure" torts such as the ones at issue in asbestos litigation are "frequently products of the deliberate policies of businesses that tailor safety investments to profit margins." In principle, this should make threats of liability more effective in reducing corporate negligence. The key is for the liability to appear large enough to deter without being so large as to produce strategies of legal delay or manipulation of information.

For corporations confronted with massive tort liability, predictability of costs and hence the possibility of effective strategic planning is crucial. For corporate officers faced with mounting tort claims over long-latent diseases, the availability of a well-managed and eventually more predictable bankruptcy proceeding might provide a more palatable course of action than fighting on and risking dissolution. At that point, executives can no longer solve the corporation's problems by changing corporate practices; they can only choose strategically among responses to the corporation's legal liability.

In the Manville case, bankruptcy makes sense when considered as part of an effort to secure compensation to victims, even though some critics argue that it impeded punishment of Manville and deterrence of future tortfeasors. Punishment and incentives for prevention were sacrificed to the achievement of compensation. Even under a negligence standard individuals had great difficulty getting a large corporation like Manville to redress (or even address) the wrongs it created; liability in individuals' suits was too ineffective to be considered a significant deterrent.

Making compensation the primary pursuit of the courts simply gives up the notion that tort law should seek to induce either corporate or individual responsibility. As both Posner (1973:214) and White (1980:235) point out, strict liability doctrines also remove some of the incentives for consumers to use products carefully, though possible financial compensation seems unlikely to make individual consumers extraordinarily careless. Whether there is any mechanism to translate potential costs into motivation for good actions is even more doubtful than in comparable cases decided on a "pure" negligence standard. The Manville case presents problems, thus, for an economic theory of tort law such as Posner's (1972) with its contention that proceedings in terms of negligence will effectively motivate prevention as well as punish wrong-doing and compensate victims. Manville's bankruptcy settlement may give pause to other corporate managers considering such a defense against tort liability. But nothing in the tort litigation itself suggests that such managers, in a situation similar to Manville's, would be poorly advised (on solely economic grounds) to hide the problem as long as possible and then fight all lawsuits vigorously. If compensation is the goal, the problems are to find and distribute funds. Corporations, their insurers, and/or the government must establish a fund; and the claims of current victims must be balanced against the rights of expected future claimants. Insurance ordinarily accomplishes this. The possibility of losing insurance coverage in cases of long-latent disease shifts the burden back to the producer and victim with a minimal actuarial buffer. As in the Manville case, private insurers will often prudently refuse protection even where businesses still operate. Where long-latent disease is at issue the law is unclear as to which insurers are liable and in what proportions (see also *Indiana Law Review*, 1982; *Harvard Law Review*, 1984). Until the law is clear, victims bear most of the burden of delayed compensation. Any attempt to "punish" the corporation by, for instance, liquidating its assets and dissolving it, will likely benefit current claimants and commercial creditors. This will be at the expense of future sufferers of asbestos-related disease, as well as of management, employees, and possible investors.

A government-subsidized fund was one possibility to avoid this sort of fix in the asbestos cases. Manville and other firms only grudgingly gave up hope for this option. Those who hold that punishment and not merely compensation must be a central goal resisted such a scheme. Such resistance was reinforced by the fact that the legislative plans put forward were grossly favorable to the company. In most imaginable cases, an "after-the-fact" legislative solution would involve either shifting a large part of the burden to the general taxpaying public or developing an almost unprecedented mechanism for close government involvement in the running of a "private" business (though see discussion in *Texas Law Review*, 1983).

Failing insurance and government backing, the corporation itself becomes the best source of funds for compensation. Where only moderate amounts are at issue, it may be possible for corporations to handle such claims as self-insurers. Where amounts are much larger, some form of legally enforced protection and reorganization may be essential to secure compensation and to save the company. Bankruptcy reorganization may be the only effective procedure available to balance the claims of future claimants against current ones, and the only means of providing a sufficiently large source of funds to meet the claims of all. It should not be thought that the bankruptcy reorganization necessarily will lead to any very different form of corporate management. The trustees will be bound by a fiduciary responsibility to victims and other creditors much like what boards of directors ordinarily have towards stockholders. Presumably this will be interpreted in the same predominantly financial terms of prudent judgment, namely, a fairly narrow seeking of profit and perhaps growth by means of standard business practices. There is little in our knowledge of corporate boards to suggest that trustees acting by similar standards would implement dramatically new management practices (Herman, 1981).

Discussion

Corporations have both caused insidious injuries and impeded individual and collective efforts to cope with them. At the same time, corporations may also be the only social actors able to compensate their victims. If the corporation did not endure and remain viable, there would often be no one to sue in a case of long-latent disease. There would be no "deep pocket" against which to make legal claims. The only remaining option would be a government-backed compensation scheme.

Similarly, just as individuals are shorter-lived than corporations, small firms are shorter-lived than large ones. Though Manville was the perpetrator (or at least the mechanism) of a large evil, its very size made it a practical source of compensation. The very corporate form and the particular size and power of Manville indeed allowed it and its agents to avoid responsibility for many actions over a long period of time. The structural asymmetry between Manville and those it wronged did contribute to the perpetuation and extension of the wrong. Ironically, however, that same asymmetry helps to provide an effective means of funding those very claims that the corporation ultimately was unable to deflect.

· · ·

Given the difficulties of using the tort law system for effective punishment or admonishment in cases of insidious injuries, we should turn elsewhere for our primary preventive measures. Central to any of these must be recognition that injuries of this sort are inevitable. We show little inclination to give up the technologies or the scale of social organization characteristic of modern production processes and commodity circulation. As a result, some significant rate of insidious injuries will continue. New products that appear benign will prove fatal; diseases will be linked to environmental or occupational exposure to toxins now unrecognized. Traditions of free business and consumer decision-making only accentuate this. In sum, with even the highest possible standards of good business behavior, insidious injuries will be discovered years after they have been caused.

It is, of course, socially desirable both to compensate the victims of these injuries and to minimize their extent. The legal system presently offers few alternatives to the use of tort law as a means of securing compensation, even where long latency periods inhibit its effectiveness. Mandatory participation in government-backed compensation insurance schemes would speed the process of providing for victims, though tort law will no doubt remain a crucial backup and goad. But tort litigation needs to be used sparingly enough to encourage corporations to act responsibly in monitoring the safety of their products and production processes. Epidemiological data needs to be collected continuously to aid in the identification of potential insidious health problems and much relevant information will have to come from firms involved in manufacturing and marketing. It is important to recognize that business corporations are fundamentally public, not private, actors. Their creation partly by contract should not be taken to impede such regulation as is needed to ensure that they gather and disseminate information on product and process safety.

Regulatory apparatuses also need to be in place to coordinate action to minimize further risks when such problems are recognized. But such efforts will be severely impeded if firms' actions are oriented substantially toward defense against future tort liability. And in the absence of an alternative compensation scheme, and especially in the presence of the possibility of claims large enough to bankrupt the country's wealthiest firms, managers are apt to follow in the footsteps of those at Manville who manipulated information, then dragged out legal defenses as long as they could. In the end, the Manville reorganization was a fair settlement, but it came much too late. We should hope that procedures for corporate reorganization will be established which are sufficiently well understood and appropriately administered that they can be used as other than a last-ditch defense. Whether handled in bankruptcy court or by other agencies, such reorganizations provide an effective way of funding both present and future claims.

References

Ackerman, Robert W. 1975. *The Social Challenge to Business.* Cambridge, MA: Harvard University Press.

Ashford, Nicholas A. 1976. *Crisis in the Workplace: Occupational Disease and Injury.* Cambridge, MA: Massachusetts Institute of Technology Press.

Berman, Daniel M. 1978. *Death on the Job: Occupational Health and Safety Struggles in the United States.* New York: Monthly Review Press.

Brodeur, Paul. 1973. *Expendable Americans.* New York: Viking.

———. 1986. *Outrageous Misconduct: The Asbestos Industry on Trial.* New York: Pantheon.

Brown, Vandiver. 1934. Letter to A. J. Lanza, December 10.

———. 1939. Letter to S. Simpson, May 3.

Calabresi, Guido. 1985. *Ideals, Beliefs, Attitudes, and the Law.* Syracuse, NY: Syracuse University Press.

Calabresi, Guido and Philip Bobbit. 1978. *Tragic Choices.* New Haven: Yale University Press.

Cater, Morrow. 1982. "Manville bankruptcy case may prompt congress to close loophole in law." *National Journal,* November 27:2029–30.

Chen, E. 1984. "Asbestos litigation is a growth industry." *Atlantic,* July:24–32.

Clinard, Marshall. 1983. *Corporate Ethics and Crime: The Role of Middle Management.* Beverly Hills: Sage.

Clinard, Marshall and Peter C. Yeager. 1980. *Corporate Crime.* New York: Free Press.

Coleman, James S. 1982. *The Asymmetric Society.* Syracuse, NY: Syracuse University Press.

Ermann, M. David and Richard J. Lundman. 1982. *Corporate Deviance.* New York: Holt, Rinehart, and Winston.

Ermann, M. David and Richard J. Lundman, eds. 1987. *Corporate and*

Governmental Deviance: Problems of Organizational Behavior in Contemporary Society. New York: Oxford University Press.

Friedman, Lawrence M. 1973. *A History of American Law.* New York: Simon and Schuster.

Galanter, Marc. 1975. "Why the 'haves' come out ahead: speculations on the limits of legal change." *Law and Society Review* 9:95–160.

Goodwyn, W. Richard. 1972. *The Johns-Manville Story.* New York: The Newcomen Society of North America.

Harvard Law Review. 1980. "Compensating victims of occupational disease." *Harvard Law Review* 93:916–28.

———. 1984. "Adjudicating asbestos insurance liability: alternatives to contract analysis." *Harvard Law Review* 97:739–58.

Hart, Gary. 1983. "Let government bear its share." *New York Times,* November 5, Sec. 3:2.

Herman, Edward S. 1981. *Corporate Control, Corporate Power.* New York: Cambridge University Press.

Hessen, Robert. 1979. *In Defense of the Corporation.* Stanford, CA: The Hoover Institution.

Hobart, George. 1934. Letter to V. Brown.

Horwitz, Morton J. 1977. *The Transformation of American Law, 1780–1860.* Cambridge, MA: Harvard University Press.

Huber, Peter. 1985. "Safety and the second best: the hazards of public risk management in the courts." *Columbia Law Review* 85:277–337.

Indiana Law Review. 1982. "Asbestos litigation: the insurance coverage question." *Indiana Law Review* 15:851.

Jackson, Thomas H. 1986. *The Logic and Limits of Bankruptcy Law.* Cambridge, MA: Harvard University Press.

Johns-Manville Corporation. 1978. *Johns-Manville Corporation Annual Report.*

———. 1982. Debtor's Petition Under Chapter 11.

Kakalik, James S., P. A. Ebener, W. L. F. Feistiner, and M. G. Shanley. 1983. *Costs of Asbestos Litigation.* Santa Monica, CA: RAND Corporation.

Kakalik, James S., P. A. Ebener, W. L. S. Felstiner, G. W. Haggstrom, and M. G. Shanley. 1984. *Variation in Asbestos Litigation Compensation and Expenses.* Santa Monica, CA: RAND Corporation.

Lewin, Tamar. 1982. "Asbestos lawyers ask court to curb Manville." *New York Times,* November 9:29.

———. 1984. "Manville bankruptcy is upheld: future claims remain issue." *New York Times,* January 24:27–32.

———. 1986. "A new set of hurdles for Manville." *New York Times,* February 17:19–21.

Lublin, Joann. 1982. "Occupational diseases receive more scrutiny since the Manville case." *Wall Street Journal,* December 20:12.

Metz, Robert. 1982. "The attraction of Manville." *New York Times,* November 2:36.

Mitchell, Cynthia F. 1986. "Manville, its bankruptcy plan in hand, girds for the long haul to pay its debts." *Wall Street Journal,* December 8:8.

Moodys' Investors' Service, Inc. 1982. *Moody's Industrial Manual*, Vol. 2. R. P. Hansen (ed.). New York: Moody's Investors' Services.

Nader, Ralph, and Mark Green, eds. 1973. *Corporate Power in America*. New York: Grossman.

Nader, Ralph, Mark Green, and Joel Seligman. 1976. *Taming the Giant Corporation*. New York: W. W. Norton & Co.

Orhnial, T., ed. 1982. *Limited Liability and the Corporation*. London: Croom Helm.

Perrow, Charles. 1984. *Normal Accidents*. New York: Basic Books.

Posner, Richard A. 1972. "A theory of negligence." *Journal of Legal Studies* 1:29–96.

———. 1973. "The theory of strict liability: a comment." *Journal of Legal Studies* 2.

Prosser, William V. 1941. *The Law of Torts*. Minneapolis, MN: West.

Roe, Mark J. 1984. "Bankruptcy and mass tort." *Columbia Law Review* 84:846–922.

Rosenberg, David. 1984. "The causal connection in mass exposure cases: a 'public law' vision of the tort system." *Harvard Law Review* 97:851–929.

Schroeder, Elinor P., and Sidney A. Shapiro. 1984. "Responses to occupational disease: the role of markets, regulation and information." *The Georgetown Law Journal* 72:1231–1309.

Selikoff, Irving J., J. Chrug, and E. C. Hammond. 1964. "Asbestos exposure and neoplasia." *Journal of the American Medical Association* 188:22–26.

Sherman, Lawrence W. 1978. *Scandal and Reform: Controlling Police Corruption*. Berkeley, CA: University of California Press.

Simpson, Sumner. 1936. Letter to F. H. Schluter, November 13.

———. 1939a. Letter to A. S. Rossiter, March 22.

———. 1939b. Letter to V. Brown, May 4.

Steiner, Henry J. 1987. *Moral Argument and Social Vision in the Courts: A Study of Tort Accident Law*. Madison, WI: University of Wisconsin Press.

Stone, Christopher D. 1975. *Where the Law Ends: The Social Control of Corporate Behavior*. New York: Harper and Row.

———. 1980. "The place of enterprise accountability in the control of corporate conduct." *Yale Law Journal* 90:1–15.

Texas Law Review. 1983. "Mass tort claims and the corporate tortfeasor: Bankruptcy reorganization and legislative compensation versus the common-law tort system." *Texas Law Review* 61:1297–1355.

Thompson, Judith Jarvis. 1986. *Rights, Restitution, and Risk: Essays in Moral Theory*. W. Parent (ed.). Cambridge, MA: Harvard University Press.

U.S. Congress, House of Representatives, Committee on Education and Labor (HCEL). 1978. "Asbestos related occupational diseases." Hearings before the Subcommittee on Labor Standards, 95th. Congress, 2d. session.

———. 1979. "Occupational diseases and their compensation, part I: asbestos related diseases." Hearings before the Subcommittee on Labor Standards on H.R. 2740, 96th. Congress, 1st. session.

——. 1981. "The attorney general's asbestos liability report to the Congress." 97th. Congress, 1st. session.

——. 1982. "Occupational health hazards compensation act of 1982." Hearings before the Subcommittee on Labor Standards on H.R. 5735, 97th. Congress, 2d. session.

U.S. Congress, House of Representatives, Committee on the Judiciary (HCJ). 1980. "Corporate criminal liability." Hearings before a subcommittee of the House Committee on the Judiciary on H.R. 4973, 96th. Congress, 1st. and 2d. sessions.

U.S. Congress, Senate, Committee of Labor and Human Resources (SCLHR). 1980. "Asbestos health hazards compensation act of 1980." Hearings before the Senate Committee on Labor and Human Resources on S. 2847, 96th. Congress, 2d. session.

Vermeulen, James E. and Daniel M. Berman. 1982. "Asbestos companies under fire." *Business and Society Review* 42:21–25.

Wall Street Journal.

——. 1985a. "Bhopal's best hope." August 12:18.

——. 1985b. "Manville reorganization delayed by appeal of plan." August 17:4.

White, G. Edward. 1980. *Tort Law in America: An Intellectual History.* New York: Oxford.

Cases Cited

Beshada v. Johns-Manville Prods. Corp., 90 N.J. 191.447 A.2d 539 (1982)

Borel v. Fibreboard Paper Prods. Corp., 493 F.2d 1076 (5th Cir. 1973)

Dartmouth v. Woodward, 17 U.S. (4 Wheat.) 518 (1819)

Dishner v. Johns-Manville Corp., No.77-518 (E.D. Va. 1978)

Eagle-Picher Indus. v. Liberty Mut. Ins. Co., 682 F.2d 12 (1st. Cir. 1982)

Flatt v. Johns-Manville Sales Corp., 488 F. Supp. 836 (E.D. Tex. 1980)

Insurance Co. of N. Am. v. Forty-Eight Insulations, Inc., 633 F.2d 1212 (6th Cir. 1980)

Johns-Manville Prods. Corp. v. Super. Ct., 27 Cal.3d 465. 612 P.2d 948, 165 Ca. Rptr. 858 (1980)

In re Johns-Manville Corp., 3 Bankr. L. Rep. (CCH) Para 69 (Bankr. S.D.N.Y. January 23, 1984)

In re Johns-Manville Corp., (Bankr. S.D.N.Y. 1983-5, various dates)

Keene Corp. v. Johns-Manville Prods. Corp., 667 F.2d 1034 (D.C. Cir. 1981)

Porter v. American Optical Corp., 641 F.2d 1128 (5th Cir. 1981)

Vogel v. Johns-Manville Prods. Corp., 363 Ill. 473, 2 N.E.2d 716 (1936)

White v. Johns-Manville Corp., 662 F.2d 234 (4th. Cir. 1981)

M. David Ermann, professor of sociology at the University of Delaware, received his B.S. from the University of Pennsylvania in 1963 and his Ph.D. from the University of Michigan in 1973. In addition to organizational deviance, his teaching and research interests include complex organizations, especially those in business and health care, and the social impact of computers. He has written and cowritten several chapters for books as well as articles in these areas, cowritten *Social Research Methods* (Random House, 1977) and *Corporate Deviance* (Holt, Rinehart and Winston, 1982), and coedited *Computers, Ethics, and Society* (Oxford University Press, 1990). Professor Ermann continues to study why some usually nondeviant organizations and their people intentionally hide hazards and thereby knowingly cause human injury and death.

Richard J. Lundman is a professor of sociology at The Ohio State University. He received his B.A. from Beloit College in 1966, his M.A. from the University of Illinois in 1968, and his Ph.D. from the University of Minnesota in 1973. Before his affiliation with Ohio State, he taught at the University of Delaware. His teaching and research interests include organizational deviance, police and policing, and juvenile delinquency. He has written and cowritten papers and books in these areas, including *Police Behavior* (Oxford University Press, 1980), *Police and Policing* (Holt, Rinehart and Winston, 1980), *Corporate Deviance* (Holt, Rinehart and Winston, 1982), and *Prevention and Control of Juvenile Delinquency* (Oxford University Press, 1993). Professor Lundman is currently examining the macro-level determinants of police arrests and the factors that shape newspaper coverage of homicide.